TRUTH AT A

TRUTH AT ANY COST

___

KEN STARR
AND THE
UNMAKING OF BILL CLINTON

Susan Schmidt and Michael Weisskopf

HarperCollins*Publishers*

HarperCollins books may be purchased for educational, business, or sales promotional use. For information please write: Special Markets Department, HarperCollins Publishers Inc., 10 East 53rd Street, New York, NY 10022.

FIRST EDITION

Printed on acid-free paper

Designed by Elliott Beard

Library of Congress Cataloging-in-Publication Data has been applied for.

ISBN 0-06-019485-5

00 01 02 03 04 ❖/RRD 10 9 8 7 6 5 4 3 2 1

For Glen, Kate, and Lacey
and for my father
—SS

For Judith, Skyler, and Olivia
—MW

TABLE OF CONTENTS

1

THE TORTOISE AND THE HARE

THURSDAY, NOVEMBER 19, 1998, was the day Independent Counsel Kenneth W. Starr was scheduled to testify before the House Committee on the Judiciary. It would be the first time most Americans got a hard look at the man who had been investigating William Jefferson Clinton for four long years, and the first time anyone heard him publicly make his case that the president had obstructed justice and lied under oath in attempting to foil Paula Jones's sexual harassment suit and hide his relationship with Monica Lewinsky. But Starr knew full well that much of the public had come to view him as a moralistic zealot, consumed by partisan disdain for his quarry and determined to bring him down no matter how problematic the evidence of high crimes and misdemeanors. Starr's motives and methods had been widely reviled, his work and character—and those of his aides—savagely attacked. Although he realized that his House testimony was an opportunity to put a human face on his office's work, Starr was a reluctant witness. He had hoped that his 453-page impeachment referral, the so-called Starr Report, would speak for itself and that he might avoid the political spectacle of testifying. He knew his appearance was risky: Everything—the fate of his entire case, his own reputation—depended on it. He hoped against hope that he would do no harm.

The pressure had been building for weeks, although, typically, he revealed little of the growing strain. Then, in early November, Starr was at a Washington dinner party with a group of old friends who began poking fun at his public image as a Bible-toting Puritan. Starr exploded with anger, his eyes growing cold in a rare display of a temper—the source of childhood tantrums—usually under firm control. Theodore Olson, one of Starr's friends from Ronald Reagan's Justice Department, went home worried about Starr's frame of mind for the upcoming testimony. The next morning, he dialed 911 for public relations: a Dallas image-maker named Merrie Spaeth who had coached Starr during the Reagan years. "It's absolutely mandatory that Ken sit down and work with you, and the rest of us are going to conduct an intervention if he won't do it," said Olson.

The emphasis of style over substance was anathema to Starr. His idea of a good performance was scoring legal points with nine justices on the Supreme Court, as he had as George Bush's solicitor general, not seducing a television audience of millions into liking him. He tended toward pedantry in a world of sound bites, toward poorly timed smiles in a medium that rewarded control and grace. But this time—with a public relations insight that had eluded him far too often in recent months—Starr knew he needed all the help he could get. He agreed to meet Spaeth on November 16, three days before his date with the House.

Spaeth showed up at the Office of the Independent Counsel at 8 A.M. with a mission, she said, to teach Starr to present a "limited, modified version of substance," echoing the "limited, modified hangout" of Watergate fame. She sat him before a video camera as her assistant, Judy Nardella, subjected him to the sort of badgering he was likely to encounter at the hands of House Democrats: "Isn't it true that this is a personal vendetta against the president of the United States and this is about your own personal beliefs of how people should lead their lives like you're the sex police?" She would ask several questions, one after another, cutting Starr off before he had a chance to answer.

Spaeth put the tape on a monitor and asked Starr to watch it. He saw himself getting angrier and angrier. "Ken, I want you to tell me whether you like this person," said Spaeth. He understood, and began to listen carefully. Remember, she told him, the viewers will hear your replies as if they are directed at them, not at the prickly inquisitors a few feet away. If you look irritated in a close-up, they will take it personally.

She worked with him on how to maintain a pleasant facial expression. She advised him to speak in headlines incorporating a fact or two, something easily digested, then to back up a point with an anecdote or a quote. She stressed the power of repetition. "Keep reminding people that what you were doing was thorough, proper, fair, and appropriate," she said. After fourteen hours, Spaeth left, believing she had made progress.

But Starr still sought more coaching. He wanted to be ready for anything. His staff compiled four three-ring binders containing every conceivable question, on subjects ranging from the investigation of the president's relationship with Monica Lewinsky to alleged conflicts of interest involving Starr's private law practice. They played the roles of key Democrats to give practice sessions a real-life flavor. And they harshly criticized Starr's performance. "You're too programmed," complained Brett Kavanaugh, author of Starr's prepared remarks, at a final rehearsal the night before his testimony.

On November 19, Starr rose early. He put on a red tie chosen by his wife, Alice, and tucked three talismans—good luck notes from each of his children—into his breast pocket. At the office, he practiced his testimony one last time. Deputy W. Hickman Ewing Jr. came in just before Starr left for Capitol Hill. He placed his right arm over the independent counsel's shoulder and prayed for him in the sun-streaked corner office overlooking Pennsylvania Avenue. "Lord, help me to guard my tongue, be swift to hear, slow to speak, and slow to wrath," intoned Ewing, an evangelical lay minister. Then Starr left for his debut before the American people.

Ken Starr had come a long way since he first laid eyes on Bill Clinton. It was 1979, and Starr had checked into the Hyatt Regency Hotel on

Capitol Hill to cram for the District of Columbia bar exam. The National Governors Conference was meeting there at the same time, and one day, Starr stepped into an elevator packed with political people. Among them was the newly elected governor of Arkansas. Starr recognized him at once. Clinton was robustly self-confident and attractive, the youngest governor in the country, his résumé bulging with credentials from Georgetown, Yale Law School, and Oxford. There was a buzz around him, an aura of potential. Everyone seemed to recognize that this was a contender, someone to be reckoned with.

Starr felt a certain kinship. He himself was a rising legal talent, a former law clerk for Chief Justice Warren Burger. He was bright, idealistic, and just four years away from becoming one of the youngest judges ever to sit on the U.S. Court of Appeals. Like Clinton, he was thirty-three, a product of the South who had idolized John F. Kennedy. Also like Clinton, he was burning with national ambition, making his own way to the center of power out of a modest past.

But in many key ways, Ken Starr was the very antithesis of the president-to-be. Clinton had always boasted a glib facility with schoolwork, for instance, while the student Starr had been a good-natured grind. In later years, he would call himself the tortoise to Clinton's hare, "moving along slowly and hopefully getting across the finish line without getting run over." And where Clinton fairly bristled with sensitive political antennae, Starr had almost none at all. From his earliest days, in fact, he had been curiously removed from the social context in which he lived and worked, possessing a kind of tunnel vision that enabled him to focus on the issues and duties at hand without much attention to wider realities. In high school, he planned his junior prom, even booking the band, but didn't go because his church frowned on dancing. In the 1960s, he seemed to sleepwalk through the social and political turmoil. He was the Washington college student who passed by Vietnam War protesters on his way to work for a Republican congressman, the Brown University graduate student on full scholarship who feared demonstrators would shut down the school and interrupt his studies.

Starr started life in a loving but austere religious household in a semirural corner of San Antonio. As a boy, he had no real toys—just clothespins to use as toy soldiers—and the only reading material in the house was religious in nature. Reading the Bible, he developed an early love of language, which led him to literature. In high school, encouraged by an interested teacher, he regularly drove fifteen miles to the public library to read Tolstoy. Few in his high school went out of state to college. But Starr had been an excellent student, and on graduation day, when his name was read off, someone mentioned that he was going to Harding College. "*Harvard?*" asked one of the city fathers, duly impressed. No, said Starr, embarrassed. Harding.

Harding was an institution in rural Arkansas, affiliated with the Church of Christ. Starr's older brother, Jerry, was an instructor there, but Ken didn't last long. He was doubtful about the church's interpretations of the Bible—its ban on alcohol, for example, even though wine abounds in the Scriptures. He wrote a column—"Starrdust"—for the college newspaper; angered by one of his efforts, Harding's president reprimanded Starr, offending his understanding of the First Amendment and underscoring his sense that Harding's worldview was too narrow for him. During his sophomore year, Starr transferred to George Washington University in Washington, D.C., where he sampled other Protestant denominations and even, for a time, considered becoming a minister like his father. In the end, however, he decided on a legal career.

Fresh out of Duke Law School in 1973, Ken Starr turned his attention from books to a real-life constitutional crisis: Watergate. He saw Richard Nixon as a study in the abuse of power, a politician who bent the presidency and the Department of Justice to serve his own interests instead of the rule of law Starr viewed as sacrosanct. Starr was clerking then in New Orleans for a Fifth Circuit federal appeals court judge. Many evenings after court, he and fellow clerks wandered into the French Quarter for a meal, after-dinner drinks, and spicy talk about the scandal of the day.

It was hardly the last time Starr was to witness the collision of politics and principle. After joining Reagan's Justice Department as an assistant to Attorney General William French Smith, for instance, he encountered the case of Bob Jones University. Under President Jimmy Carter, the Internal Revenue Service had taken away the school's tax exemption because of racially biased campus rules. It was just the kind of federal activism Reagan had campaigned against, and many in his Justice Department wanted to reverse the ruling. Starr bucked the prevailing opinion, arguing that the IRS was correct under the law. Political considerations won out, and Starr was overruled. (Eventually, the Supreme Court vindicated Starr's view, upholding the IRS.)

His years in the Justice Department did little to sharpen his political instincts. When the Reagan Justice Department was preparing to nominate Sandra Day O'Connor for the U.S. Supreme Court in 1981, Starr was charged with vetting her voting record as an Arizona state legislator. He did so with his customary thoroughness, and included a couple of O'Connor votes that could be interpreted as being in favor of abortion rights. But he failed to recognize the political ramifications of those votes and the complaints they would stir up among anti-abortion forces.

It was another example of the great divide between Ken Starr and Bill Clinton. Although both were trained in the law, it was as if they had apprenticed on different planets. Starr had nearly religious reverence for the rule of law. Clinton espoused a pragmatic, compromising approach to real-life problems. It was perhaps inevitable that Starr's absolutism and Clinton's realpolitik would violently collide.

The next time Starr crossed paths with Bill Clinton was in June 1992. Starr was traveling in Arkansas as Bush's solicitor general, and got to chatting with a state trooper assigned to drive him from a Hot Springs bar association meeting. The trooper, who often drove the governor, spoke of Clinton's informality and his easy way with voters. The governor preferred to be addressed simply as Bill, the trooper said. He liked to ride up front and argue politics with the trooper, who freely told "Bill" that he had voted against him for keeping law enforcement salaries so low.

But then the trooper launched into a detailed history of Clinton's "modern marriage" and his amorous adventures. Starr was astounded. The man who had emerged as the Democratic Party's all-but-certain nominee for president just a few months earlier had publicly denied Gennifer Flowers's claims of a twelve-year affair, casting her as a phony and a gold digger. And yet back home, it seemed, his extramarital transgressions were widely known and freely discussed.

Starr was troubled, both by Clinton's blatant philandering and by his dishonest denials. He thought of passing the information on to the Bush campaign, but he had promised the trooper that at least during the election season, he would keep his confidence. Starr mentally tucked the story away. Clinton was a complex figure, he thought, empathetic but manipulative to the core.

After Clinton swept the Republicans out of office that year, Starr left the Justice Department for the lucrative world of corporate law. But after only twenty months, he was called back to public service— to replace Robert B. Fiske, the independent counsel investigating the Clintons' financial ties to a savings and loan operator in Arkansas. Ironically, Starr had long opposed the law that allowed the appointment of independent counsels; in the Justice Department, he had led the fight to kill it. Privately, he called it "stupid, stupid, stupid," and described its creation as "malpractice by Congress." Although it was intended to ensure fair, arm's-length inquiries into wrongdoing in the executive branch, Starr thought it failed in fundamental ways, that its language was too vague. But he told associates that he would be in and out as independent counsel in short order. He fully expected the first couple to be cleared of criminal wrongdoing, and figured the task could be handled relatively quickly, certainly within a year.

The education of Ken Starr began as soon as he took the job. Just a few weeks before he left, Fiske had issued a report on the 1993 death of Deputy White House Counsel Vincent Foster, ruling it a suicide brought on by depression and job pressures. But when Starr arrived, he learned that Fiske had never been given what was arguably the most important clue to why Foster had taken his life: Foster's handwritten account of his anguish over the controversial firings of seven White House travel office workers, and the first lady's role in the affair. Fiske had relied on

White House lawyers to turn over relevant documents, and ended up issuing his report without all the evidence.

Starr and his team vowed to be less trusting of the Clinton White House. And sure enough, the Foster notebook was just the first in a succession of elusive documents that the White House only was able to find long after they were sought. They included a White House memo naming Hillary Rodham Clinton as the inspiration for the travel office firings despite her earlier denials and, even more explosive, billing records from the Rose Law Firm that showed she had worked sixty hours on a Little Rock savings and loan development project rife with fraud. Mrs. Clinton had said in statements to investigators that she did not recall working on the project, but the records turned up—eighteen months after they were subpoenaed—in her own book room in the executive mansion.

Each time an important piece of evidence surfaced belatedly, it deepened the belief in the Office of the Independent Counsel that the Clintons were skating the edge of criminal obstruction, or worse. The night the billing records were found, the Clintons' personal lawyer, David Kendall, insisted they be copied before they were turned over to Starr. Deputy White House Counsel Jane Sherburne objected. She was a no-nonsense lawyer who had come to government from the world of internal corporate investigations. Starr would want to fingerprint the records, she argued. Copying them could muck up the evidence. But Kendall would not back down. The records were copied that night. Overnight, the OIC's distrust of the White House deepened. There were bitter jokes about how Kendall thumbed through the records over a bucket of fried chicken.

But it was in Arkansas that Starr's misgivings about the Clintons reached full bloom. Starr's inquiry infuriated the state's powerful elite—the few hundred lawyers, judges, bankers, and poultry magnates who run most everything of consequence, including the Democratic Party. The investigation was training a harsh spotlight on the cozy relationships and conflicts of interest embedded in Arkansas business circles, and those in the glare didn't like it.

Starr and his team worked the hostile territory in isolation, behind drawn blinds in a gray brick building in West Little Rock they called "the Bat Cave." Combination locks secured office doors, cameras scanned the hallways. At day's end, the legal team took refuge in a garden apartment complex that became a second compound of sorts.

Their work was fruitful. The investigation led to a guilty plea from Webster Hubbell, a former Little Rock mayor and state Supreme Court judge the city had proudly sent to a top job at the Clinton Justice Department. The independent counsel then brought bank fraud charges against the sitting governor of Arkansas, Jim Guy Tucker, along with the Clintons' partners in the Whitewater real estate venture, Jim and Susan McDougal.

Hubbell liked to say, "It's not a conspiracy, it's Arkansas." But Starr came to think otherwise, thanks in part to Hubbell himself, who had embezzled hundreds of thousands of dollars from his Rose Law Firm partners and clients. Prosecuting Hubbell became one of the first big decisions for Starr, who was eager to look fair. The hulking former Arkansas Razorbacks offensive tackle was friendly and well liked. But he was also a manipulator, and he ended up suckering Starr.

A few months into his tenure, the independent counsel stood with him in court as Hubbell tearfully admitted guilt and agreed to cooperate in the Whitewater investigation. As Hillary Clinton's law partner, he was in a position to know a great deal about her legal work with the McDougals' S&L. Starr believed that Hubbell's remorse was sincere, and he treated Hubbell gently. He did not require that Hubbell state in advance what he knew about Whitewater as part of his plea deal, though requiring such a "proffer" is standard practice. He made the mistake of deferring to his high station as a friend of the president.

It was a blunder that would reverberate for years to come. Hubbell ended up offering prosecutors plenty of conversation, but little useful information. His failure to cooperate was a serious setback. Starr took from the encounter the same lesson he was learning in the Washington phase of his work: He should treat the Clintons and his associates as he would the subjects of any criminal inquiry.

His suspicions were heightened when he learned that while Hubbell was negotiating his plea agreement, he had been pocketing big checks from Clinton friends and Democratic Party donors. The money—some $600,000—was lined up by Clinton friend and Washington super-lawyer Vernon Jordan and White House Chief of Staff Thomas (Mack) McLarty, among others. For little or no work, Hubbell, disgraced as he was, raked in nearly three times more than he had earned legitimately in any year of his life. Was this hush money to buy his silence about the Clintons? Starr hauled Hubbell's benefactors before the grand jury in Little Rock, where they explained that they simply were pitching in to help a fellow in trouble.

Increasingly, Starr felt he was up against an infernal system. OIC lawyers and FBI agents continually encountered uncooperative witnesses, some hostile, some fearful. They came to believe that in Clinton's Arkansas, everything seemed geared to protect the former governor and his wife—from the local courts and prosecutors' offices to the federal judiciary.

Starr's prosecution of Tucker exemplified the problem. The presiding federal judge, Henry Woods, was one of Hillary Clinton's mentors and had been a guest in the Lincoln Bedroom. Yet he did not bother to recuse himself when he was assigned Starr's first case against then-Governor Tucker. Instead, Woods threw out the indictment in a sweeping ruling that Starr had exceeded his jurisdiction. An appeals court disagreed, and stripped Woods of the case, citing an appearance of bias in his White House connections.

From Starr's point of view, he encountered Clintonism everywhere he turned. When the OIC took Tucker and the McDougals to court in a second case—in which Bill Clinton testified for the defense—the Little Rock district attorney, under pressure from local Democratic politicians, nearly upended the prosecution by vowing to arrest Starr's key cooperating witness. Another Starr witness was fired from his municipal job. A third met with the Clintons' Washington lawyer, David Kendall, who was offering legal assistance and informal advice to witnesses interested in resisting Starr's probe. And during the trial, Kendall made no secret of his support for the defendants who potentially had the most information about the Clintons.

He dined openly with Susan McDougal and her counsel and provided assistance to Jim McDougal's lawyer.

To see the president allied with the McDougals, criminal defendants in a duly authorized federal investigation, outraged Starr and his team. They saw how Clinton clung to defendants like Hubbel and how he did not fire White House lawyer Bruce Lindsey in 1996 when a federal judge made an evidentiary finding he was part of a criminal conspiracy. Given his duty as chief executive to faithfully enforce the law, Starr thought, his loyalty to such miscreants was reprehensible.

The OIC lawyers also came to believe that the Clintons were ruthless. They operated like a crime family, expecting friends and aides to protect them even against their own best interests. Susan McDougal was Exhibit A. She spent eighteen months in jail on a contempt citation rather than tell a grand jury whether President Clinton had testified truthfully at her trial. Despite written entreaties from Starr, Clinton would not ask her to break her silence. She never talked.

By the end of 1997, Starr had arrived at the view that Clinton's conduct was lawless, his presidency a colossal moral failure. But his multiple investigations of the Clintons were drawing to a close and by summer, he was expecting to be back in private life.

At 1600 Pennsylvania Avenue, hatred of Ken Starr was pervasive. The president himself railed about the independent counsel, telling aides that he was an ambitious, none-too-bright captive of the right wing, totally out of step with modern society—a sanctimonious fraud out to destroy the administration.

James Carville, father of the campaign war room, had wanted to go after Starr as soon as he was appointed, to denounce him publicly as a right-wing hit man put in place by a judge who was a protégé of Republican Senator Jesse Helms. But calmer voices prevailed, at least initially. White House Counsel Lloyd Cutler said Starr had a sterling reputation as a federal judge and as solicitor general, and would probably be fair. In any case, it was madness to attack a duly appointed prosecutor with the power to wreak havoc. Even Kendall agreed, and he came from the Washington law firm of Williams &

Connolly, which was known for its hardball tactics with prosecutors.

But in early 1996, as the threat of Starr's probe hit home in the Tucker-McDougal trial and the discovery of Hillary Clinton's billing records, the strategy shifted. The first lady wanted to get tough. Starr had taken the unprecedented step of calling her before a grand jury to explain how her billing records had suddenly turned up. For her, the fight was intensely personal. The billing records, the travel office memo, the trial down in Arkansas—they were all big news, front-page stories for months. Starr not only posed a legal threat, his investigation also was a public relations disaster for the White House. She leaned heavily on White House damage control lawyers. Why can't you get negative stories out there on Starr? she demanded.

Deputy Chief of Staff Harold Ickes and other political aides came to agree with Hillary Clinton and Carville. Starr's investigations—Whitewater, Travelgate, Filegate—never ended. Starr, they were convinced, was a prig who felt he had a duty to rid the republic of the Clintons.

With Ickes as field marshal—and with the full endorsement of the Clintons—White House aides decided to make all-out war on the prosecutor. Ickes was a wiry blue-blood, a bracingly profane veteran of New York politics. He exhorted colleagues on his Whitewater damage control team, including Jane Sherburne and lawyer Mark Fabiani, to take Starr on. "This is a fight to the finish," he vowed. "We have to damage this asshole. Everything is fair game. All guns up and loaded." He assigned Eric Berman, opposition research chief at the Democratic National Committee, to dig up everything he could on Starr's personal background and legal work. Spare no expense, Ickes ordered.

Kendall, Cutler, and some of the other lawyers were still wary of a frontal attack. Kendall, in fact, forbade White House aides to say anything negative about Starr on the record. But behind the scenes, the lawyers helped mount a relentless campaign to wound Starr and cast doubt on the fairness of his work.

Carville organized his own Education and Information Project, which became anti-Starr central. Kendall helped him try to get information on Starr's probe under the Freedom of Information Act.

White House lawyers and senior aides faxed him ideas and materials. Soon, the research became part of Carville's political vaudeville routine, a slashing, mile-a-minute assault popular on the talk show circuit. The self-proclaimed "Ken Starr hater" pulled no punches. Starr is "one more mistake away from not having any kneecaps," Carville told the *New York Daily News*.

At the independent counsel's office, that sort of hyperbole seemed menacing. Starr had received so many death threats he needed protection by U.S. marshals. But the White House claimed to have no control over the pugnacious spin expert, even though Kendall's firm represented him, and Carville sometimes circulated advance copies of his attacks on Starr among White House aides.

One of Carville's favorite routines was tying Starr to Pennsylvania philanthropist Richard Mellon Scaife, who bankrolled many right-wing causes. Starr was "an extreme right-wing partisan," a foot soldier for Scaife, Carville claimed. Carville saw a conspiracy because Scaife had contributed to the Landmark Legal Foundation, a conservative litigation group, and Landmark had filed a brief in a case Starr handled as a private attorney for the state of Wisconsin. Starr was hired to defend the constitutionality of school vouchers, a postion also supported by Landmark. The alleged Scaife-Starr connection found traction in the media, especially after Starr announced his intention in 1997 to become dean of a new public policy school at Pepperdine University. A Scaife foundation had contributed to the new school.

In truth, Starr and Scaife had never met, and shared a mutual distrust. Scaife bankrolled journalistic ventures by far-right conspiracy theorists who believed Vince Foster had been murdered. He was contemptuous of Starr's conclusion that Foster died by his own hand. Starr believed Scaife was irresponsible, and the public suspicions he had stirred up unnecessarily dragged out his probe. Starr even thought Scaife might try to scotch his job offer from Pepperdine. As it turned out, a public furor erupted over the idea that Starr planned to quit before his investigation was complete—a furor the politically shortsighted prosecutor failed to anticipate. Ultimately, Starr said he wouldn't take the job.

Some Clinton aides mounted private campaigns against the independent counsel. Ex-journalist Sidney Blumenthal knew how to find a media outlet for virtually any assault, then used those stories to prod mainstream reporters into following up. "I can get that story placed," he would tell White House colleagues. One journalist who fed on anti-Starr stories was Little Rock columnist Gene Lyons, who passed information up the line. In one e-mail he sent to Carville "for your amusement," he said he had heard from a local lawyer who "assured me with the certitude people always bring to these things that KENNETH STARR HAS A HONEY right here in town." Starr was so straitlaced that the idea was preposterous, yet the rumor was whispered to reporters by Clinton allies.

The White House was more successful in its stealth attack on Starr for representing Brown & Williamson, one of the tobacco giants at odds with the Clinton administration's Justice Department. Armed with Democratic Party research, the White House persuaded many people that this represented a conflict of interest. As always, the Clintons were greatly aided by Starr's own public relations missteps, especially his refusal, against the advice of friends and colleagues, to quit his private legal work.

Even more critical than the campaign to discredit Starr was the legal face-off. For that, the White House adopted the tactics of modern corporate warfare: delay, obfuscate, and, most of all, litigate. To the public, the Clinton forces presented a show of weary cooperation with Starr's probe. But inside the White House, there was mighty resistance.

Every legal argument that could be made was made. Kendall and Hillary Clinton agreed that they should give nothing to Starr they didn't have to. "If they want it," Kendall would say, "they can litigate for it." They found like minds in two White House lawyers who had the confidence of the president. Bruce Lindsey, Clinton's secretive confidant from days in Arkansas, advised others not to give investigators an inch. He worked in tandem with Cheryl Mills, a bright but inexperienced young lawyer who infuriated colleagues with her sharp edges and snap judgments. These—along with Blumenthal, who brought intellectual airs to the mix, as well as a taste for below-the-belt attacks on political enemies—were the White House extremists, the "Hezbollah Faction."

Some of the more politically attuned lawyers, including Ickes, Fabiani, Sherburne, and later Lanny Davis, thought stonewalling was counterproductive, dragging out the investigation and enraging the prosecutors. It was better, they argued, for the White House to put out information on its own timetable and in its own way.

But as Starr subpoenas flowed in, the straight-arm strategy gained wider support. Contempt for prosecutors ran deep, and even prudent lawyers like Sherburne adopted what Ickes approvingly termed a "foot-dragging, fuck-you attitude" toward subpoenas.

By January 1998, a certain triumphalism was beginning to build. They had all but vanquished the independent prosecutor, the Clinton forces believed. Starr was not going to be able to take this president down. The endless Whitewater probe was going nowhere. There was every sign that investigations into the travel office firings and the mishandling of FBI files on White House personnel were going to end without indictments. The various ethics hearings in Congress were either over or hopelessly mired in minutiae.

Bill Clinton, who had easily won reelection fourteen months earlier, seemed to be on a roll. If he could just get past one last nettlesome problem, Paula Jones's lawsuit claiming he had made a crude pass at her when he was governor of Arkansas and she was a state clerk, perhaps he could put all the scandal behind him.

Despite the combat he was engaged in, Ken Starr remained outwardly calm and optimistic. But in truth, he was outraged by the White House's criticism of his probe as a vendetta. It was wildly improper, he told a former Justice Department colleague, for the president to say Starr was out to get him. If the Clinton administration can show I'm motivated by malice, he said, the attorney general should fire me.

Starr told one confidant that the worst thing about his position was its utter loneliness. Because of the secrecy of his work, he could not talk about it even to Alice, the wife he had been close to for twenty-nine years. Often, when she asked about negative stories in the press, he would say, "I don't want to talk about it," and simply shut down.

He believed in his own rectitude, and thought being unpopular was an unpleasant byproduct of doing his job. He admired, and often invoked, figures like Abraham Lincoln and Winston Churchill who had braved public scorn for doing what had to be done.

He did not realize how important it was that before the Lewinsky investigation even began, thanks in large part to the White House, he was already widely seen as a sworn enemy of the president, as a real-life Inspector Javert pursuing his prey. He did not recognize how critical public opinion is to the work of a prosecutor, whose success depends, above all, on the citizens' trust.

2

"WE HAVE SOMETHING
VERY SENSITIVE"

JACKIE BENNETT, Starr's deputy, was working late in OIC head-quarters on Monday, January 12, 1998. At 9:15 P.M., the phone rang. Stay put, he motioned to Stephen Binhak, a young prosecutor sitting across the desk. Bennett listened intently, then waved FBI agent Steve Irons into the room. Bennett's bushy black eyebrows dance when he's on to something big. Now they were in full jitterbug.

"So, let me get this right," he said slowly into the phone. "You've tape-recorded calls from a woman who had an affair with the president. She's lied about it in the Paula Jones case and is trying to get you to lie about it. People are helping her get a job to buy her silence. And Vernon Jordan is involved in it."

Binhak and Irons were as intrigued by Bennett's intensity as by what they heard of the conversation. Bennett had too much experience to get worked up about every tip that came in off the street. What Irons and Binhak didn't know was that their boss had been expecting this call. Fellow prosecutor Paul Rosenzweig had gotten the tip several days earlier from a law school friend, who had heard it

17

from a woman he did not name. Rosenzweig had gone to Bennett the previous Friday. "Is this something we'd be interested in?" he asked.

At first, Bennett demurred: "We can't have hearsay." But he kept turning it over in his mind. Pretty damn good lead, if true, he thought—more detailed than most of the wild tales that had come in over the transom. It wasn't ancient history like most of them, and it was consistent with what prosecutors had learned about how Clinton behaved and how his friends maneuvered to clean up after him. Most intriguing was the mention of Jordan, Washington's Mr. Fix-it, a seeming echo of his role with Web Hubbell.

By late Friday, Bennett decided to at least put his boss on notice. He called Starr in Aspen, where he was attending a bar conference, and told him "something's come up, but I don't want to talk to you about it on the telephone." Starr had learned he could trust Bennett's instincts. And that Monday morning, Starr, Bennett, and Mary Anne Wirth, a seasoned prosecutor viewed as the OIC's house liberal, had listened as Rosenzweig repeated the story.

Starr often joked about all the bum steers he could collect just by setting up a stand at the Little Rock airport. But this tip might be worth pursuing, he said, if the woman who had the information came to them. They should not go out chasing this story. Rosenzweig should let his classmate know that if the woman wanted to talk to Starr's team, she should call Bennett directly.

Bennett stuck around to take her call, and ten hours later, she was on the phone. She didn't identify herself at first. She spoke in hypotheticals. "Let's say," she began, "that I've got this friend who is a potential witness in a civil suit involving the president, and she knows about the president having an affair with a woman, and they're trying to get my friend to lie about it. And let's say she tape-recorded some of this stuff and it's illegal to do so in Maryland."

Jackie Bennett heard her out. If all the caller wanted was assurance that the tapes would not be used against her, that was a no-brainer. "If what you say is correct," he said, ticking off the key details—Oval Office romance, job for silence, Jordan at center stage—"the federal government will happily immunize those tapes." Immunity cost the government nothing, since there was no federal law against secretly recording conversations. Seizing the tapes would hinder prosecution by the state of Maryland, which is what the woman was apparently trying to achieve. Bennett was happy to help her ward off trouble there. He was fixed on what sounded like federal crimes: subornation of perjury, witness tampering, obstruction of justice.

To open any investigation, the OIC would have to establish jurisdiction. Jordan was the obvious hook. His activities were already under scrutiny in Starr's investigation into the payments to Hubbell—payments prosecutors suspected were intended to buy his silence. Jordan had arranged a $100,000-a-year consulting fee for Hubbell with MacAndrews & Forbes Holdings, a conglomerate where he served on the board of directors. The caller was saying Jordan had lined up a job for Clinton's girlfriend at Revlon, a MacAndrews & Forbes subsidiary. There was a striking parallel to the matter already under investigation. Who could question the right to go forward?

But Bennett wore too many scars from battles with the Clinton White House to take anything for granted. Then the caller handed him the silver bullet. "You guys know me," she blurted, warmed by the blanket of immunity thrown over her tapes.

Her name was Linda Tripp. She had been a secretary in the White House counsel's office when Vincent Foster died. In his investigation of the death, Starr had called Tripp as a witness. "You guys didn't ask me all the right questions in grand jury and these lawyers I've got wouldn't let me tell you everything," she told Bennett.

Here was another way to establish jurisdiction for this new sex-and-cover-up story. Starr was still looking into one of the controversies that might have driven Foster to suicide: the mass firing of workers in the White House travel office. Tripp was saying she knew more than she had told about the matter. She claimed to have relevant information, and now someone was leaning on her to commit perjury.

Tripp said that because of the pressure—from a woman she identified as Monica Lewinsky—she had begun taping phone calls to protect herself. But since both she and Tripp had been subpoenaed to give depositions in the Paula Jones case, Lewinsky had been worried about tapped phones, and now saved her confidences for face-to-face chats. Tomorrow they were to meet for coffee, Tripp said. Her lawyer had connections in the intelligence world and knew someone who could wire her for the meeting.

Bennett didn't like the idea of Tripp's playing detective. He feared the freelance taping would be bungled somehow, or questioned later as tainted evidence. The FBI should handle it, he thought. But he still hadn't set eyes on the informant, and he didn't remember her. He leaned into the phone. "Okay, we've gotta meet. We've gotta meet tonight." He got directions to Tripp's home. It was 10:30 P.M.

The prosecutor then dialed Starr at home in Virginia. Rosen-zweig's informant had called, he reported, and presented compelling details of an ongoing crime. "I think this is for real. We're going to go out to her house right now."

It was the first time in years of investigating Clinton that they had come upon a potential crime as it was unfolding. Starr thought his deputy must have been convinced of its legitimacy to rush out so late at night. Bennett saw a rare chance to gather evidence quietly without anyone knowing, the undercover work prosecutors thrive on. But he knew it would come at a high cost. They would be accused of treating the president of the United States like a mafia don. He was willing to take the heat for a rare snapshot of Clinton's world unobstructed by lawyers and spin doctors. He wanted to make sure his boss was, too. "We're really going to be criticized on this someday," Bennett cautioned.

If there was a single moment when Starr might have stopped and judged the wisdom of pursing sex-and-cover-up allegations against the president, this was it. He already had taken on four investigations of the Clintons, giving him the public image of a permanent hunter of the first family. His years of clashing with the White House had left him with a well-informed, though largely negative view of the president. He might have asked himself if the time had come to pass along the new and volatile charges to someone else. But he didn't. He saw only the task before him, weighing the investigative merits, not how they would play.

Go ahead, he told Bennett.

Bennett grabbed Binhak, Irons, and the office's chronic night owl, Sol Wisenberg, for the ride out to Tripp's home. On the surface, they were a motley crew: Bennett, forty-one, a tough-talking Hoosier from blue-collar stock, apolitical but vaguely Republican in outlook; Binhak, thirty-three, a cocky Ivy Leaguer from New York who had twice voted for Clinton; and Wisenberg, forty-three, a wisecracking assistant U.S. attorney on loan from San Antonio who claimed to be the only Jewish reactionary in Texas. But they were kindred spirits in prosecutorial philosophy, hard-liners who believed justice should be tough and administered evenly across the board. They were the nucleus of the office's unyielding "Likud Faction." Clinton challenged their professional pride: He flouted the rules, and maybe even the law, and despite all their efforts, he kept getting away with it. Irons fit right in. He had been the supervising agent assigned to Starr's office through the difficult investigative years in Little Rock, where he was based.

As the van headed north to Tripp's suburban home, Bennett briefed his crew. Binhak was skeptical. Wackos called in all the time with stories about the president. But he had learned as a federal prosecutor in Miami that you have to listen to them, never knowing when one will pay off.

At 11:15 P.M., the Starr aides pulled into Tripp's driveway on a cul-de-sac in Columbia, Maryland. They found a middle-aged woman with a mop of blond hair and a raspy voice. For ten minutes they sat in her antique-crammed living room making small talk. Then, between drags on one cigarette after another, Tripp led them through a drama of potentially stunning consequence.

The leading lady was Monica Lewinsky. Her dalliance with the president had started during the government shutdown of November 1995, when she was a twenty-two-year-old intern at the White House. Soon, Lewinsky had a full-time job in the West Wing, then was shifted off to the Pentagon, where she met Tripp. The two became friends, and Lewinsky shared the secret of her relationship with the president.

Starr's team listened in fascination as Tripp described Lewinsky's lovesick obsession with the head of state and their assignations in a study off the Oval Office. Tripp also recounted efforts by Clinton, Jordan, and Lewinsky to thwart the Paula Jones lawsuit. Lewinsky had been ensnared in the case when Jones's lawyers set out to find other women who might have been propositioned by Clinton in the workplace. On December 19, 1997, she had been subpoenaed for a deposition five weeks later.

The next part of Tripp's narrative got the full attention of her guests. Clinton, Lewinsky told Tripp, had advised a strategy of "deny, deny, deny." Jordan had taken a keen interest in Lewinsky's career and her legal problems, lining up job interviews for her in New York and taking her by limousine to meet a lawyer. Lewinsky had decided to ignore a subpoena from the Jones lawyers for personal items, Tripp reported. One of these especially piqued the prosecutors' interest: a photograph of Lewinsky and Clinton, which Lewinsky treasured as a reminder of an Oval Office romp. In the picture, she wore a navy blue dress that she told Tripp had been stained with Clinton's semen.

Tripp had been subpoenaed by the Jones lawyers to answer questions about a woman named Kathleen Willey, a White House volunteer who supposedly had been groped by Clinton. But Lewinsky worried that the Jones lawyers would ask Tripp about other women, including her. She had urged Tripp to lie for her own protection. If she didn't, Lewinsky warned, Tripp might lose her job as a political appointee in the Pentagon press office—and if Tripp's story didn't jibe with what Lewinsky and Clinton were saying under oath, Tripp might be accused of perjury.

Tripp said she had recorded dozens of conversations on twenty tapes in case she needed to prove her version of events. Now the Jones lawyers wanted to depose her, she said, and she feared they would subpoena her tapes, making them subject to discovery by Clinton's lawyers.

Investigators listened for more than two hours. Jackie Bennett grew concerned when he heard that Tripp had given the only set of tapes to Kirby Behre, a Washington lawyer who had represented her earlier in the Starr probe. Tripp said she had become suspicious of Behre when he suggested they share the tapes with Clinton's attorneys.

The meeting ended when Tripp repeated her plans to meet Lewinsky for lunch the next day. Investigators asked if she would wear an FBI wire, and she readily consented.

At 2 A.M., the four men piled back into Wisenberg's van for the trip back to the office. Among them they had decades of experience sizing up witnesses, and they'd just left one who seemed rational and straightforward. As they got on the road, the questions flooded out. "Is she for real? Are we getting set up?" asked Binhak. Bennett was looking ahead. "What do we do next?" he said. Wisenberg, the chronic worrier, said, "How do we make sure we don't screw it up?" They joked about what they'd tell a cop if he pulled over the van and asked where they had been. They had the blood-rushing sense of being on top of something big, breaking, and known only to them. For the first time they were gathering evidence secretly on a president who had stayed a step ahead of investigators for three and a half years.

Binhak, for one, felt overwhelmingly anxious. If Tripp was telling the truth, he thought, the implications were staggering, both for prosecutors and for the president. He realized the public would probably not distinguish the sexual aspects of the case from the criminal. Starr and his prosecutors would have to labor under that burden, he knew.

Irons asked how much he should reveal to FBI headquarters when he put in his request for emergency help. "Say no more than you need to, but enough to get this done," Bennett advised. He knew FBI director Louis Freeh would support the operation. "If it means you have to go to Louis at three o'clock in the morning, do it," he added.

Back in the office, Irons called the bureau's twenty-four-hour duty officer. "We have a very sensitive matter and we need your best people," he said. "And by the way, we need them in a few hours." A few hours later, Bennett briefed Starr. Starr gave his go-ahead for the undercover operation.

* * *

Linda Tripp was nervous when she arrived at the Ritz-Carlton Hotel near the Pentagon to meet the FBI. She felt conspicuous as she walked through the lobby. Is everyone looking, does anyone know? she fretted. In a room upstairs, a female agent taped a microphone to Tripp's inner thigh. Tripp handed over a photo of Lewinsky to help agents identify her. The agent said she had her own plans to photograph Lewinsky. Tripp panicked when she saw the camera lens sticking conspicuously out of the agent's handbag. The agent reassured her that Lewinsky wouldn't see it from a distance, but by then Tripp was drenched in sweat. This was "horrifying," a "Grisham-like experience," Tripp would write in her diary. She was terrified, she wrote, but went forward because she thought "it was the right thing to do."

Tripp worried that she would ask the wrong questions or that she'd be caught with the taping device. "Hope I don't let you down," she said as she left to meet Lewinsky in the piano bar downstairs. FBI agents watched from the lobby as the women took a table. In the room upstairs, more agents were set up to listen in and record the encounter. But the equipment that allowed them to hear the conversation as it unfolded malfunctioned. Alarmed, the agents could only pray that the conversation was being recorded. "We're flying blind," one of them told Jackie Bennett in a call to Starr's office. Two FBI agents posing as regular diners were quickly dispatched to a table near Tripp and Lewinsky and strained to hear what they could. They relayed assurances to the hotel command center that Tripp was steering the conversation as planned. "You guys are going to be happy with this," an FBI agent told Bennett. But there was no guarantee anything was being captured on tape.

Three hours later, Tripp summarized the discussion for FBI agents and Starr deputies. Then Wirth and colleague Bruce Udolf, a fairly new arrival to the office from a top job in the Miami U.S. attorney's office, drove her to her bus. They were suspicious of Tripp and her motives. On the way, they peppered her with questions that Tripp thought were intended to catch her in a lie.

* * *

As it turned out, the tape of the Tripp-Lewinsky discussion was intact. The recording was copied and sent to Starr's office Wednesday morning. Binhak was waiting with outstretched hands. He had spent the past few months working on the Hubbell payments issue and knew what to listen for.

Binhak lugged a scuffed-up boombox into his windowless office and ratcheted up the volume. The tape was hard to hear, but it bore out what Tripp had reported earlier, this time in Lewinsky's words. At each incriminating passage, Binhak scrawled notes on a yellow legal pad and flew into Bennett's office like a reporter updating his editor.

"Listen to this," he would say. "We're up to four counts of obstruction of justice, maybe conspiracy." He knew the evidence was hardening. Tripp was a witness once removed; Lewinsky was a participant with a direct tie to the White House. Not only had the president told her to deny everything, she told Tripp, he planned to do the same under oath when he was deposed by Jones's lawyers four days later.

She left no doubt how closely Jordan's job-hunting help was tied to her silence. Jordan had taken her to see lawyer Frank Carter "to make sure that I said what I was supposed to say," which Carter had drawn up an affidavit in her name denying sexual relations with Clinton. Jordan, she said, reassured her that "as long as you say it didn't happen, it didn't happen" and that "there's no way to get caught in perjury in a situation like this." But Lewinsky was no patsy. Before signing the affidavit, she wanted a job offer, a demand that she said she lofted into the Oval Office in a phone call to presidential secretary Betty Currie: "I'm not signing it until I have something."

The first strategy meeting in the Lewinsky investigation was convened late on Wednesday, January 14. The crew was small enough to fit around a conference table in a room at the far end of the independent counsel's labyrinthine offices. Starr was in his usual spot along one of the long sides. Bennett ran the meeting. His two "Likud" partners, Binhak and Wisenberg, were there as well as Rosenzweig. So were three assistant U.S. attorneys—Wirth, Udolf, and Michael Emmick—brought in in the previous year to review preliminary conclusions about earlier phases of the probe. More liberal and Democratic than many others in the office, they were genially branded the "Commie Wimps." Hickman Ewing, who had been responsible for the Arkansas phase of Starr's investigation, was on the speakerphone from Little Rock along with Robert Bittman, another deputy who was helping to wind up the work in Arkansas.

The FBI tape revealed what they saw as clear efforts to obstruct the legitimate processes of a civil case, a case in which the president was going to testify Saturday. From what they had heard, Clinton planned to lie under oath. But the prosecutors felt great trepidation. What Clinton, Jordan, and Lewinsky were trying to stifle was an extramarital affair. It may have been sleazy, it might have complicated Clinton's defense against the Jones suit, but it wasn't illegal. Starr's team had to decide whether the effort to derail a civil suit was a crime serious enough to justify going after a twice-elected president—especially when the cover-up was intended to protect actions that, in themselves, were seen by most people as private.

Wirth, forty-four, the senior woman in an office with few of them, voiced immediate concerns. She had prosecuted murders and other violent crime, including the terrorist killing of right-wing Jewish militant Meir Kahane in New York. But with her backpack and long blond hair, Wirth looked more like a folk singer than a prosecutor, and she had a tender streak. She was a devout Roman Catholic, extremely uncomfortable with the sexual content of the case. She worried about the office being accused of invasion of privacy. It was one thing, she argued, to examine the president's sex life in a perjury investigation, but quite another to expose a young woman like Lewinsky to such scrutiny. The case was a tar baby that would bring criticism and disrepute to the office, she warned.

"We're going to get killed for this," agreed Udolf. He was forty-five, a top public corruption prosecutor, a onetime rock guitarist. No matter how worthy, he said, the case would make investigators look like sex police. But he still thought the story needed to be investigated. He told colleagues that "we can go in and show that Linda Tripp is a nut, Monica Lewinsky is a nut, and all of this is bullshit, and we'll be heroes because we've shot this down."

Udolf wasn't the only one with such doubts. The only independent information the prosecutors had on Lewinsky at that point came from a 1991 *Los Angeles Times* article referring to her and other teenage girls who waited hours in a Beverly Hills hotel to get the autograph of a soap opera Lothario. Was she a groupie who had simply advanced to presidents? "We're putting our asses on the line," Udolf said at the meeting. "What if she's fantasizing and we're getting set up by these women?"

Bittman, a former state prosecutor in Maryland, argued that they should not be scared off by the inevitable criticism. As law enforcement officers, he said, "we have a duty to investigate ongoing crimes." The FBI tape was "good material," and this was a big case. He saw possible obstruction of justice, perjury, subornation of perjury, and witness tampering.

Binhak invoked basic justice. Paula Jones had the right to have the merits of her claim weighed by a judge or jury, not by the man she accused in her lawsuit. "The lowliest person in the country can sue the most exalted and get a fair day in court," said Binhak. "That's what this is all about."

Bennett said little. He had been weighing the unsavory sexual elements since Friday, when he had first heard Rosenzweig's tip. That day, he sought advice from his predecessor, John Bates, who had left the office in 1997. Bates, a highly regarded member of Washington's legal community, said that following up the allegations seemed justified, but urged caution. If it looks like a sex inquisition, he said, Starr will be attacked.

Bates spoke from experience. During his tenure, Starr had been harshly criticized after his agents questioned Arkansas troopers about Clinton confidants, including ex-girlfriends. The agents had hoped to learn more about Clinton's financial dealings from the friends. But the pillow-talk interviews were fodder for critics who accused Starr of prying into the president's personal life.

The attacks made everyone more sensitive to appearances. Someone asked if anyone from the Jones camp had ever contacted the office. Ewing recalled that one of her lawyers had known Starr at Harding College and when in Little Rock called for lunch. But he and Starr never hooked up. That was all. Or so it seemed at the time. What they didn't know was that the lawyer who initially tipped off Rosenzweig, Jerome Marcus, secretly had helped ghostwrite many of the briefs filed by the Jones attorneys. Rosenzweig knew only that Marcus had worked on a friend-of-the-court brief supporting Jones's argument that a president has no immunity from civil lawsuits, a constitutional question Starr himself had spoken out on years earlier.

Starr kept his own counsel during the long meeting. On big decisions he mentally donned his old judge's robes, trying to weigh things dispassionately. He almost always let someone else run meetings, preferring to listen to his lawyers debate. He would sip a giant Starbucks coffee, jotting notes and fielding a stream of phone messages ferried in by secretaries. Meetings like this could go on for hours, even all day, to the exasperation of some of the most seasoned lawyers, who wanted less talk and more action. But Starr wanted discussion. And while he might look like a Sunday school teacher—pink-cheeked and cherubic—he was an insistent and demanding boss. Younger attorneys especially took pains to prepare for meetings because he wanted to hear from everyone.

He was perfectly capable of making decisions by fiat, Starr told his staff. He was no Hamlet. But he believed the best decisions came out of the clash of ideas. He recognized, too, his own prosecutorial inexperience and sought the judgment of his veterans. His goal was to have the office come to a reasoned consensus.

This day Starr shared his staff's wariness. It might seem serious now, but what if Lewinsky were making it all up? Don't assume facts not in evidence, he reminded himself. "We need to keep peeling back the onion to make sure we understand all of the different layers," he told his staff. There was a collective sense that the office hadn't sought this new issue, but it was here and it couldn't be ignored or handled irresponsibly. This was an instance where he felt the need for higher guidance.

Starr had plenty of prompting. Emmick, forty-five, one of his most experienced prosecutors, argued that Attorney General Janet Reno ought to make the call. A smooth Californian with all-American good looks, Emmick had been chief of the public corruption section of the Los Angeles U.S. attorney's office and had taught prosecutorial ethics. "Run, do not walk, to the Department of Justice," Emmick pleaded. If the connection between Jordan's help for Hubbell and Lewinsky didn't pan out, he said, they'd look like they were just trolling around in the Jones case. "Somebody has to be with us in this," said Emmick, and DOJ would not be accused of being anti-Clinton. "We need cover if this goes bad."

Jackie Bennett was initially opposed to going to the Justice Department. The office had authority to look into matters "related" to those already under investigation. What could be more related than Jordan's role in this and the hush-money probe? But Bennett had another concern. He'd been a career prosecutor at Justice, and he didn't trust political appointees at the top. If the department was alerted before Clinton's deposition, he said, the odds of his hearing about it would rise astronomically. "Clinton always has the option of telling the truth whether or not he's being watched," said Bennett. But if he's predisposed to lie—as Lewinsky asserted—and was trying to get others to do the same, "why should he be entitled to a heads-up?"

Emmick had a persuasive reply. If the Lewinsky story leaked before Saturday, and the OIC was known to have been sitting on it, he told colleagues, they would end up with the worst of both worlds: Clinton would know he was under scrutiny, which would influence his testimony or decision to appear, and Starr would get clobbered for trying to set up the president.

Starr thought Emmick made sense. He had seen how quick defense lawyers were to argue that the independent counsel had no authority to investigate their clients. It was inevitable in this case, so he better be prepared. His office was a satellite spun off from the Justice Department "mother ship," as he called it. Reno should be notified, and it would be her call to drop the inquiry, give it to her assistants to handle, hand it off to a new independent counsel, or give Starr jurisdiction.

Bennett left the meeting momentarily and returned with a stricken look. He held in his hand an urgent message slip from *Newsweek* reporter Michael Isikoff. Tripp had already told them of Isikoff's past interest in the Kathleen Willey story, and now he was on the phone to the OIC. Isikoff might already know, Bennett told the group. Emmick's scenario—that the story would spill out and Starr would be accused of secretly setting Clinton up—suddenly seemed frighteningly possible.

The only question now was whom to call at the Justice Department. Starr, a stickler for protocol, said the right entry point would be Deputy Attorney General Eric Holder. Bennett had worked with him in the public integrity section years before and played pick-up basketball with him. Starr assigned his deputy to make the call.

As the meeting broke up, the prosecutors left with an uneasy feeling. "My God," said Udolf, summing up the moment. "I feel like I just got kicked in the nuts." Even Bennett, part barrister, part brawler, felt sick to his stomach.

3

"MY LIFE IS RUINED!"

WHEN DEPUTY ATTORNEY GENERAL Eric Holder got the first page from his old colleague, he figured the call could wait. But Bennett sent another about half an hour later, at 10:18 P.M., with the message "Urgent." Holder returned the call. "What's up?" he asked.

Bennett was sketchy. "We're sort of into a sensitive matter," he said, involving "people at and associated with the White House." He apologized for being vague. "No kidding," said Holder. Bennett asked for a meeting the next afternoon or evening. He asked Holder to keep it confidential. "Can I call the AG?" asked Holder.

Bennett: "I don't want to tell you not to."

Holder: "Jackie, this is Eric."

Bennett: "I know that, but this is dicey enough. I called you."

They agreed to meet Thursday, and Bennett let down his guard a bit. "I'll bring Bruce Udolf from Miami," he said. "We've played ball together." Holder hung up, mystified by the conversation. He reached Reno at about 11 P.M. and alerted her.

At 6 P.M. the next day, Bennett, Emmick, and Udolf were ushered into Holder's cavernous conference room. They sat down with Holder and an aide, and Bennett laid out the story. "There is inchoate criminality," he concluded. "It goes into the White House and very likely involves the president."

Bennett said Starr's office had a sound legal basis for everything it had done so far. But he wasn't looking for a Starr monopoly. The Justice Department could step in any time. Udolf added that the allegations against Clinton were not as clear as those against Jordan. But Jordan was not specifically covered by Starr's jurisdictional authority. "We welcome DOJ participation at this point," Udolf said. "If we get firmer evidence against the president, we could reconsider. We don't have strong feelings who, but someone needs to work the case."

If the story wasn't amazing enough, said Bennett, there was a "seriously complicating factor." Mike Isikoff had informed him that afternoon that he had the whole Lewinsky story from a friend of Tripp's and was planning to publish it in *Newsweek*'s next edition, which would be on newsstands Monday. His deadline was Saturday afternoon. Bennett had persuaded him to hold off making calls to the White House and Jordan that would expose the law enforcement effort. But, he said, "we have a very short window of opportunity to try to move this along."

Holder was stunned, but said little to the OIC team. He had plenty of front-line experience, as U.S. attorney for the District of Columbia and as a local judge. But he needed to think this through. There was no question someone had to investigate, and quickly. The undercover aspect, he thought, was absolutely critical.

Justice could not do it, Holder believed, because Reno was a Clinton appointee and the case involved Clinton. Could they get a new independent counsel in gear before Saturday afternoon? Clearly, they could not. Holder saw no alternative but to let Starr handle it.

After Starr's team left, Holder consulted with his chief of staff, Kevin Ohlson, who agreed. Ohlson also raised a concern about DOJ's own interests. If the department investigated and the case went nowhere, "everyone would say we purposely tanked it."

Holder walked across the hall to brief his principal deputy, Bob Litt. And that night he sent Josh Hochberg, deputy chief of the public integrity section, to Starr's office to listen to the FBI tape of Tripp and Lewinsky. While Hochberg was there, Starr intercepted him. If his office got the go-ahead from DOJ, Starr and his aides were planning to confront Lewinsky with the FBI tape. They hoped she would agree to go undercover to gather evidence against Jordan and Clinton. Starr wanted Hochberg in on the planning and execution of the approach to Lewinsky.

That evening Bennett stuck his head into Emmick's office to ask a question: Could they confront Lewinsky without her Jones case lawyer, Frank Carter, being present? Emmick, a nationally recognized expert on the right to counsel, said he saw no objection. Carter represented Lewinsky only in the Jones civil case; she did not yet have a lawyer in the criminal investigation. Even if she had, he argued, federal rules would permit a direct approach to her as long as she had not been indicted. Starr's team wanted to keep Carter out if possible. They suspected Carter of participating in a scheme to keep Lewinsky quiet. If she called him, he might tip off Jordan and blow any chance of undercover work.

The Justice Department would later raise questions about the way Starr handled the Carter issue. But Hochberg sat in on OIC meetings in which the issue was discussed. When the prosecutors considered how to dissuade Lewinsky from calling Carter, he did not object, and wrote in his notebook: "Helps to get Monica a new lawyer." Hochberg listened approvingly as plans were formed for confronting Lewinsky and getting her to secretly record others. He talked to his boss, Lee Radek, chief of public integrity, who registered no objection. "Lee—Okay to brace and wire," Hochberg jotted in his notepad.

Starr did not tell Hochberg that three years earlier he'd had several conversations with a lawyer named Gilbert Davis, who then represented Paula Jones. Davis had sought Starr's views as a constitutional scholar on the question of whether a sitting president can be sued. Starr believed he could be, although he had no sympathy for Paula Jones's case itself. He had spoken publicly on the issue before he was named independent counsel, and his opinions had been reported by the media. But in the crush of events in 1998, no one at the Justice Department or the OIC thought to bring up this history. When Jackie Bennett first briefed Holder, he made a point of saying "We've had no contacts with [Jones's] attorneys. We're concerned about appearances." Later, Starr would say the Davis connection never occurred to him. Davis himself had left the Jones case by then.

On Friday, January 16, Reno's top staff convened at 8:30 A.M. in her office dining room. Hochberg spoke first. He had worked through the night at Starr's office. He read from his notes, introducing Tripp and Lewinsky and highlighting segments of the FBI tape. "Monica says when she got notice of the deposition, she got nervous and called the president. He then said he would send Vernon to talk to her," Hochberg reported. He noted the Isikoff threat of publication and Starr's request for the Justice Department to okay his plans to confront Lewinsky.

The gravity of what they were being asked to do weighed heavily on everyone. Here they were, Clinton's law enforcement team, deciding on how to gather evidence that the president himself was a law-breaker. Everyone saw the allegations as serious enough to bring down the president. "This could lead to a constitutional crisis," Kevin Ohlson whispered to a colleague.

The meeting lasted just twenty minutes. Reno decided to ask the three-judge panel that oversees independent counsels to expand Starr's jurisdiction to specifically include the Lewinsky matter. Some of her deputies wondered whether this didn't reach far beyond Starr's original charge to examine the Clintons' financial dealings in Arkansas. But no one questioned his fitness to handle the job.

At 9:10 A.M., Lee Radek called U.S. Judge David Sentelle, chief of the three-judge panel, and said Reno wanted Starr to look into new, "specific and credible" allegations.

Linda Tripp had a new lawyer. She had fired Kirby Behre two days after calling Starr's office because she thought he might be close to the Clinton camp. Her new attorney, Jim Moody, was a quirky character. Legally blind, he had studied robotics and dolphin speech at the Massachusetts Institute of Technology before getting into law. Along the way, he did contract work for the CIA, the source of the cloak-and-dagger approach he brought to Tripp's case. He used the code name "Colonel Rose" when calling her, in case her phones were tapped by friends of the White House. When he picked up Tripp's tapes from Behre on January 15, Moody feared that he was being followed by "men in black." Too many people knew about the tapes, he fretted. If word got to Clinton associates, they'd have a strong incentive to deep-six them. Leaving Behre's office, he dove in and out of downtown buildings, entering through the front door and exiting through the rear.

Moody had a strong sense of the drama of the moment. In his first meeting with Starr's team the morning of Martin Luther King Day, he felt as if he was in the middle of *All the President's Men*. These are the kinds of crimes that people resign over, he thought. These are the kinds of crimes that are unacceptable for a president to commit.

His way into the Lewinsky case was a tale in itself. For much of January, Tripp had been frantic to find someone to replace Behre. She had been secretly informing the Jones lawyers about Lewinsky for three months and feared that they would subpoena her tapes. If they did, she figured, Clinton lawyer Bob Bennett would obtain them in the discovery process and she'd lose her Pentagon job. Even scarier was the prospect of prosecution for taping her friend. In December, Behre had told her that nonconsensual taping was illegal in Maryland, where she recorded Lewinsky. Tripp continued it anyway. New York literary agent Lucianne Goldberg, a friend who had urged her to tape Lewinsky as research for a book exposing Clinton's affairs, joined the search for a new lawyer.

Goldberg knew the Jones legal team in Dallas and their helper "elves," a network of conservative lawyers. Moody was a whistle-blower lawyer, and a friend of two of the elves—Anne Coulter, a conservative Washington lawyer and political commentator, and George Conway, a partner at Wachtell, Lipton, Rosen & Katz in New York. Moody was willing to take the case pro bono and they recommended him as the right person to represent Linda Tripp.

Although they all shared a common dislike for Clinton, Moody ended up working at cross-purposes with the Jones team's efforts to get Tripp's tapes. The Jones lawyers wanted them as evidence in their sexual harassment lawsuit. Moody felt to keep Tripp from losing her job and getting charged with illegal taping he had to avoid producing them in the Jones case. The independent counsel would be a shield from any Jones case subpoena.

Soon after Tripp met with prosecutors, Moody or one of the elves quietly passed on the news to the Jones lawyers in Dallas, so quietly that no one outside the small circle of Jones and Tripp advisors would know of the communication. In the days leading up to the Clinton deposition, the Jones team knew investigators would be highly interested in the president's sworn statements about Lewinsky. Starr's team, though, had no notion the elves network existed or that information was making its way back to the Jones lawyers.

Moody quickly ran into the same "complicating factor" the prosecutors faced. Tripp had been talking for months not only to the Jones camp, but to Isikoff. At the same time the reporter was calling Jackie Bennett, he was besieging Moody with messages and calls. He knew about the tapes and wanted to listen to them as evidence of Tripp's allegations. As his Saturday deadline drew closer, Isikoff became more and more threatening. He told Goldberg and Moody that unless he heard the tapes, Tripp would not be credible. "Don't you realize Linda is going to get clobbered if I can't prove how serious all this is?" he shouted over the phone to Moody. He was no less threatening in dealing with Bennett, warning that if he did not reveal some basis for intervening in the Jones case, critics of the OIC would have more reason to charge that Starr was out of control: "Unless you show me what you've got and establish the predicate for this, you're going to get roasted." The prosecutor begged Isikoff to hold off pursuing the story while the undercover investigation was in progress.

Moody himself barely had time to listen to the tapes. Thursday night, after retrieving them from Behre, he went to Coulter's apartment with Conway and played some of them on her stereo system. He made a copy of the one Tripp had recorded on December 22. Friday morning he delivered them, along with the copy, to prosecutors anxiously waiting to hear them.

Tripp was moving as fast as her lawyer. On Wednesday, Lewinsky had given her a ride home from work and handed her a typed, three-page document, headed "points to make in affidavit." It was a script for altering Tripp's account, reported in *Newsweek* the previous August, of what had happened between Kathleen Willey and Clinton. That night, Tripp handed the talking points to FBI agents. It looked like live evidence of witness tampering and subornation of perjury by Lewinsky. Tripp also told agents of two important developments: With Jordan's help, Lewinsky had been hired for a job at Revlon, and she had approved the affidavit drafted by Carter. The affidavit, said Tripp, had been "signed, sealed, and delivered." Prosecutors assigned her a new mission: Arrange a get-together with Lewinsky on Friday.

"The approach," prosecutor-speak for getting Lewinsky to cooperate, was crucial. If Starr's team had any hope of catching Clinton or Jordan in an ongoing crime, it needed Lewinsky's help. And it had to move fast to preserve secrecy.

The meeting was easy. Tripp arranged lunch with Lewinsky at the Ritz-Carlton. FBI agents would be waiting. The hard part would be turning her from Clinton intimate to informer. Starr and his aides brainstormed for two days. The strategy sessions were loosely structured, one continuous conversation carried on up and down the corridors and in half a dozen offices late into the night.

Binhak took the hardest line. In Miami's U.S. attorney's office, he had run stings on everything from drug buys to bribery, and he had a simple motto: Play by the rules, and no one can question your judgment. "If you have evidence that someone's broken the law, you should arrest them and charge them with the crime," he said in one hallway conference. Lewinsky had tried to suborn perjury with Linda Tripp. They had slam-dunk evidence of that. Binhak saw even more reason to follow tradition in Lewinsky's case, because whatever they did was certain to be minutely scrutinized.

But nearly everyone else favored a softer line. Bittman, who consulted from Little Rock, questioned whether the evidence was strong enough to arrest Lewinsky. Even if it was, he saw little advantage in jailing her. It might force her cooperation, but the publicity would blow any chance of going undercover. Starr wanted whatever it took to land Lewinsky's help, which he considered vital to ascertaining Clinton's role in any wrongdoing. She shouldn't be treated like a drug lord, he insisted. She was a pivotal witness who had to be induced to change sides.

The doves were put in charge of "Prom Night," as it came to be known. If anyone could turn an FBI encounter into a coffee klatch, it was the team of Emmick, Wirth, and Udolf, who had years of experience with witnesses. They considered what to do if Lewinsky balked at the approach: The agents could lay out the evidence, or they could have Tripp—again wearing a wire—take her aside for a heart-to-heart talk. Emmick would be the point person with Lewinsky. He was the guy who organized annual office outings and wrote poems for departing colleagues. He was also blue-eyed and handsome, and had a good bedside manner. He was the office nice guy.

At 11:30 A.M. Friday, Starr called his team—Emmick, Udolf, Bennett, Binhak, Wirth, and FBI agents Irons and Pat Fallon—to a meeting with Hochberg. They talked about what Emmick would say to Lewinsky and hashed over the Carter questions once more. A smaller group convened for a final session just before they left for the Ritz-Carlton. The group estimated it would take no more than thirty minutes to find out whether Lewinsky would cooperate. When they broke up around noon, Emmick huddled alone with Starr for one more question. It may be, he said, that she will refuse to cooperate without an explicit promise of immunity from prosecution. "Do we have the authority to offer immunity?" Starr said he would leave it to the discretion of the prosecutors on the scene.

Monica Lewinsky was still wearing stretch pants and a T-shirt from a morning workout as she entered the lobby of the Pentagon City Ritz-Carlton for her Friday lunch with Tripp. As she approached her friend, she was stopped by two FBI agents, who flashed their badges and asked her to go with them upstairs to discuss her "culpability in criminal activity" in connection with the Paula Jones lawsuit. She was not under arrest, they said, and she would not be required to make any statement. Lewinsky suggested they talk to her lawyer. The agents said the offer to discuss her legal status extended to her alone and urged her to listen to a proposal from Starr's assistants before deciding whether to cooperate or call a lawyer. She agreed to follow them.

On the way upstairs, Lewinsky realized Tripp had set her up. "Make her stay and watch," Lewinsky told the agents as they arrived in Room 1012. "I want that treacherous bitch to see what she has done to me." Lewinsky thought Tripp looked cold and indifferent, as if she were congratulating herself. Tripp recorded very different thoughts in her diary, which seemed penned for Hollywood. "I feel beyond terrible," she wrote the day before the encounter; Lewinsky is "more victim than Paula Jones," and the "emotional scarring will be permanent." Tripp was on hand in case investigators needed her, but the prosecutors quickly escorted her from the room.

Lewinsky was scared as she listened to Emmick, who was nervous himself. He sat in a chair across from her and started to explain why she was there. Tripp had recorded their conversations, he revealed. The tapes were now in the hands of investigators, and they contradicted her affidavit in the Jones case. Moody had provided that to prosecutors, too, having received a faxed copy from the Jones lawyers. With Tripp's help, the FBI also had recorded the two women at the Ritz-Carlton bar three days earlier. Emmick pulled out transcripts and photos to show her. "That's not me," Lewinsky said, studying the photos.

But Emmick pointed out those were precisely the words she had told Tripp she would use if ever confronted about her affair with Clinton. The FBI had it on tape. Emmick said she had done things that were wrong and had to think what she could do to help herself. He explained that if she did not cooperate, she could be indicted for perjury, witness tampering, conspiracy, and obstruction of justice—each carrying a maximum sentence of five to ten years in prison.

Suddenly Lewinsky began to wail. She sobbed loudly enough at times to be heard out in the hall. Emmick and the two agents in the room tried helplessly for the next hour to console her, bringing bottled water, tissues, and coffee. She would stop, bite her fingers or stare out the window trying to suppress her sobs, then begin bawling again.

"My life is ruined," cried Lewinsky. "Who's going to marry me after this?" The discussion was about to spin out of control. "All this will go away if I just kill myself," she wailed. Emmick tried to assure her the situation was not that dire. Irons, dubbed "Mr. Sensitivity" for his rough edges, found himself trying to persuade Lewinsky that that would only hurt her family and friends. Lewinsky's mood shifted from self-pity to self-defense. "Don't I have rights?" she demanded. Though she was not under arrest, an agent started to read Miranda warnings. She broke down in tears again.

Lewinsky's hysterics rattled the investigators, and had the odd effect of putting her in control of the room. Emmick tried to keep the discussion from straying too far from its purpose. He told Lewinsky there were various levels of cooperation, from telling what she knew, to testifying about it, to surreptitiously recording conversations. If she cooperated, he said, Starr's office would take that into account when deciding whether to prosecute her. He told her repeatedly that she was free to leave anytime.

The prosecutors had wanted Lewinsky to tape conversations with people close to Clinton, but they needed her help to figure out whom they should target. They would use anything incriminating they got on tape to move up the food chain toward the president. Starr's team knew from Tripp that Clinton was no longer returning Lewinsky's calls, and they thought Jordan was too shrewd to make incriminating admissions to her. They tentatively set their sights on presidential secretary Betty Currie. Tripp told them Lewinsky and Currie were friends. Currie knew about Jordan's job search for Lewinsky and the affidavit denying sexual relations with Clinton. Emmick identified subjects of the probe, including Clinton, Jordan, and Currie, but didn't single out any for bugging. He did tell Lewinsky she had to decide that night whether or not to cooperate. Isikoff had a Saturday deadline and would be calling people for comment, tipping off potential targets. "We need a quick answer," he told Lewinsky.

Lewinsky looked for negotiating room. She suggested she might be persuaded if her cooperation guaranteed no prosecution. Emmick resisted, saying they wanted to see how cooperative she would be. They had enough evidence now in the FBI tape and the "talking points" to prosecute her, he said. She was in no position to be playing the angles.

Two hours into the session, Lewinsky asked whether she could contact her lawyer. Emmick said she was free to call anyone, but that she could maximize her usefulness, and therefore gain the greatest benefit from cooperating, if she called as few people as possible, preferably no one. Irons speculated that Carter might call subjects to the probe. Emmick, the right-to-counsel expert, feared that could be interpreted as critical of Carter. He quickly headed off the discussion. When Lewinsky asked how she could get a criminal lawyer, someone offered phone numbers for the public defenders service and Legal Aid. She brushed them aside.

Time was flying by without progress. A worried Emmick consulted colleagues in the adjoining room and decided to give Lewinsky the incentive she'd been angling for: immunity from prosecution. "We're willing to offer you a guarantee, but what you have to do in exchange—just as we are taking a leap of faith—is promise complete cooperation." What about her mother?, Lewinsky asked. She had implicated her mother, Marcia Lewis, on the FBI tape as an accessory to the cover-up plot. Okay, said Emmick, they would grant immunity to her mother. He thought she'd leap at the offer. Instead, Lewinsky said she wanted to talk it over with her mother first.

Now the OIC team decided to change the dynamic. Jackie Bennett had come over from Starr's office. Famous for slashing interrogations, he was a formidable presence at six feet, three inches and 235 pounds. He was younger than Emmick, but his white mane made him appear more of an authority figure. "We're not going to sugarcoat it, Monica," he said in his Midwestern baritone. "This is serious. We have evidence of you committing various felonies. The only way you can help yourself is to cooperate."

Lewinsky was unmoved. She wanted to call her mother for advice. "You're twenty-four years old, you're smart, you don't need to call your mother," Bennett said. But Lewinsky persisted; she wanted to speak to her mother, and since she didn't trust the hotel phones, she set out for Pentagon City Mall, unaccompanied. On the way, she saw a familiar figure toting several shopping bags. It was Linda Tripp, her betrayer, calmly browsing as if she didn't have a care in the world.

"Thanks a lot," Lewinsky hissed.

Startled, Tripp lied. "They did the same thing to me, they did the same to me," she stammered.

Emmick got a little good news: Bennett said Isikoff would give them a bit of a reprieve; he was not going to make calls that could blow their undercover hopes until later that day or the next. Just as Emmick and the others were starting to make bets on whether Lewinsky would return, she showed up. She told Emmick she had reached her mother, who was "completely freaked out" and wanted to come down from New York to discuss the situation. She wanted Emmick to call her mother. He agreed. Emmick told Lewis what was happening and reluctantly agreed to wait for her to arrive. She would be taking the train. "I don't fly," Lewis said. Emmick was being worn down by inches, but he agreed to wait.

This wasn't going the way Emmick had hoped, but he needed to get Lewinsky on board and he was willing to accommodate her if he could. He conferred frequently in the next room with Udolf and, when she arrived late in the day, with Wirth. The three remained concerned that Lewinsky might have fabricated the entire story about an affair with Clinton. She hardly looked the part of a presidential paramour. Wirth said what they all felt: Something is not right here.

As they waited, Lewinsky remembered her lawyer. She was concerned that he might get an early start on the weekend and become unreachable if she decided she wanted him after all. An agent called Frank Carter's office. The lawyer was out of town, but his answering service could track him down if necessary.

Tedium set in about 5:30 P.M. Lewinsky, now feeling more in control, told a dirty joke. "Let's not go there," said Emmick. He turned on the television, but found only one cop show after another, each, it seemed, prominently featuring a snitch. He flicked again and settled on an Ethel Merman movie, *There's No Business Like Show Business.*

Lewinsky asked for coffee. Binhak ran downstairs to Starbucks and got her a cup. "If I knew you were going to Starbucks, I'd have asked for a latte," she told him when he returned.

Emmick and FBI agent Fallon took Lewinsky down to the mall, where they browsed at Crate & Barrel and had an awkward dinner at Mozzarella's American Cafe. When she insisted on paying for her own meal, Emmick took it as a bad sign. He was right. A little while earlier, Lewinsky had excused herself for the ladies' room at Macy's and was gone for twenty-five minutes. What Emmick and Fallon didn't know was that she had gone to a pay phone to call Betty Currie. There was no answer. Lewinsky was working both ends at once—trying to alert Clinton to Starr's investigation and at the same time get full credit for cooperating with the independent counsel.

Marcia Lewis, carefully coifed and bundled in fur, arrived at 10:16 P.M. She spent an hour with Emmick and Wirth, who laid out the evidence. Lewis knew of her daughter's infatuation with Clinton. She had been worried about it, and had encouraged her to find single men her own age. But she didn't see why anyone else should care. She demanded to know why Starr intended to make a criminal case of it. "What's the big deal?" Lewis asked Emmick. "So she lied and tried to convince someone else to lie." Lewis picked up negotiating where her daughter had left off. She asked Emmick to give Lewinsky immunity without doing any tape recording. Emmick said no.

Mother and daughter stepped into the hallway. They raised their voices a few times, loud enough so agents and prosecutors picked up some of what they were saying. Lewis saw clear legal danger for her daughter and urged her to cooperate, saying the prosecutors seemed reasonable. But Lewinsky was defiant. "I'm not going to be the one that brings down this fucking presidency," she yelled.

They returned and asked Emmick a few more questions. If the Paula Jones case was settled, would Starr's investigation go away? Lewis asked. Emmick said no. "What if I say I made it all up?" asked Lewinsky.

At 11 P.M., Lewis called her ex-husband in Los Angeles. She had alerted him before leaving New York, and Bernard Lewinsky had arranged for a lawyer to represent his daughter. It was his own lawyer, William Ginsburg, who was about to become the most famous medical malpractice lawyer in America. At first, Starr's team was relieved that after eleven hours of emotion, games, and stalemate, professional help was on the way. But when Ginsburg called at midnight, Emmick had new reason for worry.

Ginsburg listened to the evidence and the proposed immunity deal. "Oh, I didn't realize you were a judge," he said sarcastically, revealing his unfamiliarity with criminal law. Immunity arrangements are not just the province of judges. Emmick tried to explain and said the deal would probably be good for that night only.

"It's not in writing," said Ginsburg.

Emmick was getting frustrated. He said that four witnesses were enough to verify an offer had been made. "What do you want me to do? Go back to the office, type it in a computer, and fax it to you?"

Ginsburg said no. He couldn't decide without seeing the tape transcripts and consulting with his client. He said he would catch the first flight the next day.

Emmick had just offered a free-pass, good for one day—no charges, no trials, no penalty. Not even a "proffer" by her of what she would say in exchange for immunity. Lewinsky's new lawyer had walked away. There was nothing more Emmick could do. He told the women they could go. Both thanked him and the FBI agents for being considerate, and mother and daughter walked down the hall.

Postgame analysis began immediately in the adjoining room reserved for the backup crew. The prosecutors had lost the moment. Emmick briefed Starr, who, along with Hochberg, had received regular updates during the day but had been out of touch since the evening. Emmick presented a matter-of-fact rundown, with little emotion.

Emmick paced, cursing himself for failing to close the deal. His colleagues tried to reassure him. He had done the best he could, and Ginsburg was nuts for passing it up. But one thing was clear. The chance for undercover work was quickly slipping away. In a matter of hours,

Isikoff would begin making calls and the president would be deposed by Jones's lawyers.

Jim Moody had had a busy evening. While the prosecutors were tied up at the Ritz-Carlton, he and Wesley Holmes, a Jones lawyer in from Dallas, rode out to Tripp's house in Maryland. For weeks, Tripp had kept the Jones lawyers on tenderhooks. Now, on the eve of Clinton's deposition, Holmes was determined to interview her and get her tapes. When she left the hotel that afternoon, Tripp had told Binhak she was going to see a friend. Starr's team had no idea she was actually meeting a Jones lawyer.

When Moody and Holmes turned up Friday evening, Tripp served up pigs in a blanket and a few more tidbits about Clinton and Lewinsky. But she had no tapes. Moody told Holmes that, hours earlier, he had delivered them to the OIC.

Within an hour, Moody and Holmes were on their way back to Washington, where they planned to dine with Anne Coulter and George Conway. Instead, they went to Conway's room at the Four Seasons Hotel, arriving at 10 P.M. Holmes learned then that Lewinsky had been confronted at the Ritz-Carlton by Starr's team, and that they were hoping to get her to become a cooperating witness in their case. Moody disappeared into the bathroom to place calls to Tripp and to Starr's office. When he emerged, he pulled Conway aside and said he needed to meet with prosecutors.

The meeting took place at the Howard Johnson's across from the Watergate, the same motel where the Nixon plumbers had plotted their operation. Udolf had chosen it so that he could check on FBI agents who had set up a stakeout there of Lewinsky's mother's apartment. He hitched a ride with Bennett, and the two arrived in the Hojo's lobby around midnight.

Moody was waiting alone. Conway had spotted two men in suits, pointed the blind lawyer in their direction, then disappeared to the far reaches of the lobby, avoiding what he realized could look bad: contact between Clinton's prosecutors and a political antagonist working for Jones. Prosecutors wouldn't have known who he was even if they'd have seen him. Moody, Udolf, and Bennett headed for the back of the coffee shop. Udolf and Moody had met several times during the week to negotiate possession of the tapes, but Bennett was meeting him for the first time.

Udolf, still suspecting that Linda Tripp might be a right-winger trying to set them up, quizzed Moody about his background, asking how much criminal law experience he had and what organizations he belonged to.

But Moody's reason for being there was to get copies of the tapes he had given the OIC. He was legally entitled to them. And after several minutes of conversation, Udolf gave him the copy of the December 22 tape he'd provided that morning. When the meeting was over, Moody gathered up Conway. At 12:30 A.M., the two arrived at *Newsweek*'s Washington bureau and played the tape for Isikoff and his editors.

Did the prosecutors know what Moody planned to do with the tape? Starr's team knew the lawyer had been under pressure from Isikoff to certify Tripp's credibility. But the last thing they wanted was a story that would eliminate any chance of going undercover. Although Lewinsky had just slipped away, her lawyer had promised to be in touch the next day. There was still time to gather evidence behind the scenes.

On Saturday morning, a block-long motorcade left the White House to carry the president two blocks to the offices of his lawyer, Bob Bennett, plowing through a media horde that rivaled the crowd at O. J. Simpson's murder trial. Jones, a $6.35-an-hour state clerk when she claimed the governor dropped his pants and asked for oral sex, arrived by taxicab and was nearly crushed by the mob.

"I feel so proud to be an American, to know that this judicial system works, to know that a little girl from Arkansas is equal to the president of the United States," she said in a statement.

Upstairs, for the next six hours, Jones and her lawyers sat at a conference table with Clinton as he was questioned about the day in 1991 when, Jones alleged, he had propositioned her in a room at Little Rock's Excelsior Hotel. Federal Judge Susan Webber Wright had flown up from Arkansas to preside at the unusual session. Going in, the Clinton camp had told reporters the only question was how categorical the president would be about ever meeting Jones. He had flatly denied her sexual allegations, but he would acknowledge that his bodyguard might have escorted her to his suite.

Clinton's lawyers were fully prepared for the Jones questions, but there were more than they expected about another woman, Monica Lewinsky. She had first shown up on the witness list in early December, and the Jones lawyers told Clinton's lawyers she was a former White House intern the president had had an affair with. Clinton's lawyers found the claim utterly implausible. The idea that Clinton would have sex with a young employee in the midst of a sexual harassment lawsuit he'd fought all the way to the Supreme Court seemed ludicrous.

Bennett inquired about Lewinsky at the White House. Bruce Lindsey, Clinton's aide de camp for nearly two decades, said she was friendly with the president's secretary, Betty Currie. She had dropped off papers at the Oval Office a few times, and once a slice of pizza for the president, but there was nothing more to it. Lewinsky's own lawyer in the case, Frank Carter, had assured Bennett there was nothing between the president and the young woman.

So, after Jones lawyer James Fisher began his questioning of Clinton on Saturday, Bennett asked for a recess. He took Clinton, Lindsey, and White House Counsel Charles F. C. Ruff to his personal office. The Jones team hadn't laid a hand on the president, Ruff said. But he and the other lawyers agreed Clinton might still have to testify at a full-blown Jones trial if allegations of an affair with Lewinsky resurfaced. Why not close the loop today? They decided to introduce Lewinsky's affidavit, a copy of which Carter had given them. In it, Lewinsky flatly denied any sexual relationship with the president. Why not allow a few questions on Lewinsky to complete the record and dispense with her for good? Clinton agreed. He had read the affidavit.

Back in the conference room, Fisher resumed questioning Clinton about Lewinsky. Bennett interjected and told Wright of Lewinsky's affidavit, which, he fatefully pronounced, asserted that "there is absolutely no sex of any kind, in any manner, shape or form with President Clinton." Clinton, he said, was fully aware of the contents of the affidavit; they had reviewed it together before the day's proceedings. Clinton sat silently by his lawyer's side.

Wright allowed the questions on Lewinsky to continue and allowed the affidavit to be introduced.

Clinton was steadfast. He had seen Lewinsky when interns were running the White House during the 1995 government shutdown, he testified, but he couldn't recall any specific instance when they had been alone. He saw her again before Christmas 1997, he said, and may have made a joke about the Jones case. He wasn't aware that Jordan had talked to her about the Jones matter. He flatly denied any sexual contact with Lewinsky according to the definition given by the Jones lawyers at the outset of the proceedings.

The most detailed questions concerned gifts to Lewinsky. Did you give her a "book about Walt Whitman"? Fisher asked. It was one of the tidbits supplied by Linda Tripp just the night before. Clinton said he might have, but didn't remember. His memory improved somewhat as Fisher asked about an item from the Black Dog Cafe in Martha's Vineyard. Clinton said he shopped there on vacation and brought back gifts for the women in the office. He asked Currie to distribute them, he said, and "something" might have reached Lewinsky. Clinton stumbled for answers to oddly specific questions about Lewinsky as it became apparent that someone had been volunteering information to the Jones lawyers about him.

Bob Bittman called headquarters from his Little Rock office on Saturday morning. The Washington office was nearly deserted. Everyone had invested so much in Prom Night that its failure left them demoralized. Jackie Bennett was at home fielding calls from Isikoff and other reporters who'd heard vague accounts of what *Newsweek* was up to. Starr and Emmick were waiting for Ginsburg to arrive.

Everyone else had left for the weekend, including Udolf, who'd had to postpone a forty-sixth birthday bash in Miami so he could spend Friday with Lewinsky.

Bittman was peeved at the desertions. "Just because Monica wouldn't cooperate, the investigation doesn't stop," Bittman told Emmick when he finally reached him. He tracked down Wisenberg in San Antonio, where his family still lived. "What the fuck are people going home for?" he demanded. "We've got a lot of work to do."

Bittman, thirty-five, was stolid and organized, a Catholic school kid from Washington's wealthy suburb of Potomac. His father, William Bittman, had made a big name for himself prosecuting Jimmy Hoffa and LBJ aide Bobby Baker in the 1960s. Bob was looking for his chance, and had been maneuvering to get into the Lewinsky investigation from the first. Little Rock was winding up most of its investigative work, and the Washington office had only a dozen lawyers.

Bittman had immediately pitched in from Little Rock, reviewing Tripp's past grand jury testimony and FBI interviews for credibility and consistency. Solid marks on both, he told Washington. He asked the D.C. office to have the FBI "sting" tape and Tripp's personal collection of phone recordings flown to Little Rock for transcribing. Bittman drafted and faxed a subpoena that was served on Lewinsky Friday calling for a blue dress, computer files, tapes from her message machine, and gifts from Clinton.

Saturday morning, Bittman saw a vacuum in Washington and moved quickly to fill it. There was no investigative plan, so he drafted one and faxed it to headquarters. Tripp, he said, must be fully debriefed right away. Her tapes had to be studied and corroborated. Subpoenas had to be drafted and sent out. Calls to and from Currie, Jordan, and Lindsey had to be traced.

The next day, he boarded a plane with his transcripts and flew to Washington. He was close to Bennett and shared his prosecutorial philosophy. Emmick called Udolf in Miami and Wirth in New York. Better get back here fast, he urged—Bittman is taking over. The differences between the Likud Faction and the liberals were hardening.

*   *   *

On Monday, January 19, 1998, official Washington was in rare repose. The great halls of politics and justice had emptied for Martin Luther King's birthday, leaving the Pennsylvania Avenue power corridor as lonely as an empty battlefield. The town's long knives were sheathed, its sharp tongues silenced. Or so it seemed everywhere but Suite 490 of a modern glass tower six blocks from the White House, where the orderly world of Ken Starr was exploding.

Pressure had been building on Starr since Friday's failed approach to Monica Lewinsky. Ginsburg had not shown up Saturday as promised, but came in Sunday to hear the evidence against his client. He was planning to return with her Monday afternoon.

But Lewinsky's usefulness was fast fading. Early Sunday morning, Internet gossip Matt Drudge reported that *Newsweek* had spiked a story by Isikoff on Clinton's affair with a former White House intern. Drudge wrote that tapes of "intimate phone conversations exist." Monday, Drudge named Lewinsky as one of the women on the witness list in the Jones case. The item revealed enough to the president's associates to dash any hope of widening the OIC's undercover work. Still, as long as Starr's role was secret, prosecutors could lock down Lewinsky's story before Clinton's damage control specialists got there.

The bearded Ginsburg arrived at 5 P.M., Lewinsky in tow. He parked her in the lobby and joined Jackie Bennett, Udolf, and Emmick in a conference room. Among them, the three prosecutors had conducted scores of such "proffer sessions," which amount to auditions for people seeking immunity. Nothing had prepared them for Ginsburg.

Starr was standing by as the final arbiter. He avoided hand-to-hand combat, preferring to rely on the superior expertise of his more seasoned prosecutors.

Ginsburg wanted to pick up where Emmick had left off Friday night with an offer of full immunity. Emmick reminded him that the offer had been made when Lewinsky could still go undercover and had been taken off the table when Ginsburg rejected it. The terms had changed. Ginsburg's client was in trouble. To help cure it, Lewinsky would have to tell them everything about her relationship with

Clinton and what she knew of his efforts and those of his friends to throw the Paula Jones lawsuit off-course. She would get what criminal lawyers call a "queen for a day" letter, barring prosecutors from using against her anything she said in immunity negotiations.

Ginsburg knew more about surgical mishaps than he did about plea deals. He had brought along Nathaniel Speights, a criminal defense lawyer from Washington, but the Californian clearly was calling the shots. Ginsburg refused to submit Lewinsky for questioning until she received immunity from all charges or at least the promise of no jail time. He would stand in for her. If they had questions, he'd try to answer them after consulting her.

Bennett didn't like it. He went by the rule book, and one of the Justice Department's guidelines is that prosecutors should not make plea or immunity deals without a prior face-to-face discussion with the witness. But Emmick and Udolf were willing to make an exception to prevent Lewinsky from slipping away. This was perhaps their best chance to sign up the key witness in a case that would soon spin out of control. Bennett was quiet while his colleagues tried to square the circle.

Emmick lobbed a few questions to see how far Ginsburg would go in the role of middleman. Did Lewinsky have sexual relations with the president? Did Jordan try to buy her silence with a job? Did Clinton ask her to lie?

Ginsburg left the room to consult with his client. He returned after forty-five minutes with partial answers, which begot more questions. He did not answer the most basic question, which concerned sex with the president. Udolf tried a new tack. What about immunizing her, he suggested, but making the deal contingent on her passing a lie detector test? If she fails, the deal is off. Ginsburg seemed receptive. But Bennett had heard enough and asked to recess.

Tempers flared even before the prosecutors reached Bennett's office. Men with egos as big as their reputations, they all wanted nothing more than to "sign up" the ex–White House intern who might do for their investigation what John Dean did for Watergate. But they almost came to blows over the terms of bringing her in.

"Damn it, we're not going to buy a pig in a poke," shouted Bennett. The last place to abandon standard prosecutorial techniques, he argued, is in a case like this, where the facts were so fantastic and the stakes so high. Lewinsky had been heard professing her love for Clinton in the FBI tape. "Who's to say she'll come clean after she gets immunity?" he asked.

Udolf raised his voice just as loud. "You have to work with her," he said in the hard syllables of his native New York. "No witness will give you everything up front." He argued that the quickest way to test Lewinsky's credibility was with a lie detector. A scrappy man who carried the scalps of some of Miami's dirtiest politicians, he knew a first-rate polygrapher he could import for this. If she fails the polygraph, he said, "we'll confront her with the lies and bring her around."

"No," Bennett yelled, getting angrier as Emmick closed ranks with Udolf. "I don't trust her." She could flunk the polygraph, insist that she was truthful, and sue the office if it tore up the deal. "Everything we know about her is that she's deceptive and sympathetic to the president," Bennett argued. She sees the office begging for cooperation. Instead, "she needs to fear us," he said.

The language got harsher and more profane. Finally, Starr rushed in. Punctilious and soft-spoken, he rarely cursed, and nothing frustrated him more than hearing violent disagreement from the veterans he relied on to fill in gaps in his own training.

"Let's get Hickman on the phone," he said. Little Rock deputy Hick Ewing hadn't been directly involved in the week-old investigation, but he was the most experienced hand Starr had, and he might be able to mediate the dispute.

Bennett, whose gale-force energy fills a room, vetoed the idea. "We don't have time," he said. "Ginsburg is in the other room. The answer is no."

"We're supposed to be colleagues," Starr shot back, his face red. "There is a process, and the process is to hear people out. Let's get back to it." The injunction quieted the warring lawyers, at least for a while.

Bennett led the team back to the conference room, where the bickering resumed as they waited for Ginsburg and Speights to return. Unbeknownst to them, Ginsburg was eavesdropping, a few feet from the open door. He entered the room as confident as a legislator who had counted his votes. For ten minutes, he haggled as if he were brokering a financial settlement instead of terms for truthful testimony. Bennett finally had enough.

"I'm not comfortable with the way this is going," he said. "It's clear we're not going to make progress. Let's stop it right now and go home."

Ginsburg looked stunned and dejected. If he had promised his old friend and client, Bernard Lewinsky, that he would get his daughter off the hook, he had failed. Then, just as the long, draining day was ending, Udolf handed him a subpoena for Lewinsky's father.

"This is bullshit!" Ginsburg exploded, tossing the subpoena across the table like a Frisbee. A cup of coffee went flying. "Fuck you," he snapped, pointing his right hand like a gun at the prosecutors. "You've just made the worst enemy you've ever had. You want trouble, now you're going to see trouble."

The shouting carried into the lobby, where Lewinsky had been waiting for hours. Bob Bittman, just in from Little Rock, had joined her. They were discussing movies and life in Los Angeles when the conference room door flew open and Ginsburg charged out.

"Monica, we're going," he said. As the two headed for the elevator, Ginsburg said something in the young woman's ear. She burst into tears.

Emmick and Udolf stalked out of the office. They returned about 1 A.M. after a couple of beers to find Bennett still there. Round two of the dispute began. Bennett thought they were too eager to make a deal that could compromise the investigation of Clinton. Udolf, more outspoken than Emmick, saw Bennett and his hard-liner faction as ready to bully Lewinsky and blow the case.

"Look," Udolf said, "I believe in my bones you fucked this up tonight. You should've taken the deal. We could've gotten it. It was a good deal."

"I feel just as strongly in my bones," retorted Bennett. "We don't agree."

Starr went home that night filled with foreboding. Lewinsky's lawyer was more than boorish and threatening—he had put his client at risk of prosecution. There could be no quick and reasonable resolution now. Starr needed facts to reach the truth, and without Lewinsky, the way to get there in Bill Clinton's Washington would be perilous.

4

"DID HE HAVE AN AFFAIR?"

ON MARTIN LUTHER KING'S birthday, while Starr was secretly negotiating for Lewinsky's cooperation, Betty Currie was part of a White House search party trying to find her. At Clinton's direction, she had been paging Lewinsky, starting Sunday night and resuming at 7:02 Monday morning. "Please call Kay," she messaged. "Kay" was the code name Currie and Lewinsky had begun using in December, around the time Lewinsky had found out she was on the Paula Jones witness list and had started to worry about phone taps. Currie paged Lewinsky seven more times in two hours. At 8:44: "Please call Kay re: family emergency." At 8:51: "Please call. Have good news."

Vernon Jordan got on the phone himself that morning, paging Lewinsky three times. In fact, the man who days later would publicly portray his involvement as minimal made thirty-one phone calls that day—to Lewinsky, Clinton, Frank Carter, Betty Currie, Bruce Lindsey, and Cheryl Mills. In the afternoon, he went to the White House to talk to the president, urging him—even at this late date—to settle the Paula Jones suit. On the way out, he stopped to talk to Lindsey and Mills. "I gave it my best shot," he said. Jordan later testified that Lindsey and Mills knew about his job search on Lewinsky's behalf.

One insider who didn't know about it was Bob Bennett, Clinton's lawyer in the Jones case (and no relation to Jackie Bennett). He and Jordan had discussed the case and the need to settle it. Sometime around November 5, 1997, the day Lewinsky handed him her "wish list" of jobs, Jordan went to Bennett's home to make the case in person. Settle it, he insisted. Pay up to $1 million. Jordan even offered to help raise the money. But over the next two months, he never mentioned his legal referral and job-search services for Lewinsky.

That knowledge would have been a red flag for Bennett. Had he known about the job search, he surely would have tried to stop Clinton from being deposed January 17 and demanded that the president settle the case—something both Clintons opposed for fear it would be grist for their political enemies and ammunition for the next woman who popped up with a lawsuit.

Tuesday night, the *Washington Post* called the White House for comment on the sensational discovery that Ken Starr was investigating whether Clinton had committed perjury and obstruction in the Jones case to conceal sexual liaisons in the Oval Office with a former White House intern. By morning, former presidential aide George Stephanopoulos was on the *Today* show talking about the possibility of impeachment.

Bennett went to see Jordan at his law firm that Wednesday evening. They were two of Washington's premier legal rainmakers and their reputations, along with Clinton's, were on the line. Jordan's partner and lawyer, William G. Hundley, sat in.

"Vernon, I want to know what the hell is going on," said Bennett, still reeling. "What's all this job stuff?"

"I guess you're upset with me for not telling you," Jordan replied. He acknowledged getting Lewinsky a job. He had often done that for bright young people.

"Did he have an affair?" demanded Bennett.

"Absolutely not," Jordan insisted. He said he had put the question to both Lewinsky and Clinton, and both had denied it. Jordan said he had met Lewinsky four times, and set her up with a lawyer. That was it, he told Bennett.

"What is Clinton saying about all this?" asked Hundley. Bennett said he didn't know. Then, amid this strained encounter, Clinton called looking for his lawyer. Jordan put him on the speakerphone and affected a chipper tone: "Mr. President, looks like I need a lawyer and he's here, and so my lawyer and your lawyer are here and I think we're in pretty good hands."

But there was hemorrhaging all around the chief executive. Clinton's wobbly denials failed to steady his devastated staff. Political adviser Doug Sosnik had to push Chief of Staff Erskine Bowles to mobilize. Bowles convened a meeting Thursday afternoon of White House lawyers and top political aides, among them Paul Begala, Rahm Emanuel, and John Podesta. Clearly, both the legal and the political sides were interested in managing Clinton's defense.

At the next morning's meeting, with Kendall present, the lawyers laid down their markers. Presidential counsel Ruff announced that the legal team was in charge. He and Kendall, along with lawyers from the counsel's office and Williams & Connolly, would take complete control of the case. Political aides and the White House press operation would be out of the loop.

Within days, the lawyers got a jolt. At a meeting with the president they learned he had met with Lewinsky in the Oval Office on December 28—less than three weeks before he testified he had no recollection of being alone with her. This was a huge fact, a sign something was seriously wrong. Bennett was livid. What was he doing talking to her? he demanded of White House aides. By then, she had already been subpoenaed in the Jones case. And how could he have failed to remember the meeting? It pointed to serious problems with his entire testimony.

That post-Christmas visit by Lewinsky showed up on the White House exit and entry logs—records reporters were now demanding. Lanny J. Davis, the White House's scandal spinmaster, was impatient to get them released because they actually revealed fewer visits to the Oval Office than the thirty-seven the press was reporting.

When the lawyers emerged from their meeting with Clinton, an anxious Davis was waiting outside. Can we release the logs? he asked.

"Nothing leaves this building," said Kendall, looking shaken.

Davis was frustrated. He took his argument to Mills and others in the counsel's office. The reason for their refusal stunned him: Do you really want to take the responsibility of revealing it if Lewinsky met with the president after her subpoena?

For the first time, Clinton was in immediate legal danger. He could be impeached, maybe even indicted. Damage control took on a new meaning as Kendall and Ruff set about locking down every bit of information.

Starr rarely indulged his disdain for the Clintons, but he had displayed it momentarily on January 14, two days after the first call from Linda Tripp. The independent counsel, accompanied by prosecutors Jackie Bennett and Rod Rosenstein, had gone to the White House to take a fifteen-minute deposition from Hillary Clinton in connection with his investigation into whether the White House had intentionally obtained confidential FBI background files on Republican political appointees.

Starr was cordial, even decorous, as he always was in such situations. He greeted the first lady and introduced his two colleagues. Have we met before? Mrs. Clinton asked Bennett. No, said the deputy. Then Starr offered a bit of background. "Jack and Rod were both on the Arkansas trial team of Governor Tucker," he said cheerily. The news was certain to set the first lady's teeth on edge, yet Starr had served it up as if he was introducing medal of honor winners.

Back in the office, a bewildered Bennett stepped into his boss's office. "Do you know how that sounded?" he asked.

Starr stared up at him with a knowing smile. "Of course," he said.

Starr had the same subtle style in running the office.

Leadership, he would say, is the exercise of judgment. He didn't believe in second-guessing the professionals. He had seen Lyndon Johnson squander his presidency micromanaging in Vietnam, and he had watched another president—Ronald Reagan—delegate duty and go out strong.

He had learned those lessons. At the OIC, Starr made the final call on what to investigate and when to stop. He sat in the meetings of his prosecutors. But when it came to running the grand jury, developing witnesses, or culling documents, he left it to his generals.

Chief among them, of course, was Jackie Bennett. Starr saw him as a symbol of toughness, proof, he would say, "we're not tea sippers." Close-range legal combat was the hallmark of Bennett's career. When serving in the Justice Department's elite public integrity section, he had been sent around the country to prosecute corrupt congressmen and senators. He had grown a thick skin being attacked by local politicians as a storm trooper sent out from Washington.

He was a fearsome interrogator who challenged, intimidated, accused—whatever it took to convince a witness to cooperate. He scared the hell out of people. Defense lawyers he encountered detested him, including an influential group close to the Clinton White House. They called him a thug. When White House lawyers came over for a negotiating session, nice guy Starr had Bennett glowering from a corner.

But within his own office Bennett was a charismatic figure. He was funny and personable, the rare sort who could cite passages from a Norwegian novel one minute and curse like a longshoreman the next. His colleagues thought him less than subtle; the joke was that he had two speeds: flat-out and bull-in-a-china-shop. But he was experienced and savvy—he'd lost only one case in his career—and his fearlessness inspired confidence.

Political corruption, Bennett thought, was the worst of all crimes, because it's committed by people who hold the public's trust. But he was clear-eyed about what it took to win a case. Hired in 1995 to consider the prosecution of Bruce Lindsey for election crimes, Bennett spent several months reviewing evidence, then met with Starr. You can't do this, he told his boss. There is a theoretical case, but not a good one. You'll lose, and the office will be discredited. Starr had been assured by Bennett's predecessor that there was a case worth bringing. At first, he was angry that Bennett wanted to take a pass on the case, but in time he saw the logic of Bennett's argument. Promoting him two years later, Starr told an associate the Lindsey incident formed his judgment of Bennett. He was aggressive but prudent—and no yes-man.

As the Lewinsky case engulfed the office, creating urgent new demands, Starr needed a day-to-day manager. When Bennett suggested Bob Bittman, Starr readily agreed. There were more experienced prosecutors on staff, some more polished or creative. Bittman had come to the office after a middling career as a Maryland state prosecutor, taking on sometimes unpopular cases, like one he lost against a female teacher accused of having sex with a young male student. But Bittman considered himself "a closer," a guy who could get things done, and Starr saw him the same way. Efficient and disciplined, he had spent months in a Little Rock warehouse—"the Garage"—making sense of decades-old bank records. In 1997, Starr had made him a deputy to help wind up the Arkansas phase of the probe.

Starr wanted his lawyers to offer ideas. His college-of-cardinals structure, where every important decision was brought up for discussion by all attorneys, would be especially crucial in the Lewinsky investigation, with so much on the line. But the Lewinsky investigation was so overwhelming that it took a taskmaster to juggle assignments and set deadlines. Bittman, who could be brusque, was willing to boss people around the old-fashioned way.

Bittman's father had bested legendary Williams & Connolly founder Edward Bennett Williams in the government's high-profile case against Teamster boss Jimmy Hoffa. Now, more than thirty years later, his son would go up against one of Williams's protégés, David Kendall. And the elder Bittman was good for more than inspiration. He gave his son a closetful of his good suits and an acquaintance with some of the best criminal lawyers in Washington—two of whom would end up defending Monica Lewinsky.

Bittman had his own uniquely informed view of Bill Clinton. In the summer of 1995, as he and OIC colleague Brett Kavanaugh were playing golf at Maryland's Congressional Country Club, they spotted the president's party on the next fairway. The two young lawyers, both first-rate golfers, watched in astonishment as Clinton, who often bragged about his golf scores, shanked one ball after another, abandoning each as he went. When he finally hit the fourth one onto the green, he announced, "I'll play that one." They couldn't get over it: Clinton must be shaving his scores. The story was soon office lore.

The polar opposite of Bittman on Starr's staff was Sol Wisenberg, disheveled and disorganized. But Wisenberg was a puzzlemaster with an elephantine memory for detail, and he worked past midnight many nights, even before Lewinsky. Starr promoted him to deputy and put him in charge of the Lewinsky grand jury. Starr wanted one person to oversee everything that went on in the courthouse, someone to set the rules, to make sure there were no gaps in evidence gathering, to compare the stories of different witnesses.

Wisenberg, like Bennett, was a conservative who joked that he was the founder of an exclusive political party called SARJ—Southern Agrarian Reactionary Jews. But he formed strong friendships with office liberals, and juries liked his self-deprecating humor. Starr thought it was important to win the trust of the grand jury, especially because D.C. juries were famously skeptical of law enforcement.

Mary Anne Wirth represented the other end of the prosecutorial spectrum. Wisenberg once said her idea of sending a message was via greeting card, not indictment, and the "Hallmark" moniker stuck. Wirth was experienced, though, and her colleagues thought she knew how things would play before judges and juries. When she talked, everybody craned to hear—especially Starr, who thought her compassion for crime victims deepened her commitment to punish criminal activity.

While the office leaned to the right overall, Starr made room for liberals on the staff. One of them was Sam Dash, the part-time ethics consultant who had advised him since the beginning of his tenure. Dash, now in his mid–seventies and still serving as dean at Georgetown University Law School, had made a big name for himself as chief counsel to the Senate Watergate Committee. He was an icon in Washington's Democratic establishment, and his imprimatur gave Starr political cover.

It came at a high price. Dash knew a lot about the law and Washington's ways, but he was a prima donna. He'd spout off volubly in meetings before he knew the facts. He penciled himself in as hero of every situation. "I'm the father of the Independent Counsel Act," he would say, or "I created the Watergate investigation." Ignore his advice and he'd threaten to resign. Bennett, Wisenberg, and other senior lawyers would roll their eyes when Starr told them to consult with the man everyone referred to as "LSD"—Legendary Sam Dash.

Some senior lawyers in the office came to see Dash as a Trojan Horse for the White House. He made no secret of the fact that he regularly talked to lawyers close to the Clintons, and that he portrayed himself to them as a moderating influence on Starr. In fact, many on the OIC staff saw Dash as one of the most hawkish prosecutors in their midst—except when it came expressly to the president and his wife. Some thought Dash tried to appease his liberal friends by running interference for the Clintons.

Starr and Bennett kept Dash in the dark about Monica Lewinsky before the story broke in the press. In all the rushing around of the first ten days, they had no interest in inviting his inevitable interference. So Dash learned about Lewinsky with the rest of the world on January 21. He was furious, at first. Bennett had to talk him out of resigning.

One of the tiny circle of people who had known something about the president's interest in Monica Lewinsky before Matt Drudge informed the public was Betty Currie. Currie had won her stripes working in Carville's Little Rock war room during the 1992 campaign, then became a White House fixture, mothering aides who waited at her desk near the Oval Office for meetings with Clinton. Among them, inevitably, was Lewinsky herself.

During the president's deposition with Paula Jones's lawyers, they had asked many questions about Lewinsky—about gifts, about job help. At several points, Clinton had suggested that they ask Currie, whom he described as Lewinsky's friend and link to the Oval Office.

Suddenly, Currie was a potential witness—an important one. Mills told her she needed a lawyer. Bennett recommended one and Ruff lined him up. Sure enough, the Wednesday night after the president's deposition, an FBI agent showed up at the front door of Currie's home in Arlington, Virginia, with a subpoena from Ken Starr.

The president's secretary was scared. For most of that first week she sat at her desk quiet and puffy-eyed. On Friday morning, she got to work before anyone else. She dropped a note on the desk of Oval Office administrator Nancy Hernreich, saying she'd be meeting with her lawyers all day.

Then she disappeared.

Mid-afternoon on Friday, January 23, a secretary slipped into a meeting of Starr's legal staff with a note: A lawyer named Lawrence Wechsler had called, saying he needed to talk directly to Starr right away. "He wouldn't give me any more information," the secretary said. Starr handed the note to Jackie Bennett.

Bennett stepped out to return the call. "Starr's in a meeting," he said. "You've got to run it through me. What's this about?"

"We represent Betty Currie, the president's secretary," Wechsler replied. "I think you really want to meet with us." Wechsler had something he needed to bring to Starr's attention, but it had to be kept hush-hush. Could Starr and Bennett come to his office? "We don't do that," said Bennett. "You come here."

Soon after, Wechsler and his partner Karl Metzner showed up. Wechsler was carrying a box. He was a big man in wire-rim glasses, a name partner in the boutique white-collar defense firm of Janis, Schulke & Wechsler, which had previously represented a Clinton White House aide in the Whitewater billing records controversy. Starr and Bennett took them into a conference room and shut the door. Wechsler put the box on the table and opened it as carefully as a jeweler handling a case of precious stones. Inside were T-shirts, a photo of Lewinsky with the president, a hatpin, and a few other trinkets. All, Wechsler said, were from Clinton to Lewinsky. Betty Currie had stored the box under her bed at Lewinsky's request.

Wechsler wasn't finished. His demeanor was businesslike but his message was urgent. He needed their help. Currie, he said, would share more information of potentially great significance. What he was about to tell them, he said, did not paint the president in a very favorable light: Clinton had led Currie through a series of statements that were not true about his relationship with Lewinsky. Currie was scared. She knew how devastating for his presidency the facts of the relationship could be. At Wechsler's urging, she was staying away from the White House and her home in the Virginia suburbs. She was afraid of more pressure from Clinton retainers, and for good reason, he said. There was a very vigorous White House effort under way to reach her.

Currie and her husband were in hiding.

Starr and Bennett sat utterly incredulous. From Linda Tripp, they had heard of Betty Currie, the loyal go-between who had helped set up liaisons between Clinton and Lewinsky. The prosecutors had figured she would be hostile to their investigation. Yet here was her lawyer with evidence that amounted to a major break in the two-week-old case. After years of resistance from White House officials, Wechsler's presentation was an astonishing act of good faith. He had just handed over a cache of contraband that would be added to the mounting pile of physical evidence. And he was promising the cooperation of a woman who sat just a few feet from the president, who greeted his visitors and opened his mail.

Bennett thought they were hitting paydirt. Clinton's not going to be able to deny this, he thought.

His boss found the whole thing almost too big to fathom. This could lead to impeachment. The president, Starr thought, was actively trying to get his loyal secretary to lie for him, under oath if necessary. Starr and his team had been listening to the Tripp tapes, hearing Lewinsky discuss how Clinton urged her to conceal their affair. That was disturbing enough. Now this—the president pressuring Currie, a genteel black woman who served as an unofficial Oval Office den mother, to risk her own neck and commit perjury. Starr was stunned that he would manipulate his secretary this way. Clinton, he thought, had been extraordinarily stupid and clumsy.

Starr and Bennett said they wanted to meet with Currie that evening. Wechsler said no, it would have to be the next day, Saturday. She was tired. She had been talking to her lawyers all day, and they'd had to extract the story bit by bit.

"This is very difficult for her," said Wechsler. "She will be a very difficult witness. You're going to have to work with her."

Starr and Bennett worried they would lose Currie overnight, that she would have a change of heart and "go south" on them. They didn't want to push Wechsler too hard, though, lest he think they didn't trust him. He had been straightforward so far, and their relationship was still delicate and new. They secured a statement from him sketching out what she was prepared to say, and they agreed to begin the debriefing the next day at the Marriott in the Washington suburb of Bethesda. Currie and her husband, a government retiree, were holed up at a Hyatt across the street.

When Wechsler left, Bennett summoned the legal staff into a cramped conference room. The enormous new demands of the Lewinsky probe had turned the office into a continuous barn-raising, with workmen knocking out walls and building partitions to accommodate a tripling of the fifteen-member investigative staff. Outside on Pennsylvania Avenue, news crews staked out the building as if they were covering the Middle East peace talks. But even amid the chaos, everyone in the office knew something very big was up. Starr rarely met directly with witnesses or defense lawyers.

Bennett gave the legal staff a full briefing, reading from detailed notes he had taken during the meeting with Wechsler and Metzner.

In that moment, the world seemed to stand still. Wechsler's story had a powerful effect on the prosecutors, especially the idealists. Mary Anne Wirth nearly broke down in tears. Bittman, newly named manager of the probe, was angry. "Can you believe that asshole did this?" Bittman asked his colleagues.

And Paul Rosenzweig, who had scarcely slept since passing on the original tip about Linda Tripp from his old University of Chicago Law School classmate, felt numb with dread about what lay ahead for the investigators.

5

"I REGRET NOTHING;
I APOLOGIZE TO NO ONE!"

BETTY CURRIE WAS FRIENDLY ENOUGH as she sank onto a couch next to her lawyer in Room 618 of the Bethesda Marriott Residence Inn. But she proved to be every bit as difficult a witness as Wechsler had predicted.

Bittman and two FBI agents spent much of the weekend—five hours on Saturday, three on Sunday—coaxing facts from her. They knew how important she was to gaining leverage with Lewinsky. She could tell them about Lewinsky's relationship with the president and about her Revlon job and the Jones case affidavit. Bittman did much of the questioning himself at the urging of Currie attorney Karl Metzner, who thought the FBI agents were too cold and matter-of-fact to put Currie at ease.

Currie was halting and tentative—clearly concerned about hurting Bill Clinton. Metzner and Wechsler helped drag the story out of her. They suggested ways for Bittman to phrase his questions. They prompted Currie: "Tell them about this, Betty," or "You said something else yesterday about that." They took frequent conferences with her in an adjoining room, from which she would return saying, "I just remembered something."

In fits and starts, Currie imparted the story of a lovelorn ex-intern and the president. Lewinsky had a crush on Clinton, she said, and would come to see him in the office. The two were alone together five times or more in the Oval Office, Currie allowed, and alone in the president's nearby hideaway study about the same number of times. Lewinsky was deeply frustrated that she had been pegged as a "clutch" and moved out of the White House. It was difficult for her to see Clinton as much as she wanted. Lewinsky found the same impediments to love in *Romeo and Juliet*, which she quoted in a 1997 Valentine's Day message to "Handsome" in the *Washington Post* classifieds. Currie said Lewinsky called her to make sure the ad got noticed:

With love's light wings did
I o'er perch these walls
For stony limits cannot hold love out
And what love can do that dares love attempt.

Currie reluctantly described how the president returned Lewinsky's affections. She placed calls to Lewinsky on Clinton's behalf perhaps as many as five times. The two exchanged gifts, although a month earlier Lewinsky had turned a box full of them over to Currie and asked her to store them, saying there was too much talk going around.

Currie recounted her uncomfortable session in the White House with Clinton the Sunday after his Jones case deposition. The president had asked her a series of questions that were more like statements he wanted her to agree with: "You do remember I was never alone with Monica, right? . . . You were always here when she was here, right? . . . Monica came on to me and I never touched her, right? . . . You could see and hear everything, right?"

Currie had said "right" in response to the questions, even though she knew Clinton and Lewinsky had met privately in the Oval Office and in the president's study. Clinton was trying gauge her reaction, she said. He was concerned, and she was, too. She knew the political danger if people found out he had been alone with Lewinsky. A few days later, as the Lewinsky story was breaking in the press, Clinton had called Currie into the Oval Office and run through the questions again.

Currie seemed to take pains to minimize what she could, the significance of the gifts, the frequency of visits and phone calls. But the information was very powerful, especially given the source.

Wechsler never explained why Currie had come forward, nor did she. But prosecutors figured she had not enjoyed facilitating Clinton's sex life, and was not prepared to lie for him.

At the end of Sunday's interview, Wechsler made a surprising confession. He told Bittman he had already talked to Clinton's lawyers about what Currie was saying. "Those guys are friends of mine," said Wechsler. In fact, he said, "I'm going to a Super Bowl party with them tonight." Bittman was chagrined. He had thought Wechsler was on his side. "We ought to put a wire on you," he joked uneasily.

Wechsler had done his job. He'd kept Currie away from White House pressure long enough for her to tell her story. Even so, she'd been bombarded with pages all weekend. "Checking on you, thinking about you, page me if you need me," messaged lawyer Cheryl Mills. "You are loved," messaged another aide. "Call ASAP," implored presidential secretary Nancy Hernreich. Wechsler had shielded her from all that, and he'd gotten her on the right side of prosecutors. But that didn't mean he couldn't share everything she'd said with his friends in the Clinton camp. They would benefit by knowing how much damage she was doing. It was Ruff and Bennett who recommended Wechsler to Currie, after all.

"My philosophy is a witness can share information. A witness doesn't belong to anyone," he told Bittman. "A witness with information ought to be able to share it with the defense as well as the government."

"As long as it's not obstruction," Bittman replied. He worried that the information could allow Clinton to devise a story.

As the weekend drew to a close, Currie decided to decamp the Bethesda Hotel and go home.

* * *

On Monday, January 26, the president appeared in the Roosevelt Room of the White House. Looking straight into video cameras that would replay the moment over and over again through the next weeks and months, Clinton wagged his finger at the nation, declaring: "I did not have sexual relations with that woman, Monica Lewinsky. I never told anybody to lie, not a single time, never. These allegations are false."

The next day, Currie appeared at the federal courthouse a few blocks from the Capitol dome, the first witness in the investigation of President Clinton in the Lewinsky matter. Before the newly empaneled grand jury of twenty-three Washingtonians, Currie's memory suddenly seemed to desert her.

Even the easy areas turned tricky. Were Clinton and Lewinsky alone at times in the Oval Office? Bittman asked. "I can't remember exactly, but it's highly possible that could happen." Were they alone in the study? "I don't remember exactly, but yes, that's highly possible, too, sir."

Bittman took pains not to prod too hard. "You told us she was. Do you remember she was?"

"Yes," Currie conceded.

She forgot some highly significant details—such as when she had received the box of gifts from Lewinsky. The Jones lawyers had sent Lewinsky a subpoena for Clinton gifts in December, and over the weekend, Currie had told her interrogators that Lewinsky had called in December to ask her to store them. But before the grand jury, she couldn't recall when it had happened. The closest she could come was within the past "six months."

In her weekend interviews, Currie had remembered two Lewinsky visits to the White House after her name turned up on the Jones witness list. One was on December 6, when Lewinsky threw a tantrum at the gate after learning Clinton was meeting with another woman, Eleanor Mondale. Currie had tried to keep Lewinsky at bay that morning, telling her Clinton was out. Currie had also recounted a half-hour meeting between Clinton and Lewinsky early on the morning of Sunday, December 28.

But at the grand jury, when asked to recall those recent events, she instead described a visit in 1995, when Lewinsky had brought the president a slice of pizza—the only visit that Clinton himself had mentioned in his deposition. Only when pressed by Bittman did she recall the visits she had described so vividly three days earlier.

Remarkably, Currie had no recollection of a key exchange that she had already disclosed. Bittman asked, "Did Lewinsky say, 'As long as no one saw us, and no one did, then nothing happened'?" He repeated the question three times. Currie said she didn't remember. Only after she stepped out into the hall to consult her lawyer did her recollection improve. "My memory is a little better—but not much— that if that was said, I would have said, 'Stop, stop I don't want to hear any more' . . . I didn't want to know anything or be able to say I know anything." Bittman pressed her again. Finally she conceded: "I believe Ms. Lewinsky said that."

Prosecutors had expected some backsliding from Currie in the grand jury, since her lawyers wouldn't be in the room to bolster her. Even so, she disappointed them. "Jeez, two days ago we had a case," was Bennett's reaction when he heard the news. She had gone from "manna from heaven to reluctant witness."

Starr's team was not sure why Currie's attitude had shifted. She told them she had not spoken to anyone at the White House about the substance of her testimony. Wechsler, however, did have such conversations, as he had warned Bittman.

Prosecutors didn't know it at the time, but just before Currie's testimony, Wechsler had met in Cheryl Mills's West Wing office with Mills, Charles Ruff, and Associate White House Counsel Lanny Breuer. He had laid out for them what Currie had told Starr's team, about the gifts she stored under her bed, and about the leading questions Clinton had asked the day after his deposition. Currie had agreed with the answers Clinton seemed to want that day, Wechsler told the lawyers at the time, but she "really remembered it differently."

The leading questions particularly worried the White House lawyers. Mills even talked to Wechsler about trying to claim the conversation was legally privileged, but the idea was not pursued.

After Currie's testimony Tuesday, Bittman looked outside the courthouse and saw a restive press throng ready to descend. Bittman offered to let Currie leave through an underground exit, but Wechsler turned him down. He took his client into the crush of cameras on the courthouse steps, where she looked every bit the pitiable victim of the independent counsel's investigative might.

Currie's statements, in their entirety, were enough to convince Starr that he would have to prepare an impeachment referral to Congress. The law had a hair trigger, requiring him to report to Congress any "substantial and credible information . . . that may constitute grounds for an impeachment." What she said in the grand jury did not negate her earlier, less equivocal statements to the FBI and Bittman, he told his staff. But he couldn't go to Congress yet. First he needed Lewinsky's story—and Clinton's.

The day after Currie testified, January 28, Starr instructed Bittman to call Kendall and invite the president to appear before the grand jury. Kendall seemed surprised. "I'll have to think about it. There are a lot of issues here. I'll have to get back to you," he said. But he never did.

Of course, Starr could issue a subpoena. There were powerful arguments for subpoenaing Clinton right away, and they were advanced by Bittman and Roger Heaton, one of the most highly regarded lawyers in Starr's office—the only person on the staff who was both a career prosecutor and a top-flight legal writer. Heaton and Bittman argued that they needed to get Clinton's testimony before he found out what other witnesses were telling the grand jury. They did not want the president to be able to tailor his story.

Starr flatly opposed an early subpoena to Clinton. He told his troops that as a matter of respect and comity they should "exhaust all remedies" to get him to appear voluntarily. Clinton was in a unique bind, Starr thought, and prosecutors had to be careful about exploiting it. For practical political reasons, the president could not very well invoke the Fifth Amendment—a right exercised by ordinary citizens who found themselves targets of grand jury investigations. If

Clinton took that route, it would be seen as an admission of guilt and fuel calls for his resignation or impeachment. The power of the presidency wasn't helping Clinton here, Starr thought; it was hurting him.

The OIC followed up Bittman's oral request for the president's testimony with several letters. Only a few people within Starr's office knew of the invitations to Clinton. Some wanted to make them public, but Starr refused on the ground that prosecutors don't normally publicly announce they've invited someone to testify. Starr expected the White House to challenge a subpoena in court. When the time came, he wanted to be able to show the judge a series of spurned invitations.

With Clinton unlikely to appear soon, Starr was all the more determined to get Lewinsky's story. Investigators had gathered significant evidence—so far uncontradicted—about her and the president. But who knew what Lewinsky would say? "What if she said the moon was made of cheese," Starr fretted, "and now we've put the country through this?"

Nate Speights had forgotten more criminal law than Bill Ginsburg, the malpractice specialist, had ever learned. But before Ginsburg asked him to be his understudy, Speights had never made the big time. The glow of publicity surrounding the Lewinsky case was a welcome change from the District of Columbia criminal courts where the forty-eight-year-old African-American lawyer had spent most of his career. So after Ginsburg bolted Starr's office on January 19, Speights had stayed behind to pick up the pieces. "Let's not break things off," he said, trying to restore civility.

At the staff meeting the next day, prosecutors Emmick and Udolf suggested taking Speights up on this overture. They had tried creative methods to induce Lewinsky's cooperation, but had been overruled by Jackie Bennett, who had insisted that they needed to hear from Lewinsky directly before granting her immunity. Now they wanted to try again without Bennett. He assented, confident that they'd end up doing things his way.

"I've got plenty to do," he told the group. "Just put someone in who's a grown-up on the issue."

This casual jab at Emmick and Udolf highlighted the larger struggle. The Likud Faction, led by Bennett and Sol Wisenberg, saw no profit in bargaining with a woman who couldn't be trusted to fulfill her end of a deal. Lewinsky's performance on Prom Night had showed the limits of playing nice guy. Unless they nailed down her story first, they argued, Lewinsky would lie, mislead, and withhold information to protect Clinton as soon as she gained immunity. She had to be approached from a position of strength. They wanted to build a case against Lewinsky as they would against any criminal suspect and confront her with the evidence and the threat of a trial; only then would she tell the truth. "She's the kind of girl who needs a gun to her head," said Steve Binhak, the New York preppie-turned-prosecutor.

For their part, Emmick and Udolf argued that it made little sense to prosecute a young woman who had fallen under the spell of a powerful man. It made even less sense if they wanted to wrap up the case before it paralyzed the country. Emmick and Udolf were top public corruption prosecutors and knew ways to cut through the calculations and deceits of reluctant witnesses. If Lewinsky agreed to cooperate in exchange for immunity, Emmick said, he and Udolf would thoroughly debrief her to get the truth. The office could then proceed against the real target of their investigation, Bill Clinton.

They knew how unusual it was to grant immunity without interviewing the witness first. But this case was itself unusual—unique, in fact. Emmick argued for finesse. He and Udolf should make a friendly approach to Speights, find out what Lewinsky would say in return for immunity, and see if they could get enough assurance of her candor to justify it. Speights had a few things to recommend him. He had signaled an interest in keeping the dialogue alive. A former federal prosecutor, he knew the rules. And he wasn't Ginsburg.

Starr's preference, as always, was to delegate operational decisions such as this, so that he could ponder the big issues. But the Lewinsky question was so volatile, so central to the whole case, that he was forced to get involved directly. He would sit in a glass-enclosed conference room known as the "fishbowl" to listen, along with female FBI agents, to Lewinsky's taped interviews. He closely monitored every tip from Speights.

He knew that he risked losing strategic perspective on the case. He felt he had no time now to weigh the larger political and social consequences of his investigation, much less garner public support for it. Lewinsky would determine the outcome, and they had to bring her in.

Starr was wary of the young woman's motives. He believed it was essential for a prosecutor to look a potential witness in the eye. Why would she refuse to come forward if she had nothing to hide? But at the same time, he had no taste for pursuing a criminal case against her. In the end, Emmick's appeal seemed reasonable. He authorized Emmick and Udolf to pursue their plan.

The two were risk takers by nature. Emmick, all spit and polish as a lawyer, was a daredevil dirt biker and mountain climber with the scars to prove it. Udolf, fidgety and garrulous, willingly took on political fights. As a 1980s district attorney in rural Gainesville, Georgia, he had obtained a court order to stop the Ku Klux Klan from harassing blacks. Then he went from church to church in the black community to keep the peace.

The courtship of Nate Speights began with a phone call from Emmick and Udolf. It might still be possible to cut Lewinsky some slack, they said, but they needed to hear more of her story first. Speights restated her position: She would happily tell her whole story after receiving a free pass. Speights was not going to do anything without Ginsburg's approval. But as the phone calls continued, he seemed to open up slightly, confirming a small detail here, offering a scrap of information there. On Friday, January 23, fresh from hearing the Betty Currie revelations, the two prosecutors were invited by Speights to a late night meeting at his home just north of the District line.

On the way, Emmick checked in with Jackie Bennett by cell phone. He and Udolf still thought it remotely possible that Lewinsky had fantasized the affair with Clinton, a theory that exasperated colleagues who had no doubt that it happened. Emmick persisted, however, telling Bennett that the Speights visit might finally resolve the issue.

"Wake up and smell the coffee!" Bennett shouted.

Indeed, what Speights said that night removed any last doubt that Lewinsky had told Tripp the truth. And over the next few days, Speights confirmed other things Lewinsky had told Tripp—that Clinton had suggested she deny everything in the Jones case and scripted her lines to explain frequent visits to the Oval Office.

Emmick and Udolf thought they were making slow but significant progress. But the office hard-liners—Bennett and Wisenberg—ridiculed these gains as slim pickings. And Starr himself was increasingly wary of dealing with lawyers who had given every reason to be distrusted. It was not enough that Ginsburg had rudely stalked out of Starr's office; he seemed intent on salting the wound daily with public invective and half-truths. He complained that Starr refused to contact him, even though his partner was meeting with Starr's assistants and the OIC was calling and paging Ginsburg himself. He said Starr had received a detailed accounting of how Lewinsky would testify, although Speights actually had given only sketchy details.

Speights, too, had done his share to incur suspicion. When the FBI found a dark dress in its search of Lewinsky's apartment, he told Udolf: "That's the dress, man. It's the best present anyone ever gave you." Investigators rushed the garment to the FBI lab for semen testing. The results came back negative. But even before the OIC got them from the lab, the results were leaked to the press, making Starr look momentarily like Inspector Clouseau.

The unconventional behavior of Lewinsky and her lawyers unsettled Starr, a man of process and decorum. This was a time to go by the book, Starr thought. He kept hearing in his mind the mantra of one of his veteran staffers on dealing with grand jury witnesses: "I can deal with anything that is the truth. I cannot deal with lies."

Bob Bittman was nicknamed "Bulldog" as much for his mien as for his tenacity. In Maryland, they had called him "Maximum Bob" because he didn't like plea bargains. But on January 28, Starr assigned him to broker one of the most sensitive immunity deals in history. He brought to the task a willingness to split the difference between the office's warring factions. Bittman agreed with Wisenberg and Bennett that Lewinsky had to prove her candor before getting a free pass. But he also agreed with Emmick and Udolf that she might not have to do it in person.

The next day, Bittman called in Ginsburg and Speights. After some small talk about golf and Los Angeles, he told them the office wanted a deal, but needed more than selective tidbits from Lewinsky's lawyers if she was to avoid charges. Speights responded with a dare: "You don't have a case. Go ahead and prosecute her." Ginsburg took a different tack. For the first time, he suggested that Lewinsky might be willing to talk. "She's like a pimple ready to burst," he said, with his trademark knack for the ill-chosen phrase. But then, a few hours later, the unpredictable lawyer took everyone back to square one. Lewinsky was going to Los Angeles to see her father, Ginsburg said. There would be no meeting between her and the prosecutors.

Starr convened another meeting. The hard-liners were eager to plunge into the investigation. But it was still tempting to try to win Lewinsky's voluntary cooperation. Roger Heaton, on the speakerphone from Little Rock, suggested a new approach. If Lewinsky refused to tell her story in person, he said, perhaps she would sign a written version of it attached to an agreement granting her immunity. It would certify that the details in the statement were true and that they would be included in her immunized testimony. Even the more aggressive lawyers could live with this.

On January 29, eight days after the story broke, Wisenberg was working late as usual. The office had agreed to compile the best of Speights's offerings into a statement for Lewinsky to sign. His rival Udolf was preparing a draft and keeping Wisenberg waiting to see it. Udolf wanted the points as broad as possible so as not to scare Lewinsky or cause evidentiary problems if she later changed her story. Wisenberg argued for specificity. If she didn't commit now to incriminating details, she'd never volunteer them after getting immunity. Starr sided with Wisenberg. But Udolf got the assignment to put together the statement. Udolf finally turned over the document at

11 P.M. It was broadly drawn, missing the details of the crime. Wisenberg was furious.

"You didn't do what you were told to do," he said, raising his voice.

Udolf was angry, too. "Why don't you just write on top, 'Don't sign this'?" he shot back sarcastically.

Wisenberg left in a huff and spent a sleepless night. A few days earlier, Starr had offered him the post of deputy independent counsel. It would mean resigning his permanent job in the U.S. attorney's office in San Antonio. Now the decision was easy. He called his wife, Evangeline, in Texas at 1:30 A.M. "I'm coming home tomorrow," he said. The next morning, he walked into Starr's office to accuse Udolf of incompetence.

"I've never said this before," he told Starr. "I'm quitting."

Before Starr could respond, they were summoned to the morning staff meeting. Wisenberg resumed his attack on Udolf. "This is a violation of what we agreed to," he said of Udolf's draft statement. He insisted that it be tossed out, and that the office restore its demand for a face-to-face interview with Lewinsky.

Udolf retorted that his version had the best chance of landing Lewinsky's signature. "I apologize if I've offended anybody," he said. "It's not personal."

"Bullshit," yelled Wisenberg. No, it wasn't about personalities or politics, he declared, it was about making damn sure they ran a professional investigation. He rose, picked up his bulging briefcase, and slammed it to the floor. "I regret nothing; I apologize to no one!" he shouted. Later, his words would become a rallying cry, as prosecutors found their motives under relentless attack by the president's defenders.

But this day Starr was offended by the outburst and its suggestion of bad faith. "This is a group effort," he snapped, pointing at Wisenberg. "We used the process."

But Wisenberg had won the argument. Starr ordered Udolf's draft replaced with a half-dozen specific points drawn from interviews with Speights. After the meeting, Starr pulled Wisenberg aside. "I appreciate your honesty and I hope you'll take our offer to be deputy," he said. Wisenberg agreed to think about it.

Bittman sent the package to Lewinsky's lawyers later that day, January 30. It didn't take long for Ginsburg to call in a reply. "She didn't like the way you wrote it," said Ginsburg. She's going to write her own version of it by hand, he said.

Bittman didn't know what to make of this. It could be a problem if Lewinsky departed greatly from Speights's information. But there was also the potential to learn a lot more, especially with the chance for prosecutors to ask follow-up questions.

Then, that night, they watched Ginsburg on ABC News's *20/20.* Lewinsky, the lawyer said, was like most people who "may tell fibs, lies, exaggerations and oversell" when discussing peccadilloes. But on the whole, she's "totally reliable."

Sunday, February 1, Ginsburg was back on the air, appearing on all five major political talk shows, muddling his own message at every stop. He predicted that Clinton would remain in office and "do a good job." And he kept chipping away at his client's credibility—"all twenty-four-year-olds tend to embellish," he said—even as Lewinsky was putting pen to paper to persuade Starr's team she spoke the truth.

Her statement arrived that same day. It was more detailed and coherent than the fragments they had received from Speights and provided Starr's team with their first good look at the story from the woman who called herself "Ms. L." Lewinsky said she had "physically intimate contact" with Clinton, including oral sex, from 1995 to 1997. She described how closely he monitored her responses in the Jones case, providing a number of new leads. At first glance, it looked like just what they had hoped for.

Steve Binhak, who had spent more time than anyone analyzing the Tripp tapes, urged caution. "Take a closer look," he said. He saw where Lewinsky had interspersed enough gaps and weasel words to render the material legally all but useless.

One thing she revealed for the first time was that it was Clinton who told her she had been named as a possible witness in the Jones case. He had advised her, she wrote, that she could sign an affidavit to "satisfy their inquiry and not be deposed." Lewinsky had done that a short time later, and, of course, she had lied in the affidavit.

That raised the possibility of subornation of perjury on Clinton's part. But she did not state the president told her what to put in the affidavit, only that "in general, Ms. L should say she visited the WH to see Ms. Currie and, on occasion when working at the WH, she brought him letters when no one else was around."

Prosecutors also learned that Clinton talked to Lewinsky about the Jones case after she was subpoenaed on December 19. He invited her to the White House, she wrote, gave her Christmas presents, and shared her concern that a hatpin he had given her earlier was among the items that Jones's lawyers were seeking. Lewinsky said she had asked Clinton whether she should get someone to hold the gifts he gave her, but she did not record his response. She did say that she got a call that afternoon from Currie, who said Clinton had informed her that Lewinsky had something for her to store.

This was big news to Starr's aides. Currie had told them that Lewinsky had called *her* to pick up the gifts. Now Lewinsky was raising the possibility of the president's direct involvement in what appeared to be deliberate obstruction.

The document did link Clinton directly to the effort to find her a job in New York. The president, she wrote, promised to get Vernon Jordan to help her. She had an unproductive meeting with Jordan in November 1997, but he shifted into high gear on her behalf once she was named as a possible witness in the Jones case.

The prosecutors thought Lewinsky had taken pains to soften or qualify many of her assertions. And in case they read into it more than she intended, there was a final paragraph: "Neither the Pres. nor Mr. Jordan (or anyone on their behalf) asked or encouraged Ms. L to lie."

The OIC lawyers were at once intrigued and frustrated by Lewinsky's account. The new leads were promising. But the statement was also self-contradictory—the last paragraph, for instance, seemed to conflict with other things she said—and it omitted details Speights had given. The hard-liners called it a poison pill: Taken as is, it could kill the investigation. It cried out for the kind of clarification, Jackie Bennett said, that would only be possible if Lewinsky came in for questioning.

Bittman, Emmick, and Udolf saw it as far from perfect but fixable in another round of negotiations with Ginsburg. Everyone agreed that it was worth pursuing. On Monday, February 2, Starr instructed them to draft language that would clarify inconsistencies and cover some details not included in her account. The new package was sent to her that day.

At 6:30 P.M., Ginsburg called back. Lewinsky, he said, felt that the prosecutors were trying to put words in her mouth. Bittman took umbrage. The new points they'd sent along represented "exactly what you told us," he said. Speights, for example, had confirmed that Clinton advised Lewinsky to "deny, deny, deny" in the Jones case, yet that wasn't in Lewinsky's account. Nor did it square with her assertion that he never "asked or encouraged" her to lie. At the very least, Bittman argued, she should say he didn't "explicitly" ask her to lie.

Ginsburg agreed. Lewinsky would make that change and incorporate the "deny, deny, deny" quote. They decided that after the changes were made, Ginsburg would call Emmick's office and read them back to the three assistants.

Once the changes were made, they would go to the entire office for review—the procedure for all major decisions. If Starr approved them, Bittman would tell Ginsburg to have his client sign the agreement and send it back for Starr's signature.

"Great, I'm sure we have a deal," said Ginsburg. "It's not going to be a problem." He said he had to run the changes by his client and would call back.

They finally connected at 11:30. "What's going on?" Udolf asked Ginsburg.

"You have got exactly what you asked for," said Ginsburg. Lewinsky had made the changes along with some "minor corrections," he said. The prosecutors looked at each other and smiled. Things seemed to be coming together at last. Udolf asked what he meant by "minor corrections."

Ginsburg said he didn't have a copy in front of him. He couldn't read the new language verbatim, as promised, so he paraphrased. Her changes sounded vaguely like what the prosecutors had asked for. Ginsburg said Lewinsky also had added a "minor change" to one of the paragraphs in the earlier draft. And, by the way, he said, she had signed the immunity agreement.

The prosecutors were stunned. Bittman thought Ginsburg certainly must know nothing could be signed until Starr reviewed Lewinsky's changes. He felt he could not have been clearer in laying out the ground rules.

Udolf was doing all the talking. He asked Ginsburg about the "minor change" he referred to and Ginsburg paraphrased that as well.

There was a pause, then Udolf blurted out: "Sounds okay. I think we have a deal. Send it over." He smiled victoriously and thrust his right fist forward, thumb up.

Ginsburg, on the other end of the line, thought he had just completed a "handshake by telephone."

But Udolf's partners were taken aback. Starr gave wide latitude to his assistants. But none had the authority to sign off on a deal. Nothing Udolf said was binding, Bittman thought, and Ginsburg should know that by now. Starr and the full group would review it tomorrow.

Emmick also didn't see it as binding. He thought the statement sounded pretty good. Udolf was merely predicting that it would pass muster. He asked Ginsburg when they could start debriefing Lewinsky.

The prosecutors hung up, but before they could collect themselves, they felt the wrath of their colleagues. Wisenberg, Binhak, and another hard-line prosecutor, David Barger, had been standing outside the door, listening to the conference call. They muttered a few profanities. "How could you allow this?" one of them asked Bittman.

"We haven't agreed to anything," Bittman said. "We haven't even read it."

Wisenberg was beside himself. He called Jackie Bennett at home. "Do you know what they did tonight?" he raged. "I'm resigning over this." It was the second time in three days that Wisenberg had given notice. This time, he was so angry he threatened to issue a statement that he was quitting in protest.

Bennett tried to calm him and suggested that he call Starr at home. "We'll straighten this out tomorrow," Bennett promised.

Wisenberg hung up and joined Binhak and Barger in Barger's office. The door was closed, but Bittman walked in. "This is ridiculous," said Wisenberg. "You did exactly what you weren't supposed to do."

"If you don't like it," said Bittman, "you can quit. We don't need people with that kind of attitude."

"Consider it accomplished," Wisenberg shot back.

The agreement signed by Lewinsky arrived by fax from Speights's office a little after noon the next day. It was hardly worth the wait.

Lewinsky hadn't changed the substance of the last paragraph at all; she was still asserting no one had encouraged her to lie. She added an assertion that Clinton had told her to "deny a relationship" if anyone asked, but she placed it before she was subpoenaed in the Jones case. Speights had told Starr's team otherwise. It was far less than "deny, deny, deny" to the Jones lawyers.

And to make matters worse, she had also revised the timing of Clinton's advice on how to explain away her visits to the Oval Office. In Lewinsky's new version, that conversation, too, took place before the subpoena. This was the "minor change" Ginsburg had alluded to, but it undercut some of the case against Clinton. If he'd coached her to lie after she was called to testify, he would be more vulnerable to charges of obstructing justice, prosecutors reasoned.

Emmick tried valiantly to save the package. Yes, there were holes and inconsistencies, he said. But it represented the start, not the end of Lewinsky's cooperation. Once she had immunity, she would fill in the missing pieces.

Nearly everyone but Udolf disagreed. They concluded that the revised version was significantly weaker than the original and unacceptable in exchange for immunity.

But now there was another question hanging over them. Regardless of whether the office wanted the deal, had Udolf morally bound them to it? Udolf said he had. Starr wanted to hear from the people directly involved.

Bittman was adamant. "There absolutely is no deal," he said. Ginsburg knew of the office's decision-making process and knew it had not concluded.

Emmick said that while not legally binding, what Udolf did should be accepted by the office as a matter of honor. The deal made sense, he said. It was the only way to complete the investigation quickly.

Udolf spoke last. "I have built my career on my word," he said. "My word is my bond," he said. "We can't back out. The office is ethically bound to support us."

Udolf directed his appeal squarely at the man who had the final word. When he was invited to join the office, he said, he had made inquiries about Ken Starr. People said Starr was a principled man. That's what persuaded him to take the job. The right thing to do now was to accept the deal. "All we're left with is honor," he pleaded.

Jackie Bennett thought it was an odd time for Udolf to be invoking honor. "You knew what your marching orders were and you went beyond it because you didn't give a rat's ass," the deputy said. "We're not going to do it."

Starr listened carefully. He knew the magnitude of the decision before him. The office's cohesion was at stake, as well as the direction of his probe. This was a decisive moment, and whatever judgment he made would set events on an irrevocable course.

He was being asked, he thought, to do the unorthodox, to accept a deal that departed from normal prosecutorial practices and from his office's decision-making process. Starr thought Emmick and Udolf had a "predictive optimism" in Lewinsky and her good faith. He, on the other hand, was haunted by one of her tape-recorded statements to Linda Tripp: "I've lied all my life."

Did she deserve the benefit of the doubt? Starr wondered. Was this someone who had lived a life of rectitude, made a mistake, and at last got her heart right? He came to the answer easily. She was more intent on preserving her relationship to Clinton than advancing the truth. He had no confidence she would be honest and forthcoming.

Starr stood behind his chair and began by quoting Oliver Wendell Holmes: "Hard cases make bad law." What better time to heed the warning? asked Starr. "When the stakes are so high," he said, "why would we depart into irregular arrangements? Isn't it all the more important to turn square corners?"

He was moved by Udolf's appeal to honor. But the law imposed its own virtue here, one higher than honor—truth. "Different cultures esteem different values," he told his staff. "In the Japanese culture, honor is the most important virtue. If you are dishonored, that's the end. In my Christian culture, faith is the highest value. But in my professional life, the value I esteem above all is truth. Honor or not, this statement isn't the truth."

The next day, February 4, Bittman drafted a letter to Ginsburg and Speights; then he, Emmick, and ethics adviser Sam Dash called and read it to them. Starr's office had refused to sign the immunity agreement, they said. Lewinsky's written statement did not allow them to "reliably learn the truth." They insisted she appear for a personal interview as a prerequisite for immunity. Ginsburg responded that night. "We think we have a deal, and you're in breach of it," he said. Within days he asked a federal court to enforce it.

Starr had counted on Currie and Lewinsky to make his case quickly and convincingly. But they had moved out of range. Currie lost her direction or will. Lewinsky was suing him. There would be no easy pieces in this investigation, no single insider on whose story he could base a report to Congress. He had no choice but to prepare for a long haul.

Starr told his staff to call the best lawyers they knew and see if they'd be interested in signing up for a few months. They needed to staff up fast, and they would have to have the best litigators they could find to go up against the White House, the president's lawyers at Williams & Connolly, and Washington's resourceful Democratic defense bar. He put Bob Bittman on the phone to FBI director Louis Freeh, who agreed to dispatch twenty new agents for the office.

Ironically, Ginsburg had helped unify the office. The great divide over strategy had closed. With the investigation at full throttle, the sharp differences between the hawks and doves blurred. They had all they could handle, and a good bit more, in preparing for the struggle with the political sharpshooters at the White House.

6

"OUR CONTINUING CAMPAIGN
TO DESTROY KEN STARR"

THE POWER OF DENIAL got Bill Clinton through the initial days. He wagged his finger and sent out his wife, cabinet secretaries, and aides to reinforce the message. At least he slowed the political whirlwind. It took every last ounce of his will to halt the predictions of his imminent political demise. But by early February, he was ready to escape the worldly tempest. He invited Tony Campolo, an evangelical minister and popular author, to spend the night at the executive mansion. Campolo had prayed with Clinton periodically since 1993, but he had never seen him so somber. After dinner, they plopped down on soft chairs in the vestibule of the Queen's Bedroom for a heart-to-heart talk. "How do I set this thing right?" the president asked.

The next morning, Campolo ran into a pair of old friends at the National Prayer Breakfast in the Washington Hilton. He threw himself on the shoulders of one of them and wept. "He did it, the president confessed to me completely," Campolo said. "Hillary and the rest of the

White House are in complete denial." After he calmed down a bit, Campolo asked their advice on how he should proceed.

"You have to play Nathan," said one friend, referring to the Old Testament prophet who confronted David for killing Uriah and taking his wife. Nathan forced the king to publicly repent.

Campolo threw up his hands. "Every time I go in to play Nathan," he said, "I end up playing Barnabas"—a New Testament figure known for encouragement and comfort.

From the moment the Lewinsky scandal broke on January 21, top White House officials had been flying blind. They had not much more to go on than Bill Clinton's awkward assertion to a television interviewer that "there is not a sexual relationship" with Lewinsky, which led many to wonder whether there had been one in the past.

During the first few weeks, staffers were laying odds daily on their boss's longevity in office: 60/40 he'd resign one day, 40/60 the next. After years of almost nonstop investigations, most were furious that he had recklessly plunged them into yet another scandal that would overshadow the achievements of his presidency. They rolled their eyes when Hillary Clinton blamed the president's troubles on "a vast right-wing conspiracy." And they had no idea what they should believe, or what to tell the press.

The legal strategy was in the hands of White House Counsel Charles Ruff, a former Watergate prosecutor who in recent years had made a specialty of defending Democratic politicians. But Ruff's buttoned-up strategy frustrated the political aides. Keeping mum might be legally prudent, they argued, but it was politically obtuse. Former White House aides Leon Panetta and George Stephanopoulos were saying as much publicly—that Clinton needed to tell the whole truth. Ruff was deaf to these arguments. Senior aide Rahm Emanuel took to opening the twice-a-day Lewinsky crisis meetings in Ruff's office by needling: "So, Chuck, is there anything you can't talk to us about today?"

Part of the problem was the fact that Ruff himself was in the dark. The White House counsel hadn't been able to speak freely with his "client," as he usually referred to Clinton, because of the danger that Starr might call Ruff to testify. David Kendall, as the president's private lawyer, certainly had attorney-client privilege beyond the reach of a Starr subpoena. But Ruff was a government employee, and Starr had strong views about the obligations of people paid by the public, including lawyers. His office had fought and won a two-year battle to get hold of Deputy Counsel Jane Sherburne's notes of a conversation with Hillary Clinton. The Eighth U.S. Circuit Court of Appeals had called the use of White House lawyers in criminal defense work "a gross misuse of public assets," and the Supreme Court unanimously refused to hear an appeal by the Clinton White House.

With that definitive precedent in mind, Ruff and his team were reluctant to find out too much. As a result, they didn't even know what to make of Lewinsky's statements on the Tripp tapes. Long after the prosecutors were convinced that Lewinsky was genuine, Ruff and his staff were still dealing with hypotheticals. Was she lying, for some unguessable reason? Was she delusional? Was she telling at least part of the truth? Ruff couldn't begin to put those questions to his client unless he knew they could speak in confidence.

But he needed answers. And to get them, he paid a secret visit to Ken Starr.

On Tuesday, February 3, two weeks after the scandal broke, Ruff and Associate Counsel Lanny Breuer slipped past the press pack camped outside Starr's headquarters and took a freight elevator to Starr's offices. They were on a mission to find out how far Starr would go to penetrate White House strategy sessions.

Ruff and Starr were part of the same elite circle of Washington lawyers, and the meeting was cordial, if cool. The two eyed each other across a conference table, Ruff flanked by Breuer, a protégé he brought to the counsel's office from his old white-shoe firm of Covington & Burling; Starr, by Bennett and Bittman. What Ruff sought, he said, was for White House aides and lawyers to be able to advise the president on the Lewinsky matter. They couldn't do that if they faced the possibility of a subpoena over meetings they had with him, or even among themselves. The staff met to discuss strategy every morning and evening. Those sessions had to be protected from prosecutors' scrutiny. Otherwise, how could the president get the advice he needed during the most serious challenge to the presidency in twenty-five years?

If Ruff couldn't get Starr's assurance on this point, he said, he would seek protection from the courts. "It is inevitable that we will eventually bring up executive privilege and have to invoke it," said Ruff. He would do so despite its dark evocation of Richard M. Nixon and Watergate. He said the White House had to assume the worst, that Starr would send an impeachment referral to Congress. That threat, Ruff argued, made an otherwise private legal issue—Clinton's possibly criminal action in connection with the Jones suit—an affair of state. It was just as vital for the president to get aides' advice in confidence on this matter as on diplomatic or military affairs, the areas in which executive privilege was usually invoked.

Ruff intended to appeal to the constitutional scholar in Starr. If nothing else, his argument might get Starr to pause long enough for the president's advisers to regain their footing. They needed time to catch up to the investigators. He didn't have much to offer Starr in exchange, though, so he laid down a threat: He was prepared to refight the question of whether government-paid lawyers can advise officials under criminal investigation. Despite the seemingly definitive Sherburne ruling from the Eighth Circuit, Ruff said he thought he could get a better result in the D.C. Circuit. That would take months, or longer. Starr listened impassively. He asked a few questions, and assured Ruff and Breuer he'd get back to them promptly.

In fact, Starr had already made up his mind. Ruff's arguments, he thought, were bogus. The essence of the White House argument was that anything the president does that results in an impeachment inquiry automatically becomes official business. He consulted with Sam Dash, the old Watergate hand, who agreed that if Clinton invoked executive privilege he would be abusing the Constitution to save his own skin. "This is now a monarchy. The king is the state. This cannot be," Starr angrily told his lawyers. Should executive privilege apply if Clinton were, say, preparing false tax returns in the Oval Office? He recalled that when Lloyd Cutler had Ruff's job in 1994, he had promised that executive privilege would not be asserted in any criminal investigation of the White House.

Starr took an equally dim view of Ruff's request that he hold off subpoenaing White House lawyers. The use of government lawyers to serve the private criminal defense interests of the Clintons was corrupt. He had already spent two years proving that in court, and he wasn't about to reverse course now.

Starr wrote to Ruff the next day, politely turning down his request. In his letter, he argued that executive privilege was intended to protect communications related to the president's official responsibilities, not his private activities. Statements to the staff were of "critical importance" to the grand jury because Clinton had rebuffed an invitation to testify himself and was refusing publicly to discuss his relationship with Lewinsky.

Ruff fired back, jettisoning his respectful tone. "First," he wrote, "I want to inform you that within 45 minutes of its delivery, James Bennett [a reporter for the *New York Times*] called the White House press office asking whether I had received a letter from you concerning executive privilege." Ruff demanded an FBI investigation of this apparent leak. Starr wrote back denying he'd leaked the letter. He pointed out that Bennett didn't even cover his office, and wouldn't likely have sources there. His beat was the White House.

Starr's rejection was a serious blow to the White House lawyers, although not unexpected. It meant the battle had to be fought on Starr's terms. If they could talk to Clinton under the shield of privilege, they could find out the truth and fashion a strategy that relied on his political strengths. If they knew exactly what Clinton's legal exposure was, they could weigh the risk of confessing in public and appealing for forgiveness. But as it was, they couldn't even ask the questions without fear of being called to testify.

This meant that David Kendall was now in control of the case. And in the Lewinsky investigation, he had his own priorities. Where Ruff's goal was to protect Clinton from impeachment, Kendall wanted to keep him from criminal prosecution. Clinton would make no statements about the facts now. There would be nothing but silence from the Oval Office.

But Kendall and the White House lawyers agreed on what they needed to do next: Go after the independent counsel with every weapon they could muster. Starr had to be demonized. They had to make the investigation a referendum on Ken Starr instead of Bill Clinton. Ruff's reference to the call from a *Times* reporter was the opening shot in the next battle.

David Kendall stepped briskly down the asphalt driveway from the West Wing and stopped in front of the now permanent phalanx of camera tripods known as "Monica Beach." He wore a khaki trench coat whose military cut and epaulets underscored that he was, in effect, declaring war on Ken Starr. He stood erect, his brow furrowed with the gravity of the moment, as he read from a carefully annotated fifteen-page letter to Starr accusing prosecutors of spreading a "deluge of false and misleading information" from the grand jury. The occasion was a February 6 *New York Times* story reporting how Clinton had led Betty Currie through a series of rhetorical questions about his relationship with Lewinsky. It was "a flagrant leak from your staff," Kendall asserted, without offering evidence. He cited more than fifty other alleged leaks.

Kendall said Starr's office was employing "a calculated tactic" of "selectively leaking both information and falsehoods" intended to manipulate witnesses, deceive the public, and damage the president. He charged that Starr had "lost control" of his staff and said he would be filing a court petition to have Starr's office held in contempt.

The power of the White House to control the day's news had never been more forcefully demonstrated. Kendall's claims yanked attention away from the devastating facts of the Currie story, which strongly suggested Clinton was trying to get his secretary to lie for him in legal proceedings. The president himself followed up the attack on Starr during a news conference with visiting British Prime Minister Tony Blair. "Someone else is leaking unlawfully out of the grand jury proceeding," Clinton charged.

Clinton, vowing never to resign, was on a collision course with the independent counsel. And as his advisers saw it, public opinion could be his salvation. Presidential pollster Mark Penn was telling senior aides that not since World War II had Americans so closely hung on every twist and turn of a story. If there was a development late in the day, by morning 90 percent of the public knew about it. That was a weakness for Clinton now, but an opportunity if the story could be turned against Starr.

Penn had been sampling public opinion from the day the scandal broke. And certain aspects of the story, he found, worked to Clinton's advantage. People had no trouble believing Clinton had an affair. But they saw it as a private matter not fit for criminal investigation. Just as Starr's assistant Steve Binhak had foreseen, the public focused on the sex, not on the possibly criminal acts used to cover it up. The results rolled in: Americans don't prosecute people for having an affair; if Clinton interfered with the legal system, he did so to protect his privacy. The public was more willing to accept a philandering president than a prosecutor seeking to make crimes out of private behavior.

Clinton's advisers made use of these findings. James Carville, a deft manipulator of public opinion, mocked Starr as a hymn-singing, moralizing preacher, going down to the Potomac River "to wash all the sodomites and fornicators out of town." Kendall tapped the same concerns about privacy when he accused Starr of leaking grand jury secrets. Political aides to whom Clinton had given personal assurances of his innocence picked up the cudgel. They saw no other way to protect a presidency they had believed in.

Suddenly, the prosecutors were on the defensive. They suspected that the White House itself—possibly through Betty Currie's lawyer—had leaked the story about her and the president. This was a well-known tactic in public opinion wars: If damaging facts are destined to come out, leak them first yourself so you can put your own spin on them. In this case, it had the added advantage that the president's side could put the blame on the OIC.

There was no possibility now of cordial relations between Starr and Kendall. The distrust and mutual contempt were insurmountable. "Your role as private defense counsel and your loyalty to your client does not qualify you to lecture me on professional conduct and my legal responsibilities," Starr wrote to Kendall. "Fiercely aggressive representation, including through media grandstanding, cannot be an excuse for smearing a lawyer through reckless accusations. Let's stick to the facts. Let's find out the truth." Prosecutors had no reason to want the Currie story public. They hadn't finished debriefing her, and if she believed they were leaking what she said, she might not want to cooperate. Still, they couldn't be certain the story had not leaked from their office.

Jackie Bennett placed an awkward call to Currie's lawyer after Kendall's charges. Lawrence Wechsler, dodging a press horde eager to know what his client was telling investigators, was getting ready to leave town on a skiing trip. "Larry, you know we've got to defend ourselves on this. We don't think it was us. You told us you briefed the White House. We've got to put that out," said Bennett. Wechsler was uncomfortable. "Do what you gotta do," he said. Bittman talked with Wechsler, too, and Wechsler acknowledged he had talked to the *Times*, but only, he said, after the paper had the story in hand.

Wechsler put out a short statement that kept him in good graces at the White House. Despite what Currie had already told investigators and the grand jury, he publicly absolved Clinton of coaching his secretary. "To the extent there is any implication or the slightest suggestion that Mrs. Currie believed that the president, or anyone else, tried to influence her recollection, that is absolutely false and a mischaracterization of the facts," he wrote. Without further elaboration, he disappeared to the ski slopes.

Within hours, White House aides were on the attack again—with allegations that Richard Mellon Scaife had paid off Whitewater witness David Hale, and maybe even Starr himself. They were extrapolating loosely from an article in the weekly *New York Observer*. The story said Scaife had given $2.4 million over four years to the conservative *American Spectator* magazine, much of it to finance research into Clinton's past. Some of the money, the paper said, went for hiring private detectives in Arkansas. One of the *Spectator*'s paid

Arkansas sources was a bait shop owner who was a longtime friend of Hale, an important cooperating witness in Starr's Whitewater investigation.

On *Larry King Live*, Lanny Davis denounced Starr's purported leaks and spread his own muddled version of the *Observer*'s Scaife story. Scaife's money went to "pay anti-Clinton witnesses," he charged. Starr was "involved with" Scaife at Pepperdine University, and Scaife was even funding his prospective deanship there. "There is an interconnection between a lot of the people that have been funding efforts to destroy Bill Clinton," said Davis. "Those are the facts."

In reality, facts were the first casualty of the White House offensive. New Jersey Senator Richard G. Torricelli, one of Clinton's best friends in Congress, turned up the volume on the new charges. "Well, apparently Mr. Hale received money, which comes very close to witness tampering," he pronounced on ABC. Starr, he said, "before he became independent counsel, was preparing a brief in the Paula Jones case, for which he may have been compensated by Mr. Scaife." Torricelli wrote to Attorney General Reno, demanding an investigation.

By Sunday, White House spinmasters Paul Begala and Rahm Emanuel were free-associating conspiracy theories on the political talk shows. "We see another witness, as reported in the *New York Observer*, who changed his story after he was befriended by the head of a slush fund operated by Ken Starr's patron, Richard Mellon Scaife, who set up a $1 million teaching job for Ken Starr to move to in Malibu, California, as soon as he's finished with this investigation," Begala said. Emanuel told CNN there was now a "cloud of doubt" over Starr. He said that "one individual at this point has changed their story and that is David Hale."

In fact, Hale had not changed his story. Since September 1993, Hale had been telling first reporters, then the FBI, that Bill Clinton, while governor of Arkansas, had urged him to make a fraudulent government-backed loan of $300,000 to Susan McDougal. The *Spectator*'s "Arkansas Project" started sometime later, and both Hale and the *Spectator* denied that he had received any of the Scaife money. And Scaife was never Starr's patron. The philanthropist had been giving money to Pepperdine for decades, and his gift to the new public policy school was unconnected to the Starr offer.

But those facts never were raised in the nightly game of second-guessing by pundits and partisans who had no firsthand knowledge of Starr's probe. Cable show hosts Larry King and Geraldo Rivera interviewed lawyers from the O.J. Simpson murder case who opined on the ethics of Starr's team. Clinton, of course, was taking a savage pounding too, from late-night television comedians and even his own former staff members. But increasingly, the focus was shifting to the independent counsel.

Attacking the prosecutor is a common tactic of defense lawyers. But not since Watergate had anyone brought the formidable machinery of the president's office and party to the task. Clinton's team went after Starr with an intensity usually reserved for political enemies in a must-win election, not for government officials duly appointed by a panel of federal judges.

The OIC lawyers could scarcely keep up with the torrent of charges, working as they were late into the night six or seven days a week. And Starr did not want to wage a political war of words with the White House. He refused to hire a spokesman, arguing that prosecutors should do their talking in court, not in public. His mentor, William French Smith, had often advised, "Don't worry about what people say," and Starr frequently repeated that advice to his staff. In Starr's life, the lesson went back even further—to when his parents had warned that he might be ridiculed for his fundamentalist beliefs. One of their favorite Bible stories was the persecution of the prophets. They had urged him to shrug it off.

But not everyone thought turning the other cheek was a good idea in a fight with the White House. "Get out there and defend yourself!" Dallas PR woman Merrie Spaeth kept advising Starr. She said it over the phone and by voice mail or fax, nagging in the good-natured way a friend of twenty years can. Starr always had the same answer: "It's not what prosecutors do. It's not proper." Spaeth suggested that he turn the defense over to old friends and admirers, including former attorneys general and FBI directors, who had expressed a desire to speak up for him. She got the same answer. A few conservative activists and an occasional Republican member of Congress spoke out in Starr's defense. But they generally were no match for the Clinton surrogates.

Starr was determined not to play to public opinion, not to factor in the political and public-relations impact of each step. He deferred to veteran prosecutors on tactical decisions, failing sometimes to spot social issues they would stir up. He would make decisions according to standard prosecution guidelines, recalling a lesson from his parents to "set your face against the popular mood." But Starr's authority was tied to public support—in ways the White House understood better than he did.

That support eroded when his office summoned Lewinsky's mother, Marcia Lewis. In her taped talks with Linda Tripp, Lewinsky had implicated her mother, who supposedly suggested that Tripp fake a foot injury to avoid her Jones deposition and advised her daughter to lie about the affair for her own safety. "She keeps saying, 'Mary Jo Chappaquiddick' or whatever her name was," Lewinsky told Tripp.

Starr aides spent little time debating whether to call Lewis to the grand jury, although Mike Emmick did question the timing. Lewis would probably lie to protect her daughter, he argued. Then, if Lewinsky eventually cooperated, wouldn't she feel compelled to repeat the lie to cover for Lewis? Why not wait to call the mother? But Emmick's colleagues felt pressure to move forward and were tired of accommodating Lewinsky after her Ritz-Carlton performance and the unnerving collapse of immunity talks with her lawyer February 3.

On February 11, the second day of Lewis's appearance before the grand jury, her testimony proceeded unremarkably until Emmick tried to corroborate her daughter's nickname of "Babba" for Hillary Clinton. Lewis said she did not remember hearing it. The prosecutor asked if she knew of a Yiddish expression for grandmother that sounds like it.

"I think it's Bubah," replied Lewis, adding that her daughter was familiar with the term.

Sol Wisenberg jumped in and asked if Lewis had ever called anyone Babba. Yes, the witness said, it was a "silly family thing" used to refer to grandmothers.

Before Wisenberg could finish his next question, he noticed a change in Lewis. "Are you all right?" he asked.

Emmick intervened. "Would you like—do you need a few minutes?" he asked. "Why don't you take a break? Let's take a break. Go out for a couple of minutes."

Lewis left the grand jury room wailing: "I can't take it, I can't take it anymore. I can't stand it." Her lawyer, Billy Martin, escorted her into a cloakroom and asked the U.S. marshals to summon medical help. The courthouse nurse spoke briefly with Lewis, who declined to have her blood pressure taken and left the courthouse with Martin a few minutes later, her bottom lip quivering as if she were fighting back tears. Prosecutors thought the breakdown was staged, but that night millions of people saw a distraught and shaken mother walking from the courthouse.

Talk show guests kept the episode alive for days after, none more resonantly than Lewinsky's father, Bernard. "To pit a mother against her daughter, to coerce her to talk," he pronounced on ABC's *20/20 Friday*, "to me it's reminiscent of the McCarthy era, of the Inquisition, and even, you know, you could stretch it and say the Hitler era."

Whatever Starr did seemed to trigger totalitarian metaphors. Starr summoned White House aide Robert Weiner to determine whether he had organized a campaign to pressure Maryland authorities to prosecute Linda Tripp for taping phone conversations with Lewinsky. Weiner, spokesman for the White House drug policy office and a resident, like Tripp, of Howard County, acknowledged congratulating members of the local Democratic club for issuing a press release calling for Tripp's prosecution.

Prosecutors wanted to know whether Weiner had orchestrated the lobbying as part of a White House effort to smear and intimidate Tripp. He was subpoenaed after Bennett received a call on January 26 from the elected Republican prosecutor in Howard County, Marna McLendon, who, he said, sounded near tears. McLendon said she was under "unbearable" political pressure from local Democrats, who wanted an investigation of Tripp for violating state wiretapping laws, although she thought Tripp's federal immunity would make that difficult.

Weiner said he simply exercised his First Amendment right, then added a few strokes to the caricature of Starr as jack-booted interrogator. "It is Big Brother at its worst," said Weiner as he stepped out of the grand jury. "We don't live under the government of Nazi Germany," chimed in Weiner's wife, Patricia Berg, who also had called local Democrats. "This is the United States. We have free speech."

Starr had been one of the federal bench's most forceful advocates of the First Amendment, a Reagan appointee who had upheld the right of an air force doctor to wear a yarmulke at work. He had cast the key vote to overturn a major libel verdict against the *Washington Post*, which was represented in the case by David Kendall. But now he failed to recognize how his critics would turn evidence gathering into a fight over the First Amendment. His investigation into Lewinsky's book purchases created another furor. Starr aides sought records of her purchases from Washington's Kramerbooks and Barnes & Noble to document her statements on tape that she had bought books as gifts for Clinton (including *Vox*, a novel about phone sex). Prosecutors saw it as part of a routine effort to corroborate evidence. They had also questioned Neiman Marcus employees about a necktie she gave him, but that didn't cause a stir. The mention of books called down the wrath of publishers, authors, editors, booksellers, librarians, and civil libertarians.

These accusations, along with Ginsburg's account of Lewinsky's mistreatment during the Ritz-Carlton encounter, were difficult to refute, owing to the secrecy of the OIC's operation. Starr had Jackie Bennett provide background information to reporters to explain why they needed certain evidence, but he was no match for the army of White House backers who had cut their teeth undermining political rivals like Newt Gingrich. Soon, to many people, it began to seem as if Starr, not Clinton, should be under investigation.

One man who didn't see a percentage in demonizing the prosecutor was Bob Bennett, Clinton's lawyer in the Jones case. Quite the contrary, he considered it a huge strategic mistake. The White House might succeed in discrediting Starr's investigation, but no good could come of antagonizing the powerful prosecutor and angering congressional Republicans. Bennett was a deal-maker who believed in courting prosecutors right up until the moment they took him to trial. By pummeling Starr, he told Clinton's strategists, they were ruining chances to reach a compromise with the prosecutors.

Bennett's advice deepened his long-standing differences with David Kendall. Kendall, Bennett believed, had already mismanaged the Whitewater investigation by fostering testy relations with Starr's team. He had first made that argument in 1996, when Kendall was caught off-guard by the grand jury subpoena to the first lady over the billing records. If Hillary Clinton had had the right defense lawyer, Bennett contended, she never would have gone before the grand jury. The right lawyer would have met Starr over drinks or dinner and found some middle ground.

The independent counsel's job, Bennett thought, had been a great tragedy for Starr. He had known him for a long time; they had never been close, but never at odds, either. Starr's biggest problem, Bennett told friends, was that when he looked in the mirror he saw Jesus Christ coming back at him. Kendall had no relationship at all with Starr or his people, Bennett complained to Clinton aides. He used napalm when diplomacy would do. The Williams & Connolly ethic—rattling prosecutors and scorched-earth litigation—dangerously escalated the threat posed by the independent counsel, Bennett told colleagues. But by this time, few at the White House were listening to Bob Bennett. If he had settled the Jones case, they were saying, there would never have been a Lewinsky investigation.

Instead, Clinton aides scarcely sought to hide their efforts to discredit the independent counsel's investigation. One White House offical anonymously described it to the *New York Times* as "our continuing campaign to destroy Ken Starr." It wasn't being done from the press podium, but through leaks, tips, and criticism. Emanuel was the creative and strategic force, the person who knew which reporter to leak a story to or when to ask Torricelli to fire off a letter to Reno.

Presidential advisor Sidney Blumenthal traded information with a network of pro-Clinton reporters, including the authors of the Hale-Scaife stories, whom he invited to a party at the White House and introduced to the Clintons. He branded a half-dozen other reporters covering the Lewinsky saga for mainstream news organizations "assets to the enemy"—that is, to Ken Starr.

Blumenthal's conspiratorial outlook made senior officials like press secretary Michael McCurry and Deputy Chief of Staff John Podesta uneasy. Emanuel dubbed him "G.K.," for Grassy Knoll, and no one was quite sure what he was doing. When Stephanopoulos announced on television that unspecified Clinton "allies" were vowing to "open up everybody's closets" and "to take everybody down with him," many Clinton aides assumed he was talking about Blumenthal.

Ruff, McCurry and Podesta explicitly warned against circulating information on the personal lives of Starr's associates. Using the power of the White House to tarnish individuals would be a McCarthyite tactic. Even so, by mid-February, reporters had swamped the OIC with queries about alleged personal and professional misconduct by members of Starr's staff. The tips came directly from Clinton's camp. One reporter said a White House contact told him Starr himself was having an affair with a woman in Arkansas. Federal Judge Alex Kozinski, a longtime Starr friend, told him the same rumor was swirling among high levels of the federal judiciary. Then Helen Eversberg, the former U.S. attorney in San Antonio, called Starr to say that a private investigator was calling local ministers to find out whether Starr's long deceased father had been a member of the John Birch Society or of some weird religious sect. Blumenthal, in a speech at Harvard, ridiculed Starr deputy Hick Ewing, a born-again Christian, as a "religious fanatic." Clinton refused to denounce Blumenthal's comments, but after more than fifty congressional Republicans wrote to the president about religious intolerance, Blumenthal released a statement saying he was sorry if he had "offend[ed] Mr. Ewing's or anyone else's personal religious beliefs."

But that apology was rare. On the whole, the attacks on Starr and his team—and their corrosive effects on their targets—were intoxicating to the White House.

* * *

Mike Emmick was on the StairMaster at Gold's Gym when he saw his face looming from a television screen. It looked like an FBI wanted poster, plastered with his alleged crimes. The man Lewinsky had gotten the best of stood accused of being "callous, coercive, and vindictive" toward witnesses. Geraldo Rivera was calling him "Ken Starr's pit bull." He was accused of using "threats, deceits, and harassment" to elicit testimony in his former job as an assistant U.S. attorney.

Emmick was horrified. He felt the stares of people around him. Friends from California had been calling to say that reporters—and in one case a private investigator—had been looking for improprieties in his record, but Emmick figured he had nothing to fear. What especially stung was that the charges now being broadcast all over the country were attributed to a prominent federal judge in California, Robert Takasugi. But Takasugi had actually made the comments about someone else, another federal prosecutor in Los Angeles. He and Emmick had tried the same defendant, but in separate cases. Ironically, Emmick had good relations with Takasugi, who had called him in court "a man of great integrity." Emmick had even listed the judge as a job reference.

A year earlier, the Democratic National Committee's researchers had dug up material on the fundraising practices of the congressional Republicans who were leading the investigations into financial abuses in Clinton's 1996 reelection campaign. Now the same forces were searching for charges to hurl at Starr and his aides, who lacked the high-profile résumé and exposure of their boss. Fact sheets began emerging from the DNC with such headlines as KEN STARR'S TAINTED LIEUTENANTS and STARR'S ASSOCIATE COUNSEL [Emmick] HAS A HISTORY OF PROSECUTORIAL EXCESS.

Clinton allies considered their professional and personal backgrounds fair game, and they stirred up numerous media investigations of Emmick and Bruce Udolf. Kendall's partner Nicole Seligman gave Blumenthal a videotape of a Los Angeles television news broadcast that leveled false charges of prosecutorial misconduct against Emmick. Blumenthal had copies made, and sent them to reporters and opposition research chief Doug Kelly at the Democratic National Committee, who had his own distribution network.

Carville's operation, the Education and Information Project, gathered and disseminated some of the same material on the legal backgrounds of Starr staffers. EIP's stated goal was to "target" Starr and leading congressional Republicans "to expose their hypocrisy." Carville also made tape recordings of calls to EIP, which were subpoenaed and placed under seal in an unrelated lawsuit. The tapes purportedly contain discussions about the sexual and personal backgrounds of investigators, though Carville denied that he circulated the material.

Finally, Starr broke his usual public silence to charge that Clinton allies were spreading "an avalanche of lies" about his staff, and he designated Jackie Bennett to get the truth out. It quickly became a full-time task. Bennett was on his way home one Friday night when he passed Emmick's office and heard him pleading with a *U.S. News & World Report* reporter. The information was not true, Emmick said; the story had been looked into and abandoned by a score of other news organizations. But the reporter pressed on, saying that editorial director Harry Evans, a Clinton admirer, insisted on a story. Bennett grabbed the phone and demanded a number for editor James Fallows. Fallows said he knew nothing about the story, but that Starr and his team were public figures and therefore legitimate subjects. "But your reporter knows it's false, and she says she is being required to run it," said Bennett. Fallows made some inquiries and called back. Bennett's complaint had merit, he said. He killed the story. *U.S. News* reporters learned the next day that Blumenthal had been faxing other news organizations the same information Evans ordered them to check out.

Udolf was getting hit from all sides. The president's aides circulated information that when Udolf was a Georgia district attorney, a federal court ordered him to pay $50,000 for violating the civil rights of a man wrongfully held in jail for four days. A *Doonesbury* cartoon ridiculed him by name. Then Democratic operatives circulated a fifteen-year-old Georgia sheriff's report that mentioned Udolf's involvement in a domestic quarrel between a female friend and her estranged husband. Udolf told colleages the report had been doctored.

The attacks took a heavy toll on Udolf. Gone was the self-confident prosecutor who took criticism in stride. "This is the business we have chosen," he used to say, picking up a line from *The Godfather II*. On top of everything else, he was sick with a serious liver ailment, and colleagues thought the powerful drugs he was taking to combat it made him depressed and paranoid. At the height of the rumors about him, he called Bennett from his home in Miami and tearfully told him he wanted out. His lawyer in Miami had White House connections, he told Bennett, and was calling them to say Udolf would quit if they'd call off the dogs.

Bennett tried to reassure Udolf, telling him the office was behind him. Quitting, he argued, would play into the hands of his accusers, who would point to it as proof they were right. But Bennett was boiling. The White House, he thought, was using its might to try to intimidate prosecutors. He hung up and pounded his file cabinet. He wasn't alone in his frustration. Sam Dash advised: "Subpoena the S.O.B."-meaning Blumenthal. The next day, February 21, Bennett did.

Almost immediately, he regretted giving in to his anger. Coming now, the subpoena looked retaliatory. Bennett tried to call it back, but Blumenthal's lawyer, William McDaniel, had already begun to turn it into another First Amendment cause célèbre.

"These people have this grandiose idea that there is a conspiracy afoot by the president and the first lady and Sidney and the president's attorneys to disseminate information about Starr's office," McDaniel asserted after Blumenthal emerged from the grand jury February 26. "That is absolutely false. They just made it up. It was a fantasy." Inside the grand jury, however, his client had freely acknowledged that he fed derogatory information to reporters, including the Emmick videotape.

Emmick was miserable, too. He feared that Blumenthal would repeat damaging rumors about him to the grand jury, which in fact he did. Udolf, who had just lost the bruising fight over Lewinsky's immunity, felt that Bennett's decision to bring Blumenthal before the grand jury had hurt him more than it had protected him. But he was not in a strong position to complain. He had never recovered his standing in the office after the immunity debacle with Ginsburg. He spent time in the hospital and traveling overseas. When he returned, Starr's deputies called him in for a meeting. They told him FBI agents no longer trusted his judgment and refused to discuss investigative business in his presence. Udolf replied that it didn't matter what agents thought of him. They didn't run the investigation, he said, prosecutors did. But the deputies insisted he had lost his effectiveness in the office and took away most of his duties. Udolf had reached his limit, too. He felt marginalized, shunned because he had disagreed with the prevailing hardline approach to Lewinsky. By the end of April, he left.

The Blumenthal flap overshadowed a related controversy. During his first presidential campaign, Clinton had used private investigators to track down women from his past and control what one aide called potential "bimbo eruptions." Starr's top command suspected that the White House was using similar methods to spread around dirt on his staff, and he subpoenaed Washington investigator Terry Lenzner to testify the same day as Blumenthal.

Clinton's lawyers had assured Mike McCurry that they were not using the same tactics to dig up information on Starr's staff or Clinton critics. "No one at the White House, or anyone acting on behalf of the White House, or any of President Clinton's private attorneys, has hired or authorized any private investigator to look into the background of investigators, prosecutors or reporters," McCurry announced. But the next day, McCurry learned that he had been sent out with bad information. Kendall and Bob Bennett put out a statement saying that, in fact, they were employing Lenzner's firm, but denied investigating the personal lives of Starr's assistants. "There is public information available, which of course it is our duty as counsel to research and gather," they said. For his part, Lenzner said that if his investigators were looking into the backgrounds of Starr lawyers, "I'd say there was nothing inappropriate about that."

The White House had an important ally in District of Columbia Bar Counsel Leonard Becker, whose office investigated complaints against lawyers. Becker had already looked into Starr's job offer from Pepperdine, and whether the OIC had leaked information about Hillary Clinton to the *New Yorker* magazine. Now he informed the office that he was investigating alleged grand jury leaks by Starr's staff and whether Lewinsky had been abused by Emmick, Udolf, and Bennett at the Ritz-Carlton. When Becker learned Bennett and Udolf were not members of the D.C. bar, he forwarded complaints to the states where they had licenses to practice law—Indiana for Bennett and Georgia and Florida for Udolf.

None of Becker's investigations came to anything. Prosecutors viewed them as politically motivated hectoring to divert energy from their investigation. Starr's response on the Ritz-Carlton encounter alone resulted in a single-spaced document more than one hundred pages long. And though the bar inquiries were supposed to be kept confidential, they somehow leaked out, fueling White House efforts to discredit Starr and his staff.

One thing remained quiet, however: Becker's job search in the Clinton administration. In early 1998, while he was scrutinizing Starr's prosecutors, Becker was seeking a high-level appointment within the Justice Department as head of its office of professional responsibility, though he did not get the post.

As Clinton allies battered prosecutors publicly, the president's lawyers worked quietly behind the scenes to keep close tabs on witnesses and their testimony. The information helped determine how much damage had been done and what the president could say without contradicting other witnesses. Kendall, aided by lawyers at the White House, created some half-dozen informal joint defense agreements with witnesses and groups of witnesses. These agreements threw a cloak of attorney-client privilege over conversations among the lawyers. They allowed Currie's lawyer to freely share with Clinton's legal team what she knew of Lewinsky's White House visits. Lawyers for Lewinsky's former White House colleagues passed along the questions prosecutors had put to their clients as well as their replies.

Ruff scripted a line to help White House media handlers deflect questions on the joint defense pacts: "Defense lawyers always talk together, but I wouldn't call it an agreement." Such arrangements are commonplace in corporate litigation, but it would have been embarrassing for the president to admit he needed them. They would inevitably be viewed as screens behind which the White House was managing people's testimony.

The questioning of Ashley Raines demonstrated how the arrangement worked. Soon after the scandal broke, the FBI sought to interview Raines, a White House employee and Lewinsky confidante. She notified Ruff's assistant, Lanny Breuer. By the time FBI agents sat down with Raines on January 25, Breuer had spoken to her three times and had set her up with a lawyer—Wendy White, a former member of the White House counsel's staff. In this way, the White House learned much of what Starr was learning. Raines told the FBI and the grand jury that Lewinsky confided that she'd had a sexual relationship with Clinton. Once, Raines said, she heard Clinton's voice on Lewinsky's answering machine: "Are you there?" he whispered. "Pick up, come on, pick up. I must have missed you."

The White House counsel's office had more control when it got lawyers involved, and even marginal witnesses, such as Alex Nagy, were encouraged to hire them. Nagy, director of the White House telephone service, told the FBI that Associate White House Counsel Michelle Peterson told him to get a lawyer and said she had a list he could choose from. He didn't think he needed one and refused. But it was risky. He said he had earlier lost favor with his bosses when he talked to Starr's investigators without a lawyer present.

Ruff lined up defense lawyer Gerard Treanor to represent Nancy Hernreich, the Oval Office administrator. Treanor, Ruff, and Lawrence Wechsler, Betty Currie's attorney, were part of an old-boy network of former prosecutors. Hernreich, like Currie, was questioned many times before the grand jury, and Treanor routinely discussed her testimony with Ruff, Mills, and Breuer. Hernreich disapproved of Lewinsky, and most of the young woman's Oval Office visits occurred when Hernreich was not there. Prosecutors were zeroing in on time periods when Hernreich was off, Treanor told the White House. He told Mills what he anticipated Hernreich would be asked next, and Mills would supply Treanor with background information he could use to help prepare his client. Treanor also dealt with the president's private lawyers, telling Kendall and Seligman, for instance, what Hernreich knew of gifts Lewinsky had given Clinton.

Lawyers for other important White House witnesses—Currie, Blumenthal, Lindsey—even created rough transcripts of their clients' grand jury testimony that could be useful to the White House. Witnesses go into the grand jury room alone, but they are able to step out to confer with their lawyers at will. Blumenthal sought conferences with his lawyer after every few questions, then recreated everything he had been asked as his lawyer copied it down. Lindsey and Currie openly took notes on what they were asked.

The White House made the most of what it learned. On February 4, the *Wall Street Journal* reported in its Internet edition that White House steward Bayani Nelvis had told the grand jury he had seen Clinton and Lewinsky alone together in the president's study. The story was wrong, and Breuer quickly called Nelvis's lawyer and had him put out a denial. Then Kendall capitalized on the episode. The *Journal* story, he wrote Starr, was "extremely damaging both to the president and Mr. Nelvis. It also broadcast to the world the kind of evidence you would like to gather, inviting 'copycat' testimony and the like. That's a dangerous and destructive game to play in an alleged search for the truth."

Starr tried to make sure the grand jury saw White House tactics for what they were. On February 19, he called in Jackie Bennett to grill Bruce Lindsey. They had faced each other before over the years of investigation. Lindsey acknowledged that the White House was lining up lawyers for witnesses and receiving information from them. He was asked about the Nelvis story. Why accuse the independent counsel of leaking it? demanded Bennett.

"Mr. Bennett I do know this: I know that Mr. Nelvis' lawyer indicated he had not talked to the press. I did not know—I don't know of anyone, there may be others—besides Mr. Nelvis, Mr. Nelvis' lawyer and members of the OIC staff who would have had that information."

Said Bennett: "But you said the information was false. Why would the independent counsel leak information that's false?"

"No, you're absolutely right. I don't think we ever accused you of leaking this information," Lindsey replied.

"You don't? You want to go back and refresh your recollection on the news accounts, Mr. Lindsey?"

Lindsey was flummoxed. "Well, I can—I mean, if that's a useful exercise. But I—you know—but I mean, you know, I don't know whether or not anyone in the White House accused you of leaking this particular story or not. I just don't know."

Starr's team may have shown up Clinton officials in the grand jury, but they were taking a royal beating in the press.

7

"GOTCHA!"

BY EARLY SPRING, Starr's office—once as sedate as a corporate law firm—had the noisy bustle of a police precinct house. Two dozen FBI agents operated in a big open area known as "the Bullpen," taking telephone tips and poring over subpoenaed records. Phones rang incessantly; the copier never stopped. The mazelike hallways teemed with prosecutors and the occasional defense lawyer escorted by U.S. marshals. Locked-down security shut out the outside world. Blinds were drawn to block long-lens cameras and parabolic microphones deployed by news crews bivouacked on the sidewalk below. The elevator no longer stopped on the fourth floor without a special pass key.

Starr had stepped up the gumshoe phase of his probe after he lost hope of getting the facts the simplest way—through the cooperation of Monica Lewinsky. The OIC would have to build a case against her, then get her story. It was an unsettling task. Before they could prove that Bill Clinton had lied under oath, investigators had to establish that he and Lewinsky had had sexual relations. That meant asking embarrassing questions of her confidants, old boyfriends, and coworkers. It meant looking for evidence of an affair in White House visitor logs and in her phone records, computer files, e-mail, and receipts. It meant authenticating Linda Tripp's tape recordings. Everyone pitched in, from the young paralegals to legal writers hired for their constitutional expertise. There were thousands of records to sift, hundreds of witnesses to interview.

Everything stopped twice a day for meetings in a long windowless room. Bob Bittman ran them like marketplaces of evidence. Moving up and down a thirty-foot table, he called on lawyers and agents to discuss the day's findings. Sol Wisenberg, overseeing the grand jury, spoke on the latest testimony. Steve Binhak provided updates on debriefings of Linda Tripp. Julie Myers was piped in from Little Rock over the futuristic "Starr Trek" speakerphone. The only female prosecutor close to Lewinsky's age, Myers, twenty-eight, provided a reality check on Generation X morality and Lewinsky's credibility.

In the middle of it all was Ken Starr, taking notes and interjecting comments, a legal intellectual wading ever deeper into the investigative trenches.

Starr kept thinking back to another investigation involving a president. As a young lawyer in the late 1970s, he had tried a case with David Belin, who had worked on the Warren Commission inquiry into the assassination of John F. Kennedy. Starr asked him about the Warren Commission's finding that a single gunman had killed the president. Belin said he was haunted by criticism that the commission had rushed to judgment. Belin was certain of its conclusions, but the public was not, and in that way, he believed, the commission had failed. By not pursuing every lead and playing out every scenario, the inquiry left doubts that festered as the decades passed.

That lesson had guided Starr in his investigation of Vincent Foster's death. He took two years, ran down every theory, and produced a careful, comprehensive report pronouncing it a suicide and all but silencing the conspiracy theorists.

The Lewinsky case presented an even bigger challenge, and Starr resolved to approach it the same way. He would not leave loose strings to be woven into conspiracies by the next generation's Oliver

Stone. His report to Congress had to be definitive, "utterly impregnable," he told his assistants. History demanded it.

So did the habits of a lifetime. As a child, he believed that mastering the Bible's verses would bring him closer to God. So while other boys slept through Bible study at the Highland Boulevard Church of Christ, Starr memorized the verses so dutifully that he could summon them up at will forty years later. He applied the same rigor to his secular life, rising to the top of his high school class while working part-time at his father's barbershop snipping perfect flat tops. As a college student in the summer of 1966, he sold Bibles door-to-door in Ohio, working eighty hours a week and ringing up enough sales to earn a steak dinner bonus on most Sundays. And while Bill Clinton got through Yale Law School borrowing notes and cramming for exams, Starr never missed a class at Duke Law School, taking exquisitely organized notes and freely lending them to less dedicated students.

The self-discipline Starr showed as a student became his professional watchword. As chief of staff to Attorney General Smith in 1981, Starr had prepared detailed briefings to make sure his mentor heard every alternative to the policy choices pushed by bureaucrats. On the federal appeals bench two years later, he often researched facts and law himself so as not to be limited by imperfections in the arguments of the advocates. When he became an advocate as United States solicitor general, the government's top lawyer, Starr tried to make sure he didn't get lost in legal abstractions. To prepare his argument in a celebrated right-to-die case brought by the family of comatose patient Nancy Cruzan, Starr discussed the fate of such patients with ethicists at Walter Reed Hospital. When he argued a search and seizure case, he called in police officials to get their views.

But these qualities did not always serve Starr well as independent counsel. As a judge and litigator, Starr had deadlines. Without them— Congress had deliberately designed the post free of time or budgetary constraints—his perfectionism became an occupational hazard. Some of his veteran prosecutors grew frustrated at his insistence on turning over every rock in the Whitewater probe. They wanted to concentrate on winnable cases, but Starr had trouble giving up the pursuit of even minor figures. He was especially intolerant of lying under oath. Long-time aides argued that it wasn't worth the time and money it would take to prove some perjury cases, but Starr couldn't walk away easily. He simply put off resolution of some matters, opening him to criticism that he was dragging out the investigation of the president. "Don't let the perfect become the enemy of the good," Starr liked to tell his assistants. It was an admonition he might have directed at himself, some of them thought. Starr wanted perfect justice.

The Lewinsky matter imposed a deadline on Starr for the first time in his years as independent counsel. Congress was demanding that he move swiftly, and under Justice Department guidelines he had to complete his report well before the fall elections so as not to influence their outcome. They had to work fast, he admonished his staff. But the greater the public interest, the greater the obligation to do the case right. He wanted no shortcuts, no detours from essential fact-gathering, and, he hoped, no regrets like those of David Belin.

"Gotcha," said Steve Binhak.

He had just found crucial corroboration that Clinton had lied at least once in the Jones deposition when he said he couldn't recall being alone with Lewinsky in the Oval Office complex. Binhak had focused on that part of the president's testimony in late February after seeing a notepad that Linda Tripp had turned over to prosecutors. In it, she had recorded a history of Lewinsky's affair as she described it by phone in May 1997. One of the high points chronicled by Tripp began with a Sunday afternoon call from Clinton. He asked Lewinsky to stop by the White House later. Tripp abbreviated what followed: "Fooled around . . . Phone call from Dick Morris—head on phone."

Nine months later, Tripp had provided a full translation for prosecutors: Lewinsky had performed oral sex on Clinton as he talked to political consultant Morris. Her notes provided enough detail to date the incident: Easter Sunday, April 7, 1996.

The notes showed the two had been alone. But location was not as certain. So Binhak checked the White House visitor log for that day. Sure enough, Lewinsky had arrived at 4:56 P.M. and left at 5:28. Still, that didn't prove she had been with Clinton in the Oval Office. After all, it was a religious holiday, and he might have taken the day off. Binhak needed to know the president's whereabouts on April 7. Clinton had not yet complied with a subpoena for records of his movements within the White House, which are kept by his Secret Service detail. Binhak had to wait for the final piece of the puzzle.

Finally, on March 5, the presidential movement logs were delivered to Starr's office. Binhak flipped through until he got to April 7. There it was in tiny type: Clinton had been in the Oval Office from 2:21 P.M. to 7:48 P.M. Binhak had hit gold, a two-way corroboration of Tripp's notes. "How does the president explain this?" he wondered out loud.

More documents came in later to remove any doubt about the assignation. Phone logs for April 7 showed Morris had called at 5:11 P.M. and talked to Clinton until 5:20. All the pieces fit and added up to strong circumstantial evidence that Clinton and Lewinsky had been alone in the Oval Office. How else could she have known about the call from Morris?

Binhak had racked up an impressive trial record for a young prosecutor and wasn't shy about it. Downplaying his elite background, he adopted the argot of street cops: Criminals were "knuckleheads," their arrests "scooping them up," and their sentences "lunch on the government for the next twenty years." FBI agents, not always amused by the young know-it-all, called him "Binhak, Done That." But he enjoyed the confidence of Starr's high command, which assigned him the important task of penetrating the world of Linda Tripp.

They were an odd match. At forty-eight, Tripp was fifteen years Binhak's senior. She grew up the daughter of a high school teacher in the onetime mill town of Whippany, New Jersey. Binhak, son of a Wall Street trader, came from the well-to-do Westchester County town of Purchase. While he went to private schools, then Cornell University and the University of Pennsylvania Law School, Tripp studied at the Katherine Gibbs School for secretaries. Politics didn't bind them, either. Tripp had worked for and revered President George Bush. Binhak, who had been traveling cross-country and stopped in Little Rock the night Clinton beat Bush, celebrated at the Excelsior Hotel election bash. He watched Bill Clinton work the room that night and thought he glowed with charisma.

Now Tripp and Binhak sat at a conference table, brought together by the political investigation of a generation. Before their first formal debriefing February 20, 1998, he had plotted out his technique. She had soaked up so much detail, and he wanted to wring out every drop. She would withhold less if she knew he'd catch her. He listened to her telephone tapes until he could recite them. He studied the FBI statements and grand jury testimony she had given in the Foster and travel office investigations to figure out what triggered her memory. If she recalled things temporally, he'd bring a calendar. If places did it, he'd recreate scenes for her. Finally, he plumbed her psyche. She came across as suspicious and bitter, so he planned to let her air her fears. He had to understand her worldview to assess her story, to figure out where she was shading facts or advancing an agenda.

Binhak had reason to be suspicious. The *Washington Post* reported on February 14 that after leaving the Ritz-Carlton on Prom Night—and telling Binhak she was going to see a friend—Tripp had met secretly with Jones lawyer Wesley Holmes. She had given him enough information for the Jones team to ask several specific questions of Clinton at his deposition. And around this time investigators listening to Tripp's tapes came across a conversation between Tripp and Jones lawyer David Pyke that showed she had volunteered information to the Jones team months earlier.

From the start, Clinton allies had been trying to link the Jones and Starr teams as partners of the Republican Right, trying to damage the president through a civil case and a criminal investigation, respectively. Starr had denied the charges. Paul Rosenzweig still did not know the extent of legal work his original tipster, Jerome Marcus, had done for Jones. But now it appeared that there was a connection, unknown to the OIC, in the person of its star witness, Linda Tripp. The fact that Tripp had contact with the Jones camp didn't dictate Clinton's behavior in the affair or alleged coverup. It did cast a shadow over the motivations of his chief accuser and it gave Clinton's lawyers a big stick with which to club Starr. They quickly accused him of setting up a perjury trap for the president by sending Tripp to bait the hook.

Starr's aides were furious. Binhak placed a call to one of Tripp's lawyers, Anthony Zaccagnini. "We've got to talk," he said, and asked the lawyer to bring Tripp in for a meeting. They arrived the next day and sat down with Binhak and FBI agents. "We need to get to the bottom of this," Binhak said. "You can understand how this looks." He demanded a full description of her dealings with the Jones lawyers. He specifically wanted to know how the meeting with Holmes had come about and what was discussed. She had misled him and he felt burned. "That's not the beginning of good relations," he told her.

Tripp defended herself. She said she purposely did not tell the OIC about her conversations with the Jones lawyers because she didn't want to involve Starr's office. She then gave what still amounted to a partial account of her dealings with the Jones camp. She dated her first contacts to the previous November, when Pyke called her—a conversation she inadvertently tape-recorded and turned over to the OIC. She confirmed to Pyke that Lewinsky had had an affair with the president. Tripp suggested she would testify about it, though she needed to "look hostile" because of her Pentagon job. Her second contact, she told Binhak, was her meeting with Holmes on Prom Night. She didn't reveal it to the OIC earlier because nobody had asked, she said. Holmes already knew much of the Lewinsky story, though she told him about several gifts Clinton had given Lewinsky. If Tripp had known that Jones' camp was tipped off to Starr's probe before the deposition, she kept it from Binhak.

In retrospect, it appears clear that Tripp colluded with the Jones lawyers to set up the president. She armed the Jones lawyers with evidence to catch Clinton in lies and alerted prosecutors days before the president would lie under oath. Then someone in her camp let Clinton's interrogators know Starr would be closely watching the session.

Had Starr known of those machinations before taking on the probe, he could have factored them into his initial talks with the Justice

Department. But he didn't know the full extent of Tripp's collusion even after Binhak demanded she disclose her contacts with Jones lawyers. It would be months before prosecutors learned that Rosenzweig's tipster, Jerome Marcus, had done work on the Jones case. And they never found out that the Jones lawyers had been tipped to their investigation a few days before Clinton's deposition.

Tripp's lawyer, Jim Moody, had presented her to the OIC as a whistle-blower, but her relationship with literary agent Lucianne Goldberg and now the Jones lawyers suggested a larger and complex agenda. She hadn't lied outright to Starr's staff. But she and Moody had gone out of their way to create a misleading impression that she had done everything she could to avoid the Jones team and their sub-poenas. Still, OIC prosecutors realized they should have monitored her more closely at the start of the investigation and pressed harder to uncover her contacts with the Jones camp.

Binhak summarized his session with Tripp in a memo circulated to fellow prosecutors. Everyone had serious questions about her motives. Mary Anne Wirth saw more reason than ever to worry about Tripp as chief witness against the president. Tripp was moti-vated by animus, she said. A defense lawyer would say she conspired with Clinton antagonists to promote Jones's cause, manipulating the OIC in the process.

They all felt used, but there was no unringing the bell now. Regardless of her motives, Linda Tripp's information was proving accurate. "Saints don't swim in sewers," Binhak reminded them. And now they had Betty Currie's box of gifts and her tale of Clinton rehearsing his story with her. There was no going back. Whatever Tripp had done, Starr and his team believed, it didn't diminish Clin-ton's culpability. "Anyway you slice it, there was a crime going on," said Jackie Bennett.

Relations with Tripp would never fully recover. The lawyers and agents eyed her warily, taking extra precautions not to reveal any-thing to her about the probe. Everything she provided had to be cor-roborated in as many ways as possible. Prosecutors shared much of the larger public's distaste for Tripp and her clandestine taping of a friend's confidences. But they had an investigation to run without the cooperation of either principal. Tripp was as close as they could get.

Binhak met with her every four to five days, and between sessions, worked on her telephone tapes. The forty-six conversations recorded in the last quarter of 1997 were the most direct evidence Starr's team had of an affair and cover-up. But in their original form, they were virtually useless as proof. Tripp had never dated or indexed them. She simply tossed them in a bowl when they came to an end.

To make sense of their content, the prosecutors had to put the tapes in the right order. It was a huge undertaking. Emmick figured out the date of one tape by hearing a televised World Series game in the background. He took down the scores to find a match in the previous October's sports pages. Binhak searched the transcripts for mention of obvious hooks like the president's or first lady's travel plans, then checked their schedules for a corresponding date. When Lewinsky spoke of having something delivered to the White House, he checked receipts of the courier service she had used. He searched TV listings after hearing Tripp say that she had watched the movie *A Home of Our Own*. In Lewinsky's credit card bills, he found the purchase of a plane ticket from LaGuardia Airport to match her comments about a trip to New York City.

In her twenty-three debriefings, Tripp recalled remarkable detail from the more than one hundred hours of conversation she claimed to have had with Lewinsky on the affair. She said Lewinsky had recounted nine sexual encounters with the president from November 15, 1995, to July 4, 1997. She left one tryst with a stained dress and a suggestion by Clinton that if asked about their meetings, she could claim to be advising him on "youth affairs." Lewinsky said secretary Betty Currie facilitated the get-togethers by escorting her into the Oval Office, then slipping out the back door to avoid drawing attention. On one occasion Currie couldn't leave safely and hid in the Oval Office bathroom while Clinton and Lewinsky were in the adjoining study. Lewinsky said they had phone sex fourteen times at all hours.

What Tripp recalled of Lewinsky's words more deeply implicated Clinton in a cover-up than the statement Lewinsky had drafted for prosecutors. Tripp quoted her as saying that Clinton had urged her to deny an affair after the subpoena, not before, as she had written. And there was a difference in accounts of the night Clinton suggested an affidavit as a way to get out of the deposition. Lewinsky's written account said Clinton had suggested cover stories—delivering mail to him and visiting Betty Currie—if she was asked to explain her visits to the Oval Office. "Neither of those statements untrue," she wrote. But Tripp said she had been told the president had simply advised Lewinsky to "deny everything."

Kathleen Willey had everything Paula Jones and Monica Lewinsky lacked. She wore pearls. She was poised and mature, an attractive, fifty-one-year-old, upper-middle-class mother from Richmond, Virginia. She was no Clinton antagonist—she had campaigned for him and worked as a White House volunteer. But on March 15, Willey went on *60 Minutes* and told the nation that when she went to see Clinton in 1993 to ask for a paid job because her family was on the brink of ruin, he groped her. "It was kind of like I was watching it in slow motion and thinking surely this is not happening," she said softly. "I thought, 'Well, maybe I should give him a good slap across the face.' And then I thought, 'Well, I don't think you can slap the president of the United States like that.'" In his Jones deposition, Clinton had denied sexual contact with Willey. He lied, she said. "I just think that it's time to tell this story. Too many lies are being told. Too many lives are being ruined."

It was a devastating interview, one that had the power to rouse the feminist groups that had snubbed Paula Jones. Before the evening was over, the president of the National Organization for Women was saying that Willey's claims, if accurate, amounted to sexual assault. Republican Senator Orrin Hatch said that if her story turned out to be true, "I think this presidency would be over."

At the White House, political aides feared the worst. But Clinton and his tiny circle of advisors weren't worried. They had a secret weapon: a cache of letters and notes Willey had written to Clinton after the alleged sexual advance. Bruce Lindsey had kept them tucked away for the past eight months, since he heard *Newsweek* was preparing a story about Willey. He had collected them from Nancy Hernreich and had been waiting for just such a moment to spring them. On Saturday, the day before the *60 Minutes* interview, Clinton called his political touchstone, James Carville. His lawyers were thinking about making the letters public. What did Carville think? "It's a pretty good idea," said the old campaign war room chief.

On Monday morning, Clinton aides turned the tide. They released a batch of fifteen notes and letters from Willey, in which she congratulated Clinton on various achievements and told him she was his "number one fan." Bob Bennett went on TV that night charging that Willey was trying to cash in on a book deal. The letters worked, immediately deflating the crisis.

But putting them out was a calculated risk. On December 15, 1997, the Jones lawyers had subpoenaed Clinton for all documents related to Willey. The president's lawyers responded that they had none. By releasing the letters three months later, they virtually admitted they had defied the Jones subpoena. As usual, there was a lawyerly explanation. These were White House records, they argued, and Clinton had been asked for his personal documents. In fact, Jones had asked for documents not only in Clinton's "immediate possession, but also those over which you have custody or control." Clinton clearly had control over the letters: He ordered them released to the media.

The president faced an even more explosive allegation by Arkansas nursing home owner Juanita Broaddrick. She had told people that Clinton, as state attorney general twenty years earlier, had raped her in a Little Rock hotel room. The Jones team sought her as a witness in their case but she submitted an affidavit denying sexual contact with Clinton. When the Jones lawyers suggested that her affidavit had been coerced, Starr sent prosecutor Tom Bienert and an FBI agent to Arkansas to interview her. She told them that Clinton had assaulted her. Her affidavit was false, she said, but no one had coerced those statements. Starr's team had no jurisdiction to examine the matter further and dropped it.

Craig Lerner showed up on March 19. The thirty-one-year-old Harvard Law School graduate had been a Starr assistant until eight months earlier, when his workload lightened and he left for private practice. His ex-colleagues urged him to come back and promised him plenty to do if he returned. When he did, they handed him a thick document called "the Chron." FBI agents had combed thousands of pages of records from Clinton, Jordan, Lewinsky, and Tripp, and listed chronologically every turn in the presidential affair from first kiss to discussions of the Jones case. The listing, hundreds of pages long, provided a look at the juxtaposition of key events. But until Lerner arrived, Starr's team was too busy plotting strategy and interviewing witnesses to closely analyze it.

"There could be a smoking gun here and no one has the time to find it," Lerner told a colleague. He carefully examined the Chron, along with phone records not yet integrated into it. He found a number of threads that led to dead ends. Then he came to an entry from the visitor log of Vernon Jordan's law firm, Akin Gump. At 4:47 P.M., December, 19, 1997, Lewinsky had signed in as a guest of the firm. Lerner knew from other information that sometime between 3 P.M. and 4 P.M. she had been served a subpoena in the Jones case. He assumed she must have contacted Jordan after that to set up their meeting.

Lerner had figured out he needed to cross-check Clinton's phone records whenever he came upon an important development. He lined them up next to the Akin Gump records and found some interesting clues. Akin Gump records showed Jordan placed a call to the president at 3:51 P.M. but didn't get through. A little over an hour later, after Lewinsky had arrived at Jordan's office, Clinton returned the call. The conversation lasted for four minutes, until 5:05 P.M. A minute after Jordan said goodbye to Clinton, at 5:06 P.M., he called Frank Carter, the Washington lawyer who went on to draft Lewinsky's affidavit denying any sexual relationship with Clinton. The records suggested Clinton may have been more deeply involved than they knew in the plans for

Lewinsky to keep the truth from Jones's lawyers. Lerner ran down the hall to share his discovery.

"Check this out," he told Sol Wisenberg, shoving the records across his desk.

"Fucking-A," said Wisenberg.

This discovery was to prove crucial during Jordan's grand jury testimony, which started in early March and continued, off and on, for three months. He was a regal presence in the witness chair, towering and erect, ebony-skinned, elegantly tailored. He wasted no time in letting the grand jury know he was a figure in history and a man not to be trifled with. He and Clinton were best friends, he said, and every president in modern history had found urgent need for his counsel.

He had put Lewinsky in touch with Frank Carter, Jordan testified, because she needed a lawyer who could prepare an affidavit. He hadn't written one in twenty years. He was a rainmaker, not a nuts-and-bolts man, and had long ago graduated from billing by the hour (at last count, $450 per). When Lewinsky came to his office, he said, he summoned his driver, who serves "at my beck and call," and ferried her to Carter in his limousine.

Facing Jordan was Tom Bienert, a methodical senior prosecutor who had been recruited at Emmick's suggestion from the Los Angeles U.S. attorney's office. He had participated in big prosecutions—the Reginald Denny beating, the fertility clinic scandal at University of California, Irvine, the Orange County bankruptcy.

Jordan was a smart, tough lawyer who knew how to protect himself and did what he could to protect the president. Even so, in his first day of testimony, he recounted that he had told Clinton about Lewinsky's subpoena and demanded to know whether Clinton was having a relationship with her. If Jordan hadn't told the grand jury that he'd raised the sex question with Clinton, it might have looked as if he was getting Clinton's girlfriend a job to keep her quiet—just what the prosecutors suspected.

Jordan began by minimizing the contacts he had with Lewinsky, describing her as a nuisance who had pestered him to get her a job.

But his firm's phone records showed he had made scores of calls on her behalf, and the picture became even clearer when compared with White House logs and Lewinsky's own calling records. During his first days of testimony, Jordan doggedly insisted he had no memory of meeting Lewinsky until she came to his office on December 11, although Lewinsky had told friends of a November 5 meeting to discuss jobs. He was forced to correct himself when phone records showed a series of calls from Currie to Jordan, then Currie to Lewinsky on November 4. He acknowledged the calls could have been to set up the next day's meeting with Lewinsky. After meeting with her on November 5, he had gone to see Clinton, White House logs showed. Then he met with Bob Bennett to urge him to settle the Jones case.

As for the crucial day of December 19, Jordan testified that he didn't mention Lewinsky's subpoena to Clinton until a private moment at a White House dinner that night—well after he had arranged for Frank Carter to draw up an affidavit denying an affair. But confronted with Lerner's phone record evidence, Jordan revised his account. He had alerted Clinton to the subpoena that afternoon, while Lewinsky was still in his outer office.

Then, on December 30, Lewinsky had called Jordan to express her fears that Linda Tripp had told the Jones lawyers about her. Jordan subsequently spent twenty-five minutes on the phone with Clinton—talking, he said, about finding fund-raisers for the president's legal defense, among other subjects. Bienert spent three days in May and June with the Akin Gump records, chipping away at Jordan's story. Suddenly the confident powerbroker was backtracking. Asked why he repeatedly called Lewinsky on January 19, as the story was about to break, he first replied: "I'm certain I was not calling Monica Lewinsky to ask her about the Drudge report—absolutely not." He called, he said, as he often does, to "follow through, update, see how people are, see if she was happy." But confronted with the log documenting the extent of his contacts with the principals in the scandal, he dropped the pretense. "I wanted to ask her what she knew about the Drudge report," Jordan admitted.

Even on the defensive, he reminded the grand jury of his special status. At one point, trying to corroborate something Lewinsky had told a friend, Bienert asked Jordan if he had been out of town at the end of October. Jordan examined his calendar and warmed to his subject. "I was in Paris. I made a speech at the Benjamin Mays Academy in Detroit on Friday evening October 24th and I was picked up by private aircraft and flown to New York. I spent the night in the Hotel Regency and the next morning I took private aircraft to Paris from Teterboro Airport. And I was in Paris, according to this, I went from Paris to London and I returned from London on the Concorde at 7 P.M. and I was picked up there and flown to Chicago. . . . I left Chicago and went to the Augusta National to play golf."

Bienert stuck the needle in gently. "So you were out of town," he said.

The Lewinsky grand jury operated in secrecy. The twenty-three Washingtonians usually assembled three times weekly in an unadorned, windowless room on the third floor of Washington's federal courthouse. Presidential aide Sidney Blumenthal called it the "*Darkness at Noon* suite," an unpleasant destination for him and numerous colleagues summoned there. The entrance to the corridor of grand jury rooms was shielded from view by tall, movable screens. A U.S. marshal posted at a desk in front of the partition enforced presiding Judge Norma Holloway Johnson's prohibitions against leaning on the walls or sitting on the floor. The handful of reporters allowed on the third floor could see little but silhouettes on the shiny marble walls and feet moving beneath the screens.

Sol Wisenberg presided at the grand jury. The jurors were his flock. He cracked jokes to keep up morale. He made sure they had time to interview witnesses. And he often jumped in himself with a trenchant question. He was not, however, as solicitous of witnesses. Defense lawyers complained that he would subpoena their clients for a set time and forget he had scheduled their testimony. He'd try to save face by briefly bringing them before the grand jury, sending them home, and then calling them back. Gerard Treanor had to cut short an out-of-town visit to his mother so that he could escort his client, Nancy Hernreich, to the grand jury. But Wisenberg kept her waiting until the end of the day, then called her in for ten minutes.

The musical chairs offended Bob Bittman's sense of order, and he demanded to know why witnesses had to go before the grand jury so many times.

"What difference does it make?" asked Wisenberg.

"It makes us look like Keystone Kops," said Bittman. He worried that it fueled criticism that the prosecutors were imperious.

But there was no criticizing the case the grand jury was building. In less than a month, the jurors had enough evidence of the affair to reach critical mass. Lewinsky was remarkably consistent in the story she had told confidantes, who corroborated Tripp's version of events and added a few salacious twists. Neysa Erbland, a high school friend from Los Angeles, said Lewinsky told her she had broken the ice with Clinton while dropping off papers in the Oval Office by flashing her underwear at him. She said Lewinsky gave a detailed account of her trysts, including one episode in which the president "took a cigar from his desk and inserted [it] inside her in a sexual way."

Erbland said Lewinsky told her Clinton had ruled out intercourse because "there were repercussions to that," adding that the presidential embargo was "kind of a little bit of a let down for her."

She was initially proud to have a friend sexually engaged with "the man who runs our country," Erbland told the grand jury. "You know, it was huge." She thought "atta girl." But as Lewinsky increasingly complained of being neglected, Erbland had advised her to "move on." Catherine Allday Davis had worried from the first time her Lewis & Clark College classmate confessed the affair. Lewinsky often saw the bright side, playfully wondering if the president would "pay for the dry cleaning" of her stained dress, Davis testified. But more often Lewinsky's e-mails had reflected her unhappiness that the "Big Creep," as she called the president, hadn't paid her enough attention.

Davis said Lewinsky seemed nervous and uptight in early 1998. She had reported a late December meeting with the president in which they agreed there was no evidence to prove their affair. "I didn't want to see her being like Susan McDougal," she told the grand jury, referring to the president's former business partner who had gone to prison for refusing to testify against Clinton. "I didn't want her to lie to protect the president," Davis said.

Details lent authenticity, but they all originated from the same place as Tripp's account—Lewinsky. Prosecutors needed to be sure she wasn't fantasizing. They got closer with the testimony of Lewis Fox, a former Secret Service officer. From the first days of their probe they had heard reports of Clinton and Lewinsky sightings by the president's guards. But getting them to talk wasn't easy. Fox, who had retired a year earlier, was freer to come forward and tell the grand jury what he had seen on an autumn weekend in 1995.

Fox testified that he had been posted outside the Oval Office door early one afternoon when Clinton emerged. He said he was expecting a young woman from the congressional liaison staff office. Ten minutes later, Lewinsky approached, saying she had some papers for the president. Fox knocked and the door swung open. Lewinsky received a greeting from Clinton and went inside. Fox said no one was in the room when Lewinsky arrived. Nor did anyone join them. There are four doors inside the Oval Office. One leads to a private study. The others are passageways that at the time were locked or under guard. If anyone had entered, Fox would have known. When his shift ended forty minutes later, he said, Clinton and Lewinsky were still inside alone together.

Fox told the grand jury that other uniformed officers had openly talked about Lewinsky's weekend visits to the Oval Office. He had become chummy with Lewinsky, and other officers would tease him: "Hey, Lew, your girl's seeing the president a lot." One of his fellow Oval Office guards, Gary Byrne, told Fox in early 1996 that he had reported Lewinsky's frequent visits to Deputy Chief of Staff Evelyn Lieberman, known for regulating the decorum of the West Wing's female staffers. In a day or so, Lewinsky was sent packing to the Pentagon.

But when the prosecutors deposed Byrne, he refused to discuss anything that would suggest an affair between Clinton and Lewinsky—even whether he had ever seen her enter the Oval Office. Clinton's Justice

Department was asserting the "protective function privilege," a brand-new privilege designed to prevent the president's protectors from having to testify.

Bill Clinton had to go halfway around the world to escape Monica-mania. On March 22, he left for Africa, bringing along an entourage of more than one thousand aides—including Betty Currie—and reporters. The six-nation, eleven-day tour had been planned for months, but couldn't have fallen at a better time to change the presidential staging. Seven time zones removed from Washington, Clinton drew huge crowds and seemed to regain his footing.

The domestic scandal caught up with him in the capital of Uganda, as he posed for photos on March 24 with President Yoweri Museveni. Asked about reports that White House aides had asserted executive privilege before Starr's grand jury, Clinton replied dismissively as if it was someone else's decision: "Look, that's a question that's being asked and answered back home by the people responsible to do that." In a closed court hearing seven days earlier, White House Counsel Charles Ruff said the president personally had ordered the invoking of executive privilege.

On April 1, as the Africa tour was ending, a federal judge in Little Rock threw out Paula Jones's suit, ruling that even if Clinton had propositioned her, his behavior would have been "boorish and offensive" but not damaging to Jones. When the decision reached him in Senegal, the president thought his attorneys were playing an April Fool's joke. After making sure it was true, he celebrated in his hotel room by chewing on a cigar and beating an African drum.

Clinton aides and supporters called the ruling momentous. Prosecuting perjured testimony in a civil case had been overkill, they argued. Now that the civil case itself had been dismissed, they claimed there was no basis at all for the Lewinsky investigation. Bill Ginsburg agreed, displaying new common ground with the White House a couple of weeks after lunching with presidential lawyer David Kendall at the old-world Cosmos Club. "Now that the Paula Jones case has disappeared, the relevance, the materiality, and the importance of anything my client may have done or not done pales," he declared.

The speculation forced Starr to give the fullest public statement yet of his prosecutorial philosophy. He gathered reporters on the front lawn of his Virginia home and said the president's alleged offenses were serious enough to pursue even if they had occurred in a civil case later found to be without merit. "In that civil case, you cannot defile the temple of justice," he said. "There is no room for white lies.

"You must play by the rules. . . . And if you don't play by those rules, if you lie under oath, if you intimidate a witness, if you seek otherwise to obstruct the process of justice, it doesn't matter who wins and who loses in the civil case. What matters, from the criminal law's perspective, is: Were crimes committed?"

8

"MAKE SURE
YOU KNOW EVERYTHING
YOU CAN POSSIBLY KNOW"

THE LEWINSKY PROBE focused Starr's anger squarely on Janet Reno. The attorney general, Starr believed, had a duty to protect the integrity of his investigation just as she did any federal law enforcement activity. Instead, as the president's allies spread lies about his assistants and undermined public trust in his probe, Reno and her top officials were silent. William French Smith would have quit in protest, Starr thought. Reno, he told colleagues, was a modern-day Pontius Pilate, allowing the crucifixion of innocents. She had compromised the grand traditions of the Justice Department, he said. She had forsaken her fidelity to the rule of law and turned his beloved institution into a mouthpiece for the White House. The spirit of Richard Nixon was back.

Particularly galling was Reno's support for the Secret Service's refusal to cooperate with the OIC. The last thing Starr wanted was a fight with the Secret Service. The agents and officers who put their lives on the line for the president represented the epitome of public service, he believed. But Bill Clinton had made them witnesses to Lewinsky's unseemly comings and goings. And now Starr's staff had heard that the president had pressured his hand-picked Secret Service director, Lewis Merletti, to keep his employees from talking.

The tip came from a source connected to the Secret Service's top command. He told the OIC that shortly after the New Year, Clinton had called Merletti into the Oval Office and given him marching orders: "I want Secret Service lawyers to research the question of executive privilege. I don't want anything coming out of the Secret Service about women."

The incident would have occurred a few weeks before Monica Lewinsky burst onto the world stage, when Paula Jones was the main threat to Clinton. On December 23, Jones's lawyers had subpoenaed Secret Service work records to identify officers who might provide evidence of presidential sexual advances toward female employees. On January 13—not long after the reported conversation between Merletti and Clinton—the Justice Department filed court papers on Merletti's behalf, asking Judge Susan Webber Wright to recognize a special privilege for the service's "protective function" and block the subpoenas. Merletti had asked the department to intervene, and the decision to comply was made by Frank Hunger, chief of DOJ's civil division and Vice President Al Gore's brother-in-law.

Wright threw out the subpoenas on grounds that they were unlikely to turn up anything relevant to Jones's suit, so the question of privilege was never addressed. But her order revealed that Clinton's lawyers had supported the Secret Service motion in closed chambers. Had Clinton compromised a law enforcement agency? Starr wondered. The suspicion that Merletti had acted because of political pressure from Clinton in the Lewinsky matter hardened the resolve of Starr's prosecutors to question officers who could corroborate her frequent visits behind the closed doors of the Oval Office.

Merletti seemed determined to prevent that. Appointed by Clinton six months earlier after serving as his closest protector, his "body man," he put together a briefing for select groups of Washington decision-makers. It was a primer on assassination, complete with gory film clips to dramatize what had happened to world leaders like John Kennedy and Yitzhak Rabin when their agents were not close enough. His point was that if a president can't trust his security officers to keep his secrets, he will push them away, with potentially tragic consequences. Of course, attempts on a president's life have always occurred in public places, where he would be unlikely to do anything he'd want to hide from his security detail. Nonetheless, Merletti argued, more assassinations were inevitable unless agents were specially exempted from having to reveal their observations of the president, except when they immediately recognize a crime has occurred.

After retired officer Lewis Fox testified before the grand jury, the Justice Department informed Starr of plans to assert the "protective function privilege" on behalf of any guards called to testify. The plan had little support beyond the department's top political appointees. But Merletti pleaded for it as a safeguard against "the worst thing to happen to the service since the Kennedy assassination." Treasury Secretary Robert Rubin, whose department included the Secret Service, sent his general counsel, Ed Knight, to press the issue on DOJ.

Deputy Attorney General Eric Holder favored the decision on the ground that Merletti was the expert on security problems. But he conceded later to Jackie Bennett that the odds of this new theory's being upheld in court were no better than 5 percent. DOJ's point man on the issue, Jonathan Schwartz, was even less charitable. He told Starr deputy Bob Bittman that he feared DOJ's advocacy of the "protective function privilege" would be seen as a political exercise. The department's veteran lawyers, he said, thought it wrongheaded.

The president's support for the privilege in the Jones case had gone largely unnoticed, allowing the White House to claim it had a hands-off policy on the issue. At an April 30 news conference, Clinton said, "With regard to the Secret Service, I literally have had no involvement in that decision whatever." But this effort to block Secret Service testimony had all the markings of Clinton's survival-first politics. It played well with the public, according to Mark Penn, who reported that people were worried about turning security officers into spies on the president. And from his lawyers' viewpoint, it was coming just in time. Lewis Fox's statements to the press that Lewinsky had spent time alone with Clinton in the Oval Office had demonstrated just how damaging testimony from officers could be. Meanwhile, the prosecutors had subpoenaed two more uniformed officers and the general counsel of the Secret Service, John Kelleher.

Starr thought it odd that the head of a law enforcement agency was arguing for a special right to withhold potentially relevant information in a criminal probe. He believed the "protective function privilege" stood logic on its head: It would allow testimony from a Secret Service agent who had seen a president commit a murder, but not from one who had seen him throw a gun into the Potomac River and later learned that a murder had taken place at the White House. Precedent was on Starr's side. Officers had been questioned after Vince Foster's 1993 death to determine whether any of his papers had been removed, and also when Hillary Clinton's billing records were discovered in the White House residence. The difference this time was that investigators wanted to ask the officers specifically about what they had seen and heard the president do.

Few issues united Starr's office the way this one did. Even Mary Anne Wirth, the least aggressive of the OIC lawyers, argued that Secret Service testimony was vital—the best lever Starr had to bring in Lewinsky. She would have no reason to remain silent once officers provided direct evidence of her Oval Office visits. Starr saw the "protective function privilege" as a scheme to keep prosecutors from getting those facts. He resolved to fight it.

A month after Justice had warned it would go to court, Starr went ahead with plans to depose the two uniformed officers and Kelleher. When DOJ asked why it was necessary to summon an attorney who was never near Lewinsky, Bob Bittman cited another line of inquiry. Kelleher, he explained, was believed to know of "a directive from the president to the director of the Secret Service that may involve or lead to evidence of obstruction of justice." Justice officials informed Merletti and Kelleher, who both denied knowledge of such a directive. Kelleher showed up at Starr's office, but asserted the privilege, as did the officers. Starr informed DOJ the next step he took would be in court.

On Sunday, March 29, Janet Reno called Starr in for a meeting. The two, accompanied by aides, faced off in her vast conference room to address the most serious clash between an attorney general and special prosecutor since Watergate.

Starr didn't report to Reno, and the two had had few dealings. Reno had called him when he was appointed to pledge her cooperation and instruct him to contact the head of the criminal division if he had any business to discuss with DOJ. The few times they had met in the years since, Starr had found her warm in personal asides but grandly aloof in official matters. He thought the attorney general didn't engage unless she was challenged. For her part, Reno considered Starr sanctimonious, inclined to ascribe dark motives to anyone who disagreed with him.

This day Reno was engaged. She started by clearing the air. She had heard that Starr's aides thought the Secret Service privilege was designed to bail Clinton out of his political and legal mess. Not true, she said: She had taken the Secret Service case "for principled reasons, not because of political motivation on our part to obstruct." Merletti had initially refused to allow officers and agents to have any discussions with prosecutors. But Reno said the only information she supported withholding from Starr was their observations of the president. Even so, she knew it was impossible to avoid a court fight.

"Let's narrow the dispute," she suggested.

Eric Holder asked how far Starr intended to go in questioning Secret Service employees. He was concerned about the Kelleher subpoena because of attorney-client privilege, and Starr had signaled plans to call Merletti. Starr said he believed he had taken a "rifle shot approach," targeting only those who could provide meaningful evidence. The "protective function privilege," he argued, had no legal basis. He cited the Supreme Court ruling against Richard Nixon, which held that a grand jury subpoena trumps privilege. He said he understood the concerns of the service, which he had represented as solicitor general. He had tried to be accommodating by aiming his first subpoenas at uniformed officers posted at the White House, not at the plainclothes agents who protect the body of the president and are most privy to his private times. He had tried to avoid the adversarial setting of a grand jury by calling Kelleher and two agents to his office for depositions.

Reno and Starr agreed to look for middle ground and directed their aides—Jonathan Schwartz and Bob Bittman—to work out a compromise. Schwartz was a natural to negotiate with the wary Starr team. An assistant U.S. attorney on loan to the department, he worked for Holder but had no political ties to the White House. As a career prosecutor, he viewed privileges as impediments to evidence-gathering. He and Bittman quickly came up with an plan they thought would allow Starr to gain at least some information while the litigation proceeded. But Merletti vetoed it.

Merletti reluctantly agreed to let officers answer questions that did not involve what he considered privileged information. The Justice Department told him he had no legal right to say no. But officers were so unsure of what they were allowed to say that the depositions centered on lawyering rather than on fact-gathering. During his testimony on April 16, for example, Secret Service officer Robert Almasy left the room after almost every question to check with DOJ and Secret Service lawyers waiting outside. The session lasted six hours and twenty minutes. Almasy spent four hours and five minutes of that time in consultation with his lawyers.

The prosecutors suspected that government lawyers were trying to use the sessions to learn more about Starr's probe, a practice common among private defense attorneys "who wish to conceal relevant evidence or otherwise stonewall a grand jury investigation," deputy Jackie Bennett wrote Holder the day after Almasy was deposed. "What happened yesterday was, in my view, an effort by sworn officials of the Executive Branch to hinder this investigation."

Holder was outraged that Bennett would impugn the integrity of the line lawyer. He went to Starr's office to complain and insisted that the White House had no role in the exercise of the privilege. He urged Starr's team to bring officers in for unsworn interviews instead of formal depositions. Starr agreed.

That strategy loosened lips to some degree, and about thirty interviews followed. Prosecutors found out new details about Lewinsky, including her December 6, 1997 temper tantrum after a Secret Service officer told her TV personality Eleanor Mondale was visiting Clinton. Still, prosecutors were kept from asking questions about the president. And Clinton's lawyers, who would help shape his story, were getting a very good reading on what the officers had told them. DOJ officials suspected Secret Service brass as the conduit.

Separately, Starr's investigators spent weeks trying to corroborate Clinton's alleged Oval Office directive to Merletti. They gave up when their informant, whom they had assured of confidentiality, refused to go on the record for fear of reprisals. But Starr was more convinced than ever that the privilege was a sham intended to keep him from important evidence.

On May 14 he appeared personally before Judge Norma Holloway Johnson, asking her to compel the testimony of Secret Service officials. The privilege, he argued, would turn agents into a "Praetorian guard," serving the president rather than the people. A president would be free to "engage in criminal activity" without fear of testimony from officers who might have witnessed it. A formidable litigator, Starr relished the chance to spar with the Justice Department lawyer, Gary Grindler, who argued that forcing officers to testify would turn them into "watchdogs and video cameras." Starr responded that there would never be a reason to call them, except for grand jury probes. "We're not interested in family matters," he said. "We're interested in evidence of crimes."

The White House had already found creative ways to shield presidential aides from Starr's investigation. When Sidney Blumenthal was asked in the grand jury about talks he had with the first lady, he refused to answer, citing executive privilege, a prerogative normally construed to belong to the president alone. Deputy Counsel Bruce Lindsey had gone one step further, citing executive privilege to cover a lunch with Vernon Jordan the day after Clinton's Jones deposition. Lindsey refused to repeat the luncheon conversation about the case because "it impacts on the presidency and the president as president."

Lindsey's old foil, Jackie Bennett, said in the grand jury that he was struggling to understand how a shield for official communications between the president and his advisers could cover an adviser's talks with Jordan, who does not even work at the White House.

Because Jordan is an adviser, said Lindsey.

Does that mean "any civilian who the president happens to meet and asks for advice is an adviser of the president?" asked Bennett.

Lindsey said yes, if it has to do with "presidential issues."

Bennett was incredulous. "How about the weatherman if he wants to travel?" he asked.

The jury of talk show guests and op-ed columnists accused Starr of trying to weaken the presidency by invading the sanctity of the office, by exposing to scrutiny the president's private talks with advisers and private moments with his friends. Starr saw just the reverse. He was not making new constitutional law, he was preventing Clinton from doing so. The president, he told his aides, had invoked sacred constitutional principles as part of a "calculated effort to impede and impair" them. Clinton had used the machinery of government to "perpetuate a lie," said Starr, and when he sent out cabinet officers to assure the public of his innocence, he had gone beyond "simple mendacity about a private matter." Starr called privilege claims "extravagant and extreme."

Judge Johnson agreed, though she kept her opinions sealed because the issues came up in the context of the grand jury and could touch on its secret deliberations. In a series of orders, she ruled there was no "protective function privilege" for Secret Service agents, and she threw out the claims of executive privilege by Lindsey and Blumenthal, directing them to answer all questions asked in the grand jury. The OIC prosecutors could at least take some private satisfaction that the judge, as Starr saw it, had "rejected the excesses and pathologies of the lawyers for this particular president." But every success led to an appeal by Clinton's lawyers, and in the meantime, the OIC wasn't getting any closer to the truth.

A few days after Starr appeared in court to compel the Secret Service testimony, his assistants assembled for the daily 5 P.M. meeting, stopping at their mailboxes, as they customarily did, to look for the latest staff memo or court ruling. Inside was another letter from Grindler. He wrote to inform Starr that Bayani Nelvis, the Oval Office steward and pal of Lewinsky, would hereafter invoke the "culinary functions privilege" in further grand jury questioning about matters he may have observed while serving food and beverages to the president. "It is abundantly clear that, if presidential stewards are compelled to testify about their observations of the president that they have made while performing their culinary functions, future presidents will feel the need to distance themselves from the stewards," said the letter. "This, in turn, would have potentially disastrous effects. Presidents might find it necessary, for example, to obtain their food from private food providers, such as pizza delivery companies, rather than the White House mess. In the extreme, the president might push away the stewards to such a distance that he would be unable to eat at all, leading to malnutrition and eventual starvation. At a minimum, it should be clear that a breach of the confidentiality inherent in presidential food preparation will cause the Chief Executive increasingly to turn to fast food franchises for his nutritional needs, resulting in possible presidential indigestion, weight gain and arteriosclerosis."

Everyone was reading as they took their seats. Soon the room broke up in laughter. The letter was the work of two young litigators, Joseph Ditkoff and Mischa Travers, in despair over the continuous struggle against the Justice Department. They had cut and pasted their document onto an old Grindler letter, redated it, and had it stamped "received" by the office. No one in the office was taken in, but they would not have been shocked if it actually happened, either.

If anyone could manage the tricky task of running the Justice Department for a president who was himself under criminal investigation, it was Eric Holder. The New York–born son of a Barbadian father, Holder, forty-seven, was smooth and smart, a master of finesse. As U.S. attorney for the District of Columbia—appointed by Clinton in 1993—he had inherited his Republican predecessor's corruption investigation of Dan Rostenkowski, one of the most powerful Democrats in Congress. Holder found a safe middle course: He pressed ahead with the case, but negotiated a plea bargain. He appeared frequently at community events in the largely black city, restoring relations frayed by a decade during which white Republicans ran the U.S. attorney's office. But he also challenged the African-American community to be less complacent about fighting neighborhood crime. He became popular enough in town to consider running for mayor.

Now Holder was in an exquisitely delicate position. Just a year earlier, Clinton had tapped him for the number two job at Justice. The administration saw him as someone the White House could deal with after years of strained relations with Reno, who had commissioned six independent counsel probes that were politically embarrassing to the president. As part of his new portfolio, Holder tried to track the independent counsels. He made his office their point of contact with the department, shifting that responsibility away from career lawyers in the criminal division. At Holder's urging, Reno had rejected persistent calls from Congress and from her own line prosecutors to appoint an independent counsel to investigate questionable fundraising practices by Clinton and Vice President Al Gore in the 1996 campaign. Holder even had reason to think he might be in line for Reno's job if the attorney general, suffering from Parkinson's disease, stepped down before the end of Clinton's second term.

But the Lewinsky debacle had derailed him. Presidential aides questioned how he could have recommended Starr to run the most threatening of all the probes aimed at Clinton. Holder's once bright future dimmed the day the Lewinsky story broke.

Now, though, Holder seemed to be making amends by keeping Starr off-balance. His actions were initially so subtle that only Starr himself and his deputies knew about it. In the aftermath of David Kendall's dramatic charge that the OIC was leaking grand jury information, Starr promised an internal investigation. Holder stopped him, suggesting that he wait to see if Judge Johnson found merit in Kendall's claims. "We're going to stand down for now," he said, vetoing Starr's request for FBI agents. Starr assumed Holder didn't think Kendall's charges were worth exploring, and that was fine with him.

But Holder didn't let the matter drop entirely. He quietly called the judge and offered DOJ's help on pending issues raised by the president's lawyers, which included executive privilege and the leaks question. Johnson related the conversation to Starr during a private meeting in her chambers. Holder, she said, told her, "If there is any way we can be of help on these motions, we would be happy to do so." Johnson said she declined the offer.

That night Starr woke up at 3 A.M. with a start. *Holder was trying to insert himself into the leak investigation,* he thought. Starr felt betrayed. Holder *did* want a leak investigation—one he could control. The Justice Department couldn't investigate the case against Clinton because it was run by the president's appointees. Yet Starr believed Holder had secretly offered to take up charges leveled by Clinton's lawyer and to investigate prosecutors who threatened the president. From that point on, although they never told him they knew of his call to the judge, Starr's team saw Holder as an enemy.

Holder, who shared a background in the public integrity section of Justice with Jackie Bennett, couldn't have been more different from the aggressive, uncompromising prosecutor. He was a laid-back politician, a conciliator in the fashion of his mentor, Ron Brown, Clinton's Commerce secretary until his death in 1996. He had strong ties to the clubby world of Washington's white-collar criminal defense bar, lawyers who represented high-profile clients in the biggest congressional and criminal investigations. White House Counsel Chuck Ruff came from that milieu, as did many of the prominent Democrats who sprang to Clinton's defense, among them former Watergate prosecutor Richard Ben-Veniste, ex-White House Counsel Lloyd Cutler, and Abbe Lowell, who eventually became chief Democratic counsel for the House Judiciary Committee. These were the oracles of Sunday morning, the talking heads who were accustomed to molding public opinion whenever scandal erupted on the political landscape. To the general public, they appeared to be impartial observers. But as Democrats, it was natural for them to side with a popular Democratic president, and as defense lawyers, it was logical that they would be critical of Starr's prosecutorial pursuits. They worked behind the scenes as well, circulating tips to friendly reporters, helping to shape coverage favorable to Clinton—and adverse to Starr.

The Democratic legal establishment also had a long-standing dislike of Bennett, going back to his years in the Justice Department. In 1992, he had been sent to San Antonio to prosecute Douglas Jaffe, a wealthy Texas businessman accused of making illegal campaign contributions. Jaffe was a political patron of former House Speaker Jim Wright, and the local hostility toward the case was reflected by the U.S. attorney, who went so far as to refuse to let Bennett use his copying machines. Jaffe's lawyer was Reid Weingarten, a leading white-collar defense attorney in Washington and a pal of Holder's from public integrity. Weingarten accused Bennett of roughing up witnesses.

Lowell had originally represented Jaffe, but was forced to step down after Bennett complained he had a legal conflict. Bennett tangled with Lowell partner Stanley Brand on the witness stand, aggressively questioning him about legal advice he had given Jaffe on campaign contributions. Brand responded with hostility as Weingarten glowered from the defense table. In the end, Jaffe was acquitted, and the judge blasted Bennett, demanding he tell his bosses in Washington not to bring any more "rinky dink" cases. But Bennett kept going. The Jaffe matter was the prelude to a bigger case, a racketeering indictment against Democratic Representative Albert Bustamonte of Texas. Bennett and his colleagues convicted Bustamonte of taking bribes, including one from Doug Jaffe. In 1994, Bennett received the Justice Department's top honor, in recognition of the unfriendly venue and difficulty of the prosecution. He also won the permanent enmity of powerful Democratic political forces in Washington and Texas.

More and more, it seemed to Starr and Bennett, Holder was adopting his friends' view of the case against Clinton. Despite his own role in launching the probe, the deputy AG had begun to question its legitimacy. He didn't go as far as presidential lawyer David Kendall, who had publicly accused Starr of colluding with the Paula Jones camp to entrap Clinton. But Holder did tell associates he now believed Starr's team might have had a more extensive relationship with the Jones lawyers than Bennett revealed when he sought authority to look into Linda Tripp's story. In retrospect, Holder said, he believed Bennett had been maneuvering from the beginning to take control of the case.

On March 20, 1998, Bennett was back at DOJ attending a retirement party for an old colleague when his office paged him with an urgent message. Eric Holder wanted to talk to Starr right away. Starr was in court, so Bennett returned the call. A few minutes later, he was face to face with Holder two floors up in the deputy attorney general's elegant office overlooking the dome of the Smithsonian's Natural History Museum.

The normally placid Holder was agitated. "Merletti's ready to go nuclear on you guys," he said. The Secret Service director had just learned that Starr's FBI agents had interviewed his predecessor, Eljay Bowron, without clearing the interview with him. He was prepared to call a press conference to blast Starr and the FBI, said Holder, pacing the room. That sort of interagency warfare would be ugly.

"We did something Merletti didn't know about, that's why he's upset," said Bennett. Still looking for a way around Merletti's objections to calling agents before the grand jury, Starr had dispatched investigators to question Bowron about his resignation in 1997. There were persistent rumors that he had left because Clinton insisted on relaxing security to allow big campaign contributors, some of them with criminal histories, into the White House for fundraising coffees. The relaxation of security might cast doubt on Merletti's assertions that that was his paramount concern. Bowron told the FBI that he had left for financial reasons. But Merletti was still angered by the visit.

Bennett challenged Holder: "You're telling me you don't want us to do this."

"No, no, you do what you have to do," Holder responded.

But Bennett was in no mood to make peace. Holder, he believed, was actively undermining Starr's probe. Bennett said he knew Holder had quietly disparaged Starr's team to the media. He complained bitterly that the department had done nothing to stop the attacks by the White House and its allies on Starr's lawyers, including several high-ranking prosecutors on loan from the Justice Department. Starr and

Bennett himself had been vilified by the White House and its allies, he said, and Mike Emmick and Bruce Udolf—both longtime assistant U.S. attorneys—had nearly been destroyed.

Holder dropped his usual conciliatory manner. "You guys are just too thin-skinned," he said dismissively. "This is the big leagues."

Bennett was enraged. What did Holder know about the big leagues? he thought. He had never lived though anything like this. "You have a duty to come forward and defend them!" Bennett yelled. Emmick and Udolf had been criticized for work performed for the Clinton Justice Department before joining Starr's office, said Bennett. "At a very minimum if the White House is criticizing the conduct of somebody who did work on its behalf, you have an obligation, Janet Reno has an obligation, to say, 'That's it. You just crossed the line, White House. We will not have you deprecating the work somebody did on your behalf just because they are now on loan to the OIC.'" Defense lawyers, Bennett said, might be able to use the White House–sponsored criticism to try to reverse convictions won in the past by Emmick and Udolf.

Holder said he hadn't thought of it like that. He agreed to bring it up with Reno. Privately, he thought Bennett had been way out of line, jumping to unfounded conclusions about DOJ's motives. But for now, at least, he wanted to calm things down.

Three weeks later, he was ready for war. On April 9, Holder sent a letter to Starr calling for an investigation into whether Arkansas Whitewater witness David Hale had been paid by conservative philanthropist Richard Mellon Scaife to discredit the president in Starr's probe. Holder added a jab at Starr, suggesting that Scaife's role might present a conflict of interest for him. In that case, he said, DOJ could take on the investigation. Then Holder took the unusual step of releasing the letter to the press.

Holder's demand rested on the strange and shifting stories that an Arkansas tarot-card reader and her teenage son had given to the Internet magazine *Salon* and to the weekly *New York Observer*. The conduit for the payments, they said, was Arkansas bait shop owner Parker Dozhier, the fortune-teller's ex-boyfriend. In their account, Dozhier received the money from a Scaife-funded project linked to the *American*

Spectator and passed it on to Hale. But their stories varied in the telling. The woman first said she'd seen money changing hands, then that she had not actually witnessed payments. Her son gave different accounts of how much money he claimed to have seen passed from Dozhier to Hale.

On the basis of those wispy stories, DOJ had publicly signaled a lack of confidence in Starr. And Clinton lawyer Kendall immediately seized on the shadowy allegations, sending his own letter to Starr a day after Holder's. "You have well-publicized connections to Richard Mellon Scaife," wrote Kendall. "I do not think you or your office can credibly or appropriately conduct this investigation."

Starr appeared on the steps of the federal courthouse on April 16 to announce his reply to Holder. He said his Little Rock office was convinced that no such payments to Hale had occurred, at least while he was under its jurisdiction as a cooperating witness. The alleged payments, Starr said, if they occurred at all, would have happened when Robert Fiske was running the Whitewater investigation under the auspices of the Justice Department. Starr said he would have a neutral third party investigate. Eventually, with Reno's concurrence, he chose Michael J. Shaheen, for twenty-two years the head of the Justice Department's office of professional responsibility.

Starr had another major announcement. He had informed Pepperdine University that he would not be taking a deanship there, ending the controversy over his accepting a job at an institution to which Scaife had been a benefactor. Starr said he made the decision because he would not be in a position to leave his post anytime soon. The end of his investigation, he told reporters, was "not yet in sight."

Ever since Betty Currie had met his team in January, Starr had known his investigation would probably end up in Congress. Under the Independent Counsel Act, he was required to refer to the House any "substantial and credible information that may constitute grounds for an impeachment."

But the statute provided no guidance on the content and timing of an impeachment referral. What was it supposed to look like? Raw evidence? An indictment? Something different? Nowhere else in American law is "substantial and credible" the standard for legal judgment or action. Grand juries bring indictments on "probable cause," and juries convict when they find proof "beyond a reasonable doubt." The Independent Counsel Act was an anomaly, one of the reasons Starr had opposed its enactment in the first place. And its impeachment provision had never been triggered.

For ideas on what Congress had intended, Starr had none other than Sam Dash, the self-proclaimed "father" of the act as chief counsel to the Senate Watergate Committee. Dash often told Starr and his team that anything Clinton had done in the Lewinsky case was insignificant compared to Watergate: "When you compare it to Watergate, on a grading of 10 being the most serious, I give it a 1." Still, he believed that the Lewinsky investigation was important and had to be pursued. "It involves the president of the United States as the chief law enforcer of the country attempting to destroy the judicial process," he told colleagues.

Dash wanted Starr's investigation to bring credit to the already controversial statute, not damage it further. That was the reason he had signed on as ethics counselor in the fall of 1994. In those early days, he lectured Starr's new team on investigative techniques—how they had done it in Watergate, by moving out from their target to gather evidence in widening circles. An independent counsel, Dash advised, had to be thorough and comprehensive, turning over every rock, running down every lead.

Dash's advice had as much to do with his view of those in Congress as with his understanding of the law. "Take your time," he told Starr. "Make sure you know everything you can possibly know before you send it." There should be no wiggle room, he insisted. Otherwise, he warned, Congress would "pick it apart, shove it aside, and overlook the fact that what we are talking about is perjury, obstruction of justice—serious federal crimes, as opposed to 'I misled my wife about an extramarital affair.'" Congress, Dash predicted, "will not behave boldly or bravely."

But at this point, Starr's worry was getting the referral to Congress, not what Congress would do with it. The congressional elections a half-year away loomed large. Justice Department guidelines explicitly cautioned prosecutors against indicting a politician too close to an election.

Everyone in Starr's office had his or her own views of what the law required. The career prosecutors reacted reflexively. They wanted to build a powerful, airtight case like the ones they took to trial. The idea of sending up a referral without first gathering all the evidence simply contradicted all their training and experience. Mike Emmick, for one, argued that moving too fast might weaken the case Congress would consider. The office might have enough "substantial and credible information" to trigger a referral, he said, but the strongest evidence so far was against Lewinsky. Most of what they had on Clinton was hearsay, albeit extensively corroborated. Congress would want Lewinsky's testimony and probably grant her immunity to get it, making any criminal prosecution of her extremely difficult and thus reducing her incentive to tell the truth. Emmick and the other veteran prosecutors wanted Lewinsky's testimony before Congress got the case.

Staff lawyer Mischa Travers occupied the other end of the OIC spectrum. He argued that they already had met the standard of "substantial and credible" information, and should simply send Congress what they had. The investigation was a political hot potato, and it was time to throw it to someone else. "Just send it up," urged Travers, a corporate lawyer brought in to work on legal briefs. Get a truck and haul all of it up to Capitol Hill—the records, the grand jury testimony, the tapes, the gifts.

Starr dismissed that idea as "irresponsible." As he saw it, the law required him at a minimum to carefully assemble the information and provide a legal analysis.

The independent counsel had had a dry run at impeachment a year earlier. Then, the question had been whether there was "substantial and credible" information of perjury by Clinton in his testimony at the trial of Arkansas Governor Jim Guy Tucker and onetime Clinton business partners Jim and Susan McDougal. Starr had concluded that the case against Clinton didn't meet the credibility standard because the witnesses would have been a pair of convicted felons, Jim McDougal and David Hale. He made his decision after reviewing a hundred-page memo prepared by the Little Rock staff. In the process, he had thought extensively about the statutory threshold. And this time, he knew he was past it.

His duty, Starr felt, was to present a document that was careful and accurate. It was not his job to build a persuasive case for impeachment. That was up to Congress. House Judiciary Committee Chairman Henry Hyde and his colleagues on the House Judiciary Committee might decide that a referral did not merit action. Starr wanted only to ensure that there were no legal or factual flaws in the report he set before them.

"Congress has placed this responsibility upon us," Starr told his staff. "There is not a single word in the statute or its legislative history that says 'thou shalt prosecute,' but we are sitting on this information, and each day that goes by is a day that the country, for better or worse, does not have this information. This is an express statutory responsibility uniquely imposed on independent counsels to report. It's very true the statute doesn't say when. But the very idea of the possible impeachment of a president of the United States is pregnant with the demand that you act quickly when you have it."

Starr often reminded his staff that under the Independent Counsel Act, "prosecutorial discretion is discretionary. My impeachment duty is mandatory." He said he did not want to repeat the folly of Union General George McClellan, forever marching and drilling his troops instead of crossing the Potomac to join the battle. He did not want to keep bringing in more witnesses to massage and perfect the evidence.

The debate over how much information would suffice began in March, and would last for several months. Starr first set a May 15 deadline for completing the referral. But in May, he had to agree with what almost everyone else in the office believed: Two witnesses were missing.

They needed testimony from Clinton or Lewinsky—preferably both—to meet their statutory duty to Congress.

9

"WE'VE GOT TO MAKE A STAND"

KEN STARR'S POLITICS were complex, rooted in the Texas of the 1950s—a place and time dominated by Senate Majority Leader Lyndon B. Johnson. LBJ was a hero to many Texans, but Bill Starr, the upright Church of Christ minister, saw him as a grasping and devious hack who would let nothing stand in the way of amassing power. Absorbing his father's attitude, Ken Starr would forever abhor the unprincipled, unscrupulous side of politics. He would also idolize those he thought rose above it.

The first of these was John Kennedy. The televised Kennedy-Nixon debates were Starr's first political texts. He started to read national news magazines and got involved in student government. The Cuban missile crisis and Kennedy's vow to beat the Russians to the moon captured his imagination and expanded his horizons. Someday, Starr decided, he would work in Washington D.C.

His first job there, during his undergraduate days at George Washington University, gave him an insider's view of politics in the United States Congress, then roiling with some of the most passionately fought issues of the twentieth century. Starr signed on to handle constituent mail for Bob Price, a libertarian Republican from the

Texas panhandle. Price was an unusual political mentor, a stubborn maverick who disdained polling and insisted on voting his conscience even if it meant opposing agricultural subsidies for his own constituents. "If they don't like it, they can go fuck themselves," he told his young aide. Starr was impressed with Price's independence—even after the congressman's constituents rewarded it by voting him out of office.

By the time Starr went to work for Ronald Reagan, he had become a Republican, but he was never the hard-right ideologue later portrayed by Clinton allies. He supported Robert Bork's nomination for the Supreme Court in 1987, and was appalled at the contemptuous treatment Bork received at the hands of Senate Democrats. But Starr also angered conservatives by arguing that the right to privacy covers contraception, a contentious issue in the Bork confirmation hearings. During the Bush administration, Starr was on the short list of likely Supreme Court candidates, but his judicial championing of First Amendment rights and past scrapes with conservatives kept him from being nominated.

At various points in his career Starr had considered electoral politics, weighing a run for Texas attorney general at one point. Just a year before he was named independent counsel, he had considered challenging Oliver North in Virginia's Republican primary for the Senate. Starr wanted to deny the nomination to North, whom he regarded as an unscrupulous lawbreaker and a disgrace to the Reagan administration. North heard of Starr's interest and asked him to lunch. "I am determined," he told Starr, boasting of his campaign war chest and the political commitments he'd amassed. His message had its intended effect: Starr left the table more disgusted than ever with North but convinced that a challenge would be futile.

He had no more appetite for political warfare in the job of independent counsel. He saw the law as his shield and refused to engage with critics and opponents. He would not discuss James Carville's damaging and oft-repeated story that in 1993 Starr had approached him at an airport and said, "Your boy Clinton is going to get rolled." A conversation did occur, though to anyone who knew Starr the comments attributed to him seemed out of character. But he never took on Carville in a public spat, even after leaving office. The consultant and White House sponsors understood what Starr did not, that in politics, the unanswered charge sticks.

As allegations about Starr accumulated, it became more and more difficult for his supporters in Congress to come to his defense. And as his public image darkened, so did congressional prospects for action on his referral. The day after Marcia Lewis collapsed at the grand jury, Clinton's pollster announced at the White House's morning staff meeting that Starr's public approval numbers had crashed. "He's down in Gingrich-land," Mark Penn said, referring to the House speaker's dismal poll ratings.

When the topic of polling came up, Starr pointed to Abraham Lincoln. "We would not be one nation if Lincoln followed the opinion polls," he often said. Like his first boss, Bob Price, he thought of worrying about popular sentiment as a substitute for real leadership. The nation was built in part on "counter-majoritarian influences," like the Bill of Rights and the unelected judiciary, he would say. He told his staff they had been asked to perform a legal function, not public policy. "It is simply clear: facts and law."

Some of Starr's friends realized the danger prosecutors face if they lose public support. Bob Vagley, a Washington lobbyist who was close to Starr and his wife, was kept awake nights thinking about how his friend was being demonized. As the head of an insurance trade association, Vagley understood the city's political dynamics. He tried to advise Starr on the basics of public relations, urging him to sever his ties to his law firm, Kirkland & Ellis. Starr had been designated to handle a long-scheduled appeals court argument for Meineke Discount Muffler, which was trying to overturn a company-busting $400 million judgment. He was under enormous pressure from Meineke and his law partners to go through with the argument and rejected Vagley out of hand. "I am not going to break my promise to them," he snapped.

Vagley had another suggestion. He pleaded with Starr to hire an experienced media adviser, someone who could head off embarrassments. "If you undercut the credibility of the prosecutor, nobody will believe what he says in the end," Vagley argued. When Starr said the issues were legal, not political, his friend responded: "It's both political and legal if impeachment is involved."

Secretly, Vagley enlisted a key ally in his public relations rescue effort. Alice Starr had been her husband's world-wise guide and protector since they met at a summer school Spanish class at Harvard in 1968. He was the brainy but provincial minister's son from far-off San Antonio, she the sophisticated, well-traveled Jewish daughter from a well-to-do suburb of New York City. Alice Mendell took him to Trader Vic's in Manhattan and taught him to dance, and his days as a summer Bible salesman were over. They married two years later.

Now Alice Starr was an executive for a large Virginia commercial development company, at ease dealing with local politicians and the public. Vagley didn't have to convince her that her husband needed help. Not only had the investigation taken a personal toll on him, it had taken over their lives. The Starrs' home on a quiet suburban street in Virginia was under twenty-four-hour federal guard because of death threats. Starr had two U.S. marshals escorting him full-time. The second of their three children, Carolyn—a Stanford University student, along with Chelsea Clinton—had also been the target of serious threats, and she, too, was under guard. Their son, Randy, an undergraduate at Duke, was so upset by his father's travails that he was rethinking plans for a career in the law. Alice Starr teared up when she talked of the assaults her husband had endured. She quietly urged Vagley on.

Vagley called Stuart Taylor, a legal affairs writer whose work he admired. Taylor thought Starr's investigation was important, but had criticized him for maintaining his private legal practice and for other blunders. Vagley learned Taylor had been first in his class at Harvard Law School. He knew that would impress Starr. He persuaded Taylor to think about working for the independent counsel. Then he sprang the idea on Starr, acknowledging, "You may hate me for this."

Starr had resisted earlier suggestions, but was intrigued by this one. He began a courtship of Taylor that lasted several weeks, telling him the office needed a "strategic thinker" to prepare for Congress. "There is no margin for error," he said.

Taylor was interested at first, then changed his mind. Frantic, Vagley and his wife, Holly Rudkin, tracked him down by phone at a Colorado ski resort in late March. Rudkin, an actress, knew Taylor loved Shakespeare. She exhorted him with the Saint Crispin's Day speech from *Henry V*—"We band of brothers." It got Taylor back in the game briefly, but he ultimately backed out, fearing he would not be able to return to journalism.

But by now, Starr was persuaded that he did need help. Within weeks, he hired lawyer Charles Bakaly, who had served as spokesman for Independent Counsel Donald Smaltz. Flying back to Washington after a meeting in Little Rock, Starr and Bakaly talked about ways to improve the office's public image. Should they enlist surrogates to publicly explain their position on issues like executive privilege? Should Starr try to get to know individual reporters? Bakaly said when he worked in the Reagan administration, he used to invite reporters over to his home. Starr was dubious. Given all the pressure and attention, he said, it would be hard to have reporters over for "libations," the minister's son's word for what most people in Washington called "drinks."

The conversation was overheard by someone seated nearby and reported in a *Washington Post* gossip column under the headline, STARR CATCHES A FLACK. The new public relations effort had a long way to go.

Before Starr could turn his attention entirely to the impeachment referral, he had to determine the fate of Hillary Clinton. On the morning of April 27, all of his attorneys, including the skeleton crew from Little Rock, gathered in Washington to conclude the Arkansas phase of the investigation. In twelve days, the Whitewater grand jury in Little Rock would expire. It was time for a decision: Either indict the first lady, decide not to do so, or empanel a new grand jury for the next eighteen months, dragging the long-running investigation to the year 2000. It was up to Little Rock deputy Hick Ewing to lay out the evidence.

Ewing, a fifty-six-year-old former U.S. attorney, had racked up a long list of public corruption convictions in his native Tennessee.

Since the fall of 1994, he had been with Starr, investigating the Clintons and their relationship to Jim McDougal's freewheeling savings and loan. In the early days of the Whitewater case, he had served as Starr's guide through the unfamiliar terrain of criminal probes. He had became Starr's closest friend in the office, though their lives in the law could not have been more different. Ewing specialized in developing witnesses and charting out investigative trails. Starr much preferred wrangling with constitutional issues.

But they were from the same part of the country and shared a deep religious faith. They discussed the meaning of Bible passages and occasionally attended church together. Often, when they shared lunch in the office, one of them would say grace. Ewing heard the biblical echoes in Starr's favorite aphorisms—such as "you reap what you sow"—that others in the office took as commonplace expressions.

They shared another powerful experience as well, though they never discussed it. Like people they had pursued in Arkansas, close family members of Starr and Ewing had swindled money. Starr's brother, Jerry, seven years his senior, had pleaded guilty in 1985 to taking $30,000 in a phony land deal. He received ten years' probation and was ordered to repay the money to his victims, two San Antonio women who were friends of the Starr family. The onetime economics instructor at Abilene Christian College returned to the family trade of barbering. At the time of his brother's ignominy, Starr was rocketing to the top of his profession. Just the year before, he became one of the youngest men ever appointed to the federal appeals court.

Ewing's father had been a legendary high school coach in Tennessee. Appointed Shelby County clerk, he developed a drinking problem and embezzled $38,000 in taxpayer funds, and in 1965, he was sent to prison for more than a year. The younger Ewing, serving in Vietnam at the time, was devastated by his father's conviction, and was able to talk about it only after his own religious awakening a decade later. His father died in 1996 at eighty-three, just hours before his son delivered the closing argument in one of the Whitewater bank-fraud trials.

Ewing and Starr shared an intolerance for people who lied under oath. Both were stubborn about keeping investigations going, no matter how problematic the evidence, as long as they were convinced that crimes had been committed. Starr's Washington staff had long pushed Ewing to wrap up his business in Arkansas, but he refused to be rushed. The Little Rock team was indicting targets and winning cases, with fourteen convictions to their credit, including the sitting governor. But in 1998, Ewing complained, most of his staff had been "raptured away" to Washington by the Lewinsky probe. His Whitewater resources were depleted as the grand jury neared the end of its term. "Monica," he told colleagues, "was a blessing in disguise for the Clintons."

For the April 27 presentation, Ewing and his team detailed the evidence against Hillary Clinton in a three-inch-thick memo. Ewing, compact and athletic, began his presentation at 8:30 A.M. He paced the room for more than three hours, recalling the facts from memory in his distinctive Memphis twang. He spoke passionately, laying out a case that the first lady had obstructed government investigators and made false statements about her legal work for McDougal's S&L, particularly on the thrift's notorious multimillion-dollar Castle Grande real estate project. McDougal had used the Little Rock thrift to engineer fraudulent land schemes that ultimately brought it down at a nearly $60 million cost to taxpayers.

Ewing described how Hillary Clinton had prepared papers on a real estate option at Castle Grande that allowed a Madison insider to drain $300,000 from the tottering thrift, a transaction presented to federal regulators at the time as perfectly proper. He drew heavily from Hillary Clinton's long-lost billing records, which showed the work she had done on the Castle Grande project. Before the records mysteriously turned up in 1996, federal banking investigators had questioned the first lady several times about her work for Madison. She said then she did not know anything about Castle Grande. Even after a secretary found her billing records in the White House residence, she insisted she had not lied, saying she knew the Castle Grande project under the name of its former corporate owner. But prosecutors believed she was well aware of the name. Her own former client, Jim McDougal, had been accused of bank fraud in 1990 in a highly publicized trial that centered on the Castle Grande transactions.

Ewing presented a clear outline of false statements and putative obstruction, while conceding that there were weaknesses in the evidence. The biggest problem was the unexpected death a month earlier of Jim McDougal, who had been serving time in prison for bank fraud. Without him, prosecutors would have a hard time describing the S&L dealings they suspected Hillary Clinton had lied about. And they did not have the proof to charge her with potentially the most obstructive act in the entire investigation—concealing her billing records. The FBI had interviewed more than five hundred people, including Secret Service officers, to find who might have had the missing records during the two years they were under subpoena. But everyone, including Hillary Clinton in her grand jury testimony, denied knowledge of their whereabouts.

After Ewing laid out the evidence, the afternoon was devoted to discussion. Virtually everybody concluded that the first lady had lied but that the evidence was not strong enough to convict her. Starr asked for comments from all five Little Rock lawyers who had worked on the prosecution memo. Not one was in favor of going forward with an indictment, including a somber Ewing, who spoke last.

One of the loudest opponents was Sam Dash, who had tried to head off the meeting altogether. Starr told him there was substantial evidence and they should "hear Hick out." Dash listened and confirmed to himself that the evidence was insufficient. "I was very strong on it," he would say later. "When I finished speaking and analyzed all the evidence and showed it was a bunch of nothing, I won over most of the staff." But Dash notwithstanding, the outcome had been all but a foregone conclusion. Several weeks earlier, Bittman and Bennett had vetoed Ewing's proposal that they inform Hillary Clinton that she was a target of their investigation and invite her to testify before the grand jury—the kind of moves that precede a criminal indictment.

By evening, Starr's team turned its attention to the two most intractable witnesses of the Whitewater investigation: Webster Hubbell and Susan McDougal. They decided not to bring another case against

Hubbell in Arkansas but discussed reindicting him in Washington on charges of making false statements and evading taxes.

The McDougal debate was more contentious. Her testimony was considered vital to determine whether Bill Clinton had lied at her 1996 bank-fraud trial, when he denied that he had urged David Hale to lend her $300,000 in government-backed funds. Some of that money had gone to the benefit of the Whitewater Development Corporation, jointly owned by the Clintons and the McDougals. Susan McDougal had refused to answer the grand jury's questions about Clinton's testimony and portrayed herself in the media as a martyr to Ken Starr's zeal.

Her defiance was a crime on its face: She had no right to refuse to answer questions about a crime for which she already had been convicted. But McDougal had already spent eighteen months in jail for civil contempt and had begun her two-year sentence for bank fraud. Some prosecutors thought reindicting her on a criminal contempt charge would look too heavy-handed. Bob Bittman said an indictment would give her more opportunities to play the victim. But Brett Kavanaugh, arguing that she had made a mockery of the legal system, insisted she had to be charged, even if a jury refused to convict her. A narrow majority favored indicting her on charges of criminal contempt. Starr agreed with them.

Starr had tried a different tack to get McDougal to break her silence the previous year. If Clinton were innocent, Starr reasoned, he had nothing to lose from her testimony, and he should ask her to tell the truth to the grand jury. Starr wrote five times to White House Counsel Chuck Ruff, asking the president to urge McDougal's cooperation. But Clinton refused to intervene, and he had refused even to rule out pardoning her. While McDougal was in jail for civil contempt in 1996, the president was asked publicly what he thought of her claim that Starr did not care about getting the real truth from her. "There's a lot of evidence to support that," Clinton replied. Starr complained to Ruff that the statement only "reinforced Ms. McDougal's intransigence." Ruff disagreed. It would be "entirely inappropriate" for Clinton to intervene with Susan McDougal, he said. Ruff added that the president had always urged everyone to tell the truth.

*   *   *

Starr and his team were growing impatient to hear the truth—especially from Clinton himself. Getting his story would be the fastest way to move the Lewinsky matter to Congress. Bittman and a few others had argued from the very first week that he should be subpoenaed. But Starr insisted on giving the president every opportunity to testify voluntarily. Since asking him in January to meet with the grand jury, he had issued five more invitations. But every overture was rejected by David Kendall.

The longer Kendall could put off the president's testimony, the more he could learn from news reports or friendly defense lawyers whose clients had testified. The more Kendall learned, the better he could prepare Clinton. Ideally, he would wait for Lewinsky's testimony to determine how much the president would have to admit. The worst scenario for Clinton would be if he testified first and said something that leaked out and angered Lewinsky.

The only thing Clinton could hope to accomplish by going before the grand jury was to persuade it to shut down. But Kendall knew it was too late for that, and anything Clinton might say would be used against him. So he rejected all Starr's offers. When Kendall claimed Clinton was too busy, Bittman noted in a letter that in the weeks since the scandal broke, the president had found enough time to squeeze in golf, basketball games, political fund-raisers, and a ski vacation. Bittman offered to do whatever was necessary to preserve presidential dignity and security. "Nothing," he wrote, "should stand in the way of the truth's coming out."

Kendall countered with his most pointed criticism to date. The Starr probe, he wrote March 18, "may not, in fact, be an even-handed search for justice but rather may be, for whatever reason, a campaign to embarrass and harass the President." He suggested a meeting to discuss his concerns, which deepened with the next day's editions of the *Washington Post*. The front-page story said House Speaker Newt Gingrich and Judiciary Committee Chairman Henry Hyde had agreed to send a small group of House members at the appropriate time to examine Starr's evidence to determine if there was any basis for impeachment.

On March 20, Kendall and Bittman met on neutral grounds for a rare and decisive face-off. In the lawyers' lounge of the federal courthouse, one floor above the grand jury, they shook hands and sat at a small table. For the next twenty minutes, they angrily talked past each other as White House Counsel Chuck Ruff and prosecutor Roger Heaton looked on.

Bittman got right to the point. "Is the president going to testify?"

Kendall demurred, saying he questioned the legitimacy of his probe. Starr, he said, had failed to fully inform the Justice Department of Linda Tripp's credibility problems, including those arising from her illegal taping of telephone conversations. Until that issue was resolved, he could not advise Clinton to cooperate.

Bittman replied that the attorney general had not second-guessed Starr's authority to proceed, so why should he?

Kendall changed the subject. He questioned whether Starr should have been relieved of the investigation in light of reports that a Kirkland & Ellis partner had aided the Jones legal team.

The discussion began to feel like bait-and-switch to Bittman. "If we answer all your concerns, will the president testify?" he asked.

"We'll have to see what the answers are," replied Kendall. "I don't know."

Starr had worked with Kendall once before to ease a politically sticky situation. The issue had arisen just before the 1996 election, as prosecutors sought White House lawyer Sherburne's notes of a legal discussion with Hillary Clinton. Kendall intended to claim executive privilege for the notes, but he feared that a closed-door hearing in Little Rock a week before the election would draw the attention of reporters and lead to inevitable comparisons to Richard Nixon. Starr agreed to move the hearing to Batesville, a remote hamlet in the Ozarks where no reporters would recognize the lawyers.

Kendall's professionalism in that earlier matter seemed sharply different from the caustic tone of his grand jury RSVPs. To Starr, the change suggested that Kendall had something to hide and that the president had no intention of testifying voluntarily. There would be no more invitations. But Starr wasn't ready to subpoena Clinton just yet.

*   *   *

One question Starr's team examined was whether Clinton should be considered a target for prosecution. The Justice Department had the last word on presidential immunity during Watergate, when then-Solicitor General Robert Bork ruled that a sitting president cannot be indicted. The Constitution vested in him the "power to control prosecution," Bork wrote, including the right to get rid of prosecutors who displease him. On that basis, Richard Nixon had ordered the firing of Watergate Special Prosecutor Archibald Cox. But Bork's opinion had been issued twenty-five years earlier, and Starr was uncertain whether it still applied.

Ron Rotunda, a constitutional scholar at the University of Illinois, had been a consultant to Starr when the question of indicting a sitting president arose in connection with Whitewater. As decision time neared in the Lewinsky case, Starr asked Rotunda to present his preliminary findings.

Lawyers filled the conference room for the May 12 presentation. Rotunda was a brilliant academic with a politically ecumenical résumé; he had been assistant Democratic counsel on the Senate Watergate Committee and also coauthor of a friend-of-the-court brief supporting Paula Jones's right to sue Clinton. Regarding claims of presidential immunity, he was aggressive even by the standards of Starr's hard-line prosecutors. The Independent Counsel Act of 1978, he said, weakened the president's control of prosecutions. The independent counsel was accountable not to the president but to the judges who appointed him. Constitutional doubts about the act had been quelled by a Supreme Court decision in 1988, which undercut the core argument of Bork's memorandum. Not even a sitting president is above the law, Rotunda said. The Supreme Court had ruled that the president could be sued while in office, he noted. What would be the logic of subjecting him to civil law but exempting him from the even more important criminal process?

Starr had devoted little time to the question of indicting Clinton. He saw it as separate from the impeachment track. But he listened carefully to Rotunda's three-hour briefing. At the end, Starr said he had been persuaded, at least in theory: The president could be indicted during his term.

Bittman focused on something else in the briefing. Rotunda had cited other sitting presidents, including James Monroe and Gerald Ford, who had testified after receiving a subpoena, though none had appeared before a grand jury. In that, Bittman found support for his long campaign to get Clinton's testimony.

On May 26, he circulated a detailed memo mentioning the legal history and Clinton's voluntary testimony in the Whitewater probe. In the memo, and at a follow-up meeting, Bittman said the goal of showing respect to the office of the presidency had been satisfied by the six invitations to Clinton. They were running out of witnesses to interview and leads to follow, he argued, and Starr was setting referral deadlines. They had lost the chance to get the president's story before he could tailor it to match the testimony of other witnesses. But if Clinton intended to challenge the subpoena in court, why not force him to start now? "We've got to make a stand," he pleaded.

Starr wanted everyone on board for such a momentous decision. His insistence on forging consensus was intended for occasions just like this one. He believed that collective decisions would tamp down excessive zeal and protect him from accusations of bias.

On this issue, though, his office was far from consensus. Bittman won over a few colleagues, but others were gun-shy about such a dramatic step. A few feared the inevitable litigation over a subpoena and its drain on manpower. But the largest concern was investigative. There would be one shot at questioning Clinton. Why not wait for witnesses who could sharpen the inquiry? The Secret Service had seen Lewinsky disappear into the Oval Office for long blocks of time. She was the big trophy. Prosecutors wanted her story before they confronted the president.

By spring, Lewinsky had gotten as far away from Starr as she could. While he waited for her story, she mugged for a *Vanity Fair* photo spread on the beach in California, peering teasingly from behind a pink boa like a fan dancer. The shoot, with celebrity photographer Herb Ritts, had been arranged by Ginsburg, her attorney, who intended it as a way to boost her morale. Lewinsky's "libido" had been suffering, he said. "She's been imprisoned like a dog for four months, and she's angry at all the gossip writers who say trashy things about her. The press and gossip columnists are all snakes, always making things up. So, yes, I pamper her when I can. It was a way of saying, 'Honey, you're beautiful and sweet, and we want the world to know it.'"

For months, Starr's team couldn't get near her. They had to wait until Ginsburg's immunity claim had been litigated. The standstill ended May 1. Judge Norma Holloway Johnson ruled that no agreement had been reached between Ginsburg and the prosecutors on the night of February 2. She said a last-minute revision in Lewinsky's proffer that Ginsburg had described as "minor" represented a "material change" in the draft agreement; it altered the timing of Clinton's suggestion of a cover story. Starr had not approved it, said Johnson, so there was no accord. That ruling was affirmed two weeks later by the U.S. Court of Appeals, freeing Starr to go after Lewinsky's testimony.

His team settled in for a long debate over their options. The most obvious tactic was a deal: a negotiated statement of what Lewinsky would say under oath in exchange for a plea agreement or immunity. This had the same appeal as in the beginning, offering a running start at a cooperative relationship with the only witness capable of directly implicating the president. But by now, Starr and his prosecutors had no trust in Ginsburg. At a closed hearing in March, he admitted lying to the media about Starr's position on the immunity agreement, saying his policy was to do "what is necessary to protect my client at all times as a vigorous advocate." Ginsburg had become more hostile to Starr, all but daring him to indict Lewinsky, confident Starr would never risk that public relations nightmare.

Starr and Mary Anne Wirth at first favored limited immunity as the best option. The OIC would summon Lewinsky to the grand jury and stipulate that she would not be prosecuted for anything she admitted in her testimony—which meant she couldn't refuse to answer their questions on the ground of self-incrimination. Since this course didn't involve striking a deal, Lewinsky would not be suspected of selling out Clinton to save her own skin. But compelled testimony had risks. It had to be delivered in person to the grand jury, a formal, adversarial process not as conducive to eliciting detail as the easy give-and-take of prosecutor interviews. And if she lied, Starr was stuck. He could charge her with perjury, but that would discredit his only direct witness against the president.

The final option was charging Lewinsky. This was the hawks' favorite, based on the premise that she would respond only to force. If she were indicted, she would have to cut a deal to avoid a criminal trial—or, if tried and found guilty, she could be jailed for contempt if she refused to testify before the grand jury. Hard-liners considered the courtroom one way to bring out the facts about Clinton. They weighed the idea of indicting Lewinsky for conspiracy and naming Clinton as an unindicted coconspirator. The trial would show how she plotted with the president to conceal their affair from the Jones lawyers, with Vernon Jordan a leading witness. Jurors might refuse to convict Lewinsky, out of sympathy for her or because they liked Clinton, but the facts would be on the record, beyond the reach of spin and political posturing. Of course, there was a big downside. The case could take eighteen months to try in Washington, obliging Starr to send a report to Congress without Lewinsky's testimony.

One alternative was to try her in northern Virginia, where the smaller federal courthouse was known for its "rocket docket," moving cases very quickly. Starr had venue there because Lewinsky had tried to get Linda Tripp to lie at a Ritz-Carlton in the state. Prosecutors calculated the PR costs of leaving a largely black, Democratic jury pool for a whiter, more conservative one. Steve Binhak reminded them of what happened after the politically correct move of the O. J. Simpson trial from Santa Monica to Los Angeles. "It's better to take a hit on race than lose," he argued.

The consensus was to keep all options open and ready to be exercised. In mid-May, Starr directed Mike Emmick to prepare a prosecution memo to lay out a case against Lewinsky. Emmick had often disagreed with Starr, but he had mastered the chronology and evidence against Lewinsky in Linda Tripp's tapes and in phone records from the White House and Jordan's office. Starr valued his even-handedness. He had even regained the trust of the hawks, who once called him a "commie wimp," by coming up with a novel idea for charging Lewinsky with aiding and abetting Clinton's perjury and obstruction. That would allow prosecutors to inject Clinton into her trial.

Meanwhile, Bittman drafted a plan with a dual purpose: to help Emmick make a case for indictment and to signal Lewinsky that her chance to trade her testimony for leniency was fast slipping away. Bittman called for "action driving events," including a subpoena for a blue dress with stains. He believed the garment existed despite denials by Ginsburg and a fruitless FBI search of Lewinsky's apartment. If they had the dress and it was marked with Clinton's DNA, they would have smoking-gun evidence against Clinton and they would be in a strong position to force Lewinsky's cooperation.

Bittman also wrote to Ginsburg demanding Lewinsky's fingerprints and samples of her voice and handwriting. There were plausible investigative reasons for the request. Fingerprints were needed to trace Lewinsky's handling of gifts, the handwriting to validate her letters to Clinton, voice samples to confirm her side of the Tripp tapes. But Bittman had another reason for the exercise: disabusing Ginsburg of the notion that Starr would never prosecute his client. These steps suggested an indictment was on the way.

It was 8:15 A.M. on May 28 when Lewinsky arrived at the Federal Building in Los Angeles. She was in a foul mood, having had to fend off a media mob at an hour when she should have been lingering over coffee. In the FBI fingerprint room, she rolled each digit from inkpad to white paper, then blackened her palms, fronts, and sides of her hands for imprints. Her father watched from the doorway as Ginsburg paced the small space. Finished, she threw up grimy hands, grimacing. She was taken to a nearby sink to wash.

It was Lewinsky's first direct contact with Starr's team since the

Martin Luther King holiday—an encounter followed by nearly five months of dizzying notoriety, isolation, and fear. When Ginsburg agreed to the session, he promised that if the OIC sent someone to Los Angeles, avoiding the need for a trip back to Washington, "we'll give you whatever you want." Prosecutor Ed Page was chosen. He was polite and so low-key that his office nickname was "Mr. Electricity." As Bittman saw it, he was "the perfect straight man" to face the emotional Lewinsky and her stormy lawyer. Page had experience with the girl-friends of powerful men. He had recently convicted the ex-mistress of Henry Cisneros, Clinton's first secretary of Housing and Urban Development, for helping to falsify documents to conceal Cisneros's payments to her.

Page left the fingerprint room with the Lewinsky party as they headed for the seventeenth floor office of the FBI's supervising agent. Upstairs, Lewinsky took a seat at the head agent's large mahogany desk. She was given three pens and told to use each to write the alphabet and numbers one through ten. She complied, then was asked to sign her name on the photocopy of a blank check to compare against actual payments for various gifts to Clinton. Ginsburg objected. He said it would take a court order to get her to sign anything that could be used as evidence against her. "We will not create an exhibit," he said.

FBI agent Pat Fallon shot Ginsburg a look that suggested he'd be only too happy to serve Lewinsky with a subpoena. He had little patience for Ginsburg's refusal to follow routine procedure. But Page, who had a longer fuse, was determined to get something out of the long journey from Washington. He offered to let Ginsburg initial the blank check to remove any doubt about its origin.

Ginsburg declared that he would only accept promises signed by Starr. The disastrous immunity negotiations with Starr's aides still chafed at him. And he had another condition. Before negotiating, he wanted to take handwriting samples from the independent counsel. Page and Fallon were taken aback by this bizarre demand. Tension filled the room. Lewinsky suggested that her father leave to avoid being subpoenaed as a witness. Bernard Lewinsky was seething. On the way into the building he had shouted to reporters, "Kenneth Starr is trying to use her as a pawn to get to the presidency. This is unfair. This is totally un-American." He left, and Page called a time-out.

Outside, a female FBI agent approached Page and Fallon. Lewinsky, she said, might be on medication. She showed little of the anxiety most people do when they are fingerprinted. Page called FBI headquarters in Washington to find out if medication can alter a witness's handwriting. The reply was a qualified yes. So when they returned to the interview room, Fallon asked Ginsburg if his client had taken any drugs that morning.

Ginsburg was irritated by the question. No, he said. But after Lewinsky pulled him aside, he modified his denial. She had taken "no narcotic, benzodiazepine, or other medication" that would affect her coordination or alertness, he said.

Ginsburg now seized control. He vetoed requests for Lewinsky to write a sentence taken from one of her letters to Clinton and a phrase from the statement she wrote during the February immunity talks. He did allow her to sign paper strips cut in the shape of checks, but stopped her from including dates and dollar amounts.

At 11:05 A.M., the examiners called off the session. Fallon handed Ginsburg a subpoena for Lewinsky to complete the exercise on June 4. Next time, it would be under court order on Starr's turf, in Washington.

And next time, it would be without Ginsburg. Lewinsky was increasingly angry about his tasteless off-color remarks and his taunting of the prosecutors who had the power to send her to prison. The last straw was an article he wrote for a California legal journal two days before her handwriting session. In a piece entitled "Open Letter to Kenneth Starr," he all but conceded what Starr had spent months trying to prove. "Congratulations, Mr. Starr! As result of your callous disregard for cherished constitutional rights, you *may* have succeeded in unmasking a sexual relationship between two consenting adults." It could have been a lot worse, though. At Lewinsky's insistence, Ginsburg had cut this line out of his first draft: "Now Mr. Starr, thanks to you, we will know if another's lips aside from the first lady's have kissed the president's penis."

A month earlier, Lewinsky had shared a dinner with Ginsburg and friends at Legal Sea Foods in Washington. Sipping red Bordeaux, Ginsburg was expansive about his new fame and the prospects of a TV career. "Yeah, you'll have plenty of time when I fire you," Lewinsky cracked. By May, it was no joking matter. Ginsburg had failed to persuade a judge that she had an enforceable immunity agreement with Starr. And while he blustered that Starr would never indict her, Lewinsky read the recent reindictments of Susan McDougal and Webster Hubbell as evidence that Starr acted without fear of public opinion. At the fingerprinting session, she was unnerved that Ginsburg had to call long distance to tap the criminal law expertise of co-counsel Nate Speights. That session had achieved Bittman's goal. Lewinsky saw it as the first step toward her indictment.

Her mother's lawyer, Billy Martin, agreed and pushed hard to replace Ginsburg. By Memorial Day, the Lewinsky family finally decided Ginsburg had to go.

Martin brought in several premier lawyers for Lewinsky to interview. The two who impressed her most were doyens of the defense bar, Jake Stein and Plato Cacheris. Separately, they told Lewinsky they'd either get immunity for her or go to trial. "I won't go into court and plead you guilty," said Cacheris, whose big-name clients had included Oliver North's secretary, Fawn Hall, who had escaped prosecution in the Iran-Contra scandal. Martin suggested to Stein and Cacheris that they work as a team, and they agreed.

Stein and Cacheris specialized in the subtle interplay of media, politics, and law that characterized Washington. Stein, like Ginsburg, favored bow ties, but all similarity ended there. He was seventy-three, elegant and silver-thatched. His office resembled an old-fashioned library, lined with floor-to-ceiling bookshelves and lit by a single desk lamp. He was a skilled litigator, well known to most judges in town. Outside court, he liked to keep his listeners off-balance by driving home a point with a reference to an obscure Danish proverb or a Shakespearean sonnet. But there was nothing offbeat about his practice. He had been getting high-profile clients out of trouble since Watergate. He knew how specially appointed prosecutors worked. He had been one in the 1984 probe of Ed Meese, then Ronald Reagan's attorney general–designate.

Cacheris, sixty-nine, was gregarious and well positioned to plug into the buddy system of defense lawyers who were accustomed to sharing what their clients had told prosecutors. He was a close friend of Bob Bennett, the president's lawyer in the Paula Jones case, and Bill Hundley, his former law partner who represented Vernon Jordan. But as a former assistant U.S. attorney, he also knew how to talk to prosecutors.

On June 2, the phone rang in Bittman's office. On the line was Cacheris, who had known Bittman's father for years and had employed his older brother as a law clerk. Cacheris asked if he and Stein could pay a visit. Twenty minutes later, Stein and Cacheris were sitting with Bittman and fellow deputies Bennett and Wisenberg. Cacheris did the talking. "We're here to tell you we represent Monica Lewinsky," he said.

"We have an extremely strong case against her," said Bittman.

Cacheris extended an olive branch. He and Stein hoped to have professional relations with the office. "We're not Bill Ginsburg," he said. "We're going to be different." He didn't advertise his interest in a deal, but indicated an openness to talks.

A week later Stein and Cacheris returned for a negotiating session, this time with Starr and his three deputies. Bennett started off with an offer: Lewinsky would have to plead guilty to a felony and cooperate with investigators; in exchange, Starr would recommend a lenient sentence and not prosecute her for other offenses. The offer was less generous than Starr negotiators offered Ginsburg in February. But prosecutors had much more independent evidence against her now. And hardliners like Bennett believed perjurers had to accept responsibility to salvage their credibility as government witnesses. Then, if defense lawyers tried to impeach their testimony by citing past perjury, the witnesses could say they made a mistake and paid for it.

But Cacheris cut off the discussion. "No plea will be offered by us," he asserted. "We are either going to get immunity or there will be a trial."

Stein seconded it. "I have one good trial left and I'm willing to devote it to Monica," he said.

Bittman said before they offered anything, prosecutors had to test Lewinsky's truthfulness in a face-to-face meeting. But his demand led to the same kind of standoff that occurred in the Ginsburg era. Cacheris said she would not come forward without a commitment to give her immunity if she proved credible in an interview.

Cacheris was playing a hunch. He thought it might be too late to stop an indictment of Lewinsky. But he knew that Starr needed her. His hope for full immunity was based on precisely the opposite calculus of prosecutors. She would be less credible as a witness if she pleaded guilty, he thought, because her testimony would be discounted as a bid to lighten her sentence.

He changed tack, dangling an incentive. "We have material evidence that would strongly corroborate her testimony," he said. Bittman thought it could only mean one thing: the stained dress. He asked for more details.

"We have to work out a deal first," Cacheris replied.

Bittman's suspicion was correct. Lewinsky had revealed in her first meeting with Cacheris and Stein that the dress existed and was in her mother's apartment in New York. She wasn't sure if the stain was semen. They told her to bring it back to Washington. They considered having it analyzed but decided not to. If the findings turned out negative they could be accused of tampering with evidence.

At the White House, lawyers went into mourning for Ginsburg. They joked that as the investigation unfolded, they first saw him as a savant, then as an idiot savant, and finally just as an idiot. But as long as Ginsburg kept his client from Starr and undermined her credibility, he was doing Clinton's bidding. When Chuck Ruff learned of the new team, he was heard telling assistant Lanny Breuer, "I always like it when there are good lawyers in a case." But Breuer didn't think much of it. "It's terrible," Breuer told colleagues. "With Ginsburg in the case, it was working. He was nuts, but it was great. The more he was on TV, the more I liked it. He was making his client look horrible, and he was confusing the record terribly. Plato and Jake will do it right and save their client."

They would also close an open channel to the Clinton camp. Ginsburg's co-counsel, Speights, had kept Kendall's partner Nicole Seligman informed about Lewinsky's thinking. Speights remained on the Lewinsky team, but her new lawyers shut him out of their decision making.

Clinton had no choice but to wait it out. Mark Penn reported that Lewinsky had the profile of a celebrity: plenty of public interest and no sympathy. The worst thing Clinton's team could do was criticize her before she decided whether to deal with prosecutors. But they might need to do that down the road, and Clinton's lawyers had private eye Terry Lenzner do a background investigation that could be used to undermine her credibility.

Ken Starr had heard rumors that Ginsburg would be replaced, and he had feared Lewinsky would turn to David Kendall's firm of Williams & Connolly, with its take-no-prisoners style. He was elated to learn she'd hired Stein and Cacheris. "This is divine intervention," he said. He had known both men for years and worked with Stein on the Senate Ethics Committee's sexual harassment investigation of Bob Packwood.

Overnight, the odds for a deal rose, capping a streak of good news for Starr. He was cleaning up in the courts. Johnson had not only denied Ginsburg's claim to an immunity deal, she had cleared Starr's office of misconduct allegations arising from the Ritz-Carlton encounter. His aides did not improperly deny Lewinsky access to her lawyer, Johnson ruled. She did raise concerns about the discussion of an immunity arrangement without Lewinsky's lawyer present, but declined to take action.

More bouquets came from the appellate bench. Its judges set a brisk timetable for hearing the Secret Service and attorney-client privilege cases. On the question of executive privilege, Starr had faced down the

White House. It dropped its claim after Starr asked the Supreme Court to hear Clinton's appeal on a emergency basis, which had not occurred in the high court since Watergate.

For the first time all year, Starr was getting the breaks. Perseverance seemed to be paying off. Perhaps, Starr thought, he'd soon be finishing his work.

10

"I HAVE NO EXCUSES"

THINGS WERE GOING so well that Ken Starr took off his first Saturday in nearly six months. On June 13, he piled his family into a minivan and drove to Philadelphia for an afternoon show and sightseeing with friends. They had just reached their first stop at historic Christ Church when the office paged him. Sol Wisenberg said he had bad news.

The inaugural edition of *Brill's Content*, a journalism review, had turned an interview with Starr into a purported confession of illegal grand jury leaks. The magazine claimed to have gotten Starr to admit that he and deputy Jackie Bennett regularly informed reporters of what investigators had learned from witnesses. Starr, the article said, justified this practice based on faulty readings of the grand jury secrecy law and ethical guidelines laid down by the Justice Department. Editor-in-chief Steven Brill, a legal writer turned press critic, cited several major news stories from the first three weeks of the scandal as proof that the media had become an "enabler of Starr's abuse of power." "There is a lot more evidence of Starr and some of his deputies committing this felony," Brill wrote, "than there is of the president or Vernon Jordan committing a felony."

"This is just ridiculous," Starr told Wisenberg. Brill had misconstrued his remarks and leaped to unfounded conclusions. Starr had endured too many attacks to panic, and this one seemed manageable. He ordered up a strong denial. "This is over the top, squash it," he said. Put out a press release correcting the record. In the meantime, why spoil a nice day? He went on with plans to visit the Betsy Ross home and take in a Stephen Sondheim musical, *Merrily We Roll Along*, starring family friend Holly Rudkin. The tour ended at Valley Forge, where George Washington's frigid and starving army barely survived the bleakest winter of the Revolutionary War.

Ever since February, when David Kendall had charged Starr with a "deluge" of grand jury leaks, the issue had lurked in the background. Now a seemingly independent critic had given it new life. As Starr toured Philadelphia, the White House seized on the Brill article, not yet even on newsstands, and declared "grave concerns" about Starr's entire probe. It called for an outside investigation of Starr's "pattern of violating grand jury secrecy laws." The Starr statement, released late on Saturday, gave no quarter. Brill, Starr said, had "recklessly and irresponsibly" accused him of wrongdoing in an article replete with "false and misleading statements." Starr had not admitted leaking grand jury material, he said, nor had he or his aides talked to reporters about anything other than nonsecret subjects.

But there was no stopping this story. The *New York Times* gave it front-page prominence under the headline STARR ADMITS ROLE IN LEAKS TO PRESS, teeing up the issue for Sunday's TV talkathons. White House aide Rahm Emanuel proclaimed Brill's piece a "bombshell" on NBC's *Meet the Press*, and the author, in turn, handed more ammunition to Clinton backers on CBS's *Face the Nation*. He said Starr had used a "loophole" in secrecy rules to defend leaks, even though "every court" that had looked into the law "flatly contradicted" Starr's interpretation of it.

Starr passed up watching the talk shows to prepare for a conference of appellate judges he had agreed to cohost in New York. When one of the judges mentioned Brill's TV appearance that morning, Starr rolled his eyes. "Look, the guy is trying to sell a magazine," he said. "Big deal.

We'll overcome it." Not until his Metroliner ride home Monday afternoon did Starr recognize how big a deal it was. His office called him on his cell phone. Judge Norma Holloway Johnson had scheduled a conference for 4 P.M., giving just one hour's notice—too soon for Starr to attend.

Brill had extrapolated a good deal from the comments he claimed Starr made during their April 15 interview. Starr, he wrote, told him he occasionally talked to reporters on a not-for-attribution basis and that Bennett spent "much of his time briefing the press." From that, Brill concluded that Starr was giving out secret information, based on the assumption that any briefing by prosecutors amounted to improper disclosures to the press. "Aren't those apparent leaks violations of the federal law?" Brill wrote, as if he had posed that question to Starr. He then quoted what appeared to be a direct response from Starr: "Well, it is definitely not grand jury information, if you are talking about what witnesses tell FBI agents or us before they testify before the grand jury." Starr said later he was speaking theoretically, not describing office practice. But Brill seized on the statement as if Starr had confessed to leaking witness accounts prior to their grand jury appearances. And if Starr thought such accounts were not secret, Brill had news for him: Courts view even prospective testimony as part of the grand jury process. The impression left by Brill was that Starr had leaked grand jury material to reporters without knowing it.

In fact, Starr left press contacts to his aides. He couldn't monitor every conversation they had with reporters to know whether they leaked grand jury material. But there were questions of law, policy and process not covered by secrecy rules that he did want conveyed to the press. As the scandal broke in January, both the OIC and the Justice Department disclosed the expansion of Starr's mandate to investigate alleged obstruction of justice by Lewinsky and others. Later, Starr's staff talked about the dilemma of dealing with uncooperative witnesses like Lewinsky and the need for face-to-face interviews in immunity negotiations. They complained about her lawyer Ginsburg's strident and erratic statements and about White House delaying tactics and mudslinging. They explained the standard prosecutorial practice of subpoenaing family members like Marcia Lewis. They discussed their reasons for fighting privileges asserted by the White House and Secret Service. When the Jones case was dismissed, they explained why they still had jurisdiction to pursue allegations of perjury. And as impeachment referral headed to Congress, they laid out their understanding of the evidentiary standard.

But when "Pressgate" hit, the media and a riveted public were too swept up in the sensationalism of Brill's charges to detect how he transformed such routine briefings into illegal leaking. Starr's aides did see the journalistic alchemy, but they were almost as angry at their boss as they were at Brill.

Few of them had known about the interview in April, and none could comprehend why Starr had granted it, much less gotten into a sensitive topic with someone clearly out to make a splash in his new magazine. It looked to Starr's staff as if he had blundered into a trap, putting the whole investigation at risk. It is a crime for prosecutors to disclose grand jury material. It was bad enough that Starr had lent credence to Brill's attack and put himself at professional risk, but he had implicated Jackie Bennett, as well. Why did Starr jeopardize so much for so little, aides wondered. How were they going to pick up the pieces? Was this investigation jinxed? The staff vacillated between fury and despair.

Starr couldn't blame them. He had mistakenly trusted Brill. Twenty years earlier, Brill had interviewed him for the launch of his *American Lawyer* magazine, and Starr had admired the results. When Brill asked for a meeting to discuss his latest venture, Starr didn't see the danger. He knew Brill was politically liberal, but thought of him as fair-minded. The day of the interview was Charles Bakaly's first day as the new spokesman for OIC, and Bakaly was apprehensive about the meeting. Starr almost never spoke to reporters. But Starr would not be talked out of it. "We can talk to people like this," he said.

When Brill challenged Starr on the scope of secrecy laws, the independent counsel had considered begging off the discussion. But he enjoyed the clash of ideas. Always the litigator, he decided to debate Brill's reading of the law. Now as he traveled home toward trouble, Starr thought Brill had deliberately set him up for an assault on the integrity of the office. He was shocked at what the journalist had done, but he was even angrier at himself. He had made a colossal mistake, engaging Brill out of pride.

What Starr didn't see as clearly was that this fit a pattern of self-destructive choices on his part. Too often, he plunged into decisions he deemed "right" despite obvious dangers and the pleas of those closest to him. His long refusal to sever his ties with Kirkland & Ellis, for example, had set him up for charges of conflict of interest because of the law firm's diverse client base. By agreeing to speak at Pat Robertson's law school in 1996, he had helped political enemies tie him to the religious right. It was that same hubris that led him to ignore Bakaly's warning about Brill.

Shortly before four o'clock, Bob Bittman and Paul Rosenzweig entered Judge Johnson's courtroom. The Clinton lawyers had already arrived—in high spirits. In the back sat Monica Lewinsky's new legal team, Plato Cacheris and Jake Stein. Bittman was taken aback. Their predecessor, Bill Ginsburg, had joined the White House's legal effort to sanction Starr for alleged grand jury leaks. But Bittman had been working with Cacheris and Stein in hopes of gaining Lewinsky's cooperation. Now they were part of the den of thieves, he thought, eager to see whether Starr was mortally wounded. "What are you guys doing here?" he asked. Cacheris replied: "We were invited."

Johnson had become chief judge of the U.S. District Court a year earlier, a black Democrat named by President Jimmy Carter. Her eighteen-year tenure had been marked by generally pro-prosecution rulings and intolerance for corrupt politicians. So far, in presiding over the grand jury, she had lived up to her reputation, favoring Starr in most decisions. Kendall's earlier protest about leaks hadn't moved her. By spring, she was focusing on more important matters, including the debate over Lewinsky's claim of a binding immunity deal. She had reviewed much of Starr's evidence and knew the strength of the case against the president.

When Johnson entered the courtroom Monday, June 15, she

brought a new attitude. She looked coldly past the Starr aides. The Brill story, she said, had reminded her of the leaks issue and convinced her "the sooner I get this accomplished, the better." She now believed a hearing was "absolutely essential" for Starr to show why he should not be held in contempt for leaking grand jury secrets.

Kendall asked for the right to depose prosecutors in preparation for the hearing. Johnson promised to rule on that request in a few days.

Bittman had little to say, other than to argue that the Brill article was inaccurate. He found himself unable to look at Kendall. The president's lawyer was arguing for the right to grill government prosecutors like common criminals.

Rosenzweig felt as if he had been kicked in the stomach. He was cerebral and proper, not used to being upbraided by a judge. He had handled the leaks litigation for Starr, and since the first Kendall complaint in February, he had been assuring Johnson that there was nothing to it. Rosenzweig thought she saw the prosecutors as the good guys in this case. Now the tone of her voice, her body language conveyed an unmistakable message: She felt betrayed. The judge wanted answers and wanted them soon. Rosenzweig saw doom rushing toward him, and it was too late to move.

Rosenzweig and Bittman left the courthouse in emotional tatters. They decided to walk back to the office. Halfway there, the clouds loosed a drenching summer rain. They arrived bedraggled. Everyone was waiting in the conference room, and as soon as Starr came in, Bittman reported: "I've been in a lot of bad situations in my life, including when I was arrested as a kid for reckless driving. But I've never, ever felt as low and small as I did in that hearing." Then he and Rosenzweig played back the courtroom events.

The room went silent. All eyes turned to Starr. He seemed to shrink in his chair, as penitent as a felon on sentencing day. He removed his glasses and wiped his eyes. The words came slowly, preceded by a sigh. "Let me apologize to each of you personally for the damage I've done to the office and the investigation," he said softly. "I have no excuses." He did have an explanation, though, and told the group how Brill's interview came about: "I made the mistake of engaging him. I never said we had done those things. I said, academically, even if we had, it would not have violated 6(e)," the federal rule that bars prosecutors from discussing matters before the grand jury.

No one had seen Starr this way before. He was almost always upbeat with his staff, advising them to stay focused despite public criticism. He would agonize over decisions, but once they were made, he never looked back. Second-guessing was not his style. Nor was making errors of this magnitude, and he acknowledged it with rare self-criticism. Jackie Bennett, who stood to lose the most from his boss's terrible misjudgment, thought Starr was in as much agony as anyone could possibly be in.

But that did not ease Bennett's pain. Not even his enemies had ever challenged his integrity. His credo was to fight for every advantage but play by the rules; such an aggressive prosecutor simply had to be above reproach. Now he was being accused by a national magazine of violating the law he had taken an oath to uphold.

He had seen trouble coming ever since the day of the interview. Bakaly had sat in on most of it and reported to Bennett that "it didn't go that well." When Bennett spoke to Brill, he found out just how badly. The journalist accused him of repeated leaks. Bennett denied leaking grand jury material and refused to go beyond what Starr had said. When Brill demanded to know which reporters he had talked to and about what, Bennett said, "I don't think it's any of your business." For the next two months, he had brooded and waited. Now the article said Starr "all but fingered Bennett as 1998's Deep Throat." Before the staff meeting, Starr had gone to Bennett privately and apologized for mentioning his name. But Bennett was in despair, reflecting the general mood.

The lawyers ended their meeting without a pardon for Starr, but with a sense of resolve. Kendall had a gun pointed at their investigation. They had to fight back to save it. The first step was a comprehensive rebuttal of Brill. Rosenzweig was assigned to draft it. He stayed up all night and produced a nineteen-page letter to Brill, signed by Starr. It accused Brill of a "reckless and irresponsible attack" that "borders on the libelous." It said Brill took Starr's view of secrecy rules out of context and erroneously assumed his office released the contents of witness briefings that had occurred outside the grand jury. It went on to list fourteen factual errors and unfair inferences in the article.

Brill's premise was that Starr was not as ham-handed at public relations as he seemed, but rather a maestro who used leaks to control the press. Journalists, Brill claimed, became "a cheering section" for "a prosecutor in search of a crime." He didn't go so far as to accuse reporters of felonies, but said the press was "corrupted to its core." Brill trumpeted that his conclusions had been based largely on "what reporters or editors at six different news organizations had told me."

But journalists from three operations—*Time*, the *Washington Post*, and the *Wall Street Journal*—denied saying what Brill had attributed to them.* Reporters at *Newsweek*, ABC News, and NBC News disputed his critique of their work, including his charge that ABC had been reckless in reporting that Lewinsky kept a dress stained with the president's semen—the "vanishing dress," as a skeptical Brill described it. Brill brushed off the criticism, correcting only his description of a *Journal* story after reporter Glenn Simpson informed him he had a tape recording of his telephone interview with Brill.

Brill's objectivity also came under fire. In criticizing the prosecutors investigating Clinton, he failed to disclose that he and his wife had given $2,000 to the president's 1996 reelection and $4,000 to three Democratic congressional candidates. But perhaps more important than any appearance of conflict was the tendentiousness of the account itself. Brill wrote as if Starr had a monopoly on information. In fact, Starr knew less in the early days of the scandal than Linda Tripp, her attorneys, and her friend Lucianne Goldberg, not to mention the Jones camp and the Lewinsky entourage. By the first weeks, Clinton's lawyers also

---

*Author Susan Schmidt of the *Washington Post* was one of the journalists who denied statements Brill attributed to her. *Time* magazine managing editor Walter Isaacson, a colleague of Michael Weisskopf, was another.

knew a great deal from the lawyers for Lewinsky's friends and White House aides who had spoken to investigators.

Still, Brill concluded that many stories "could only have come from" Starr's office. He named as a favored recipient *Newsweek*'s Michael Isikoff, who had held off making phone calls to Vernon Jordan and others in January to give Starr's office more time to make a move on Lewinsky without alerting the White House. Brill suggested that in return, Starr aides made sure Isikoff had the "best seat in the house as they continue to trickle out the alleged contents of the tapes they made of Tripp and Lewinsky." He cited as an example a *Newsweek* article on what Lewinsky had told Tripp about her demands of Jordan: a job in return for signing the affidavit denying sex with Clinton. Starr's office was hardly alone in possession of that information. *Newsweek* could have gotten it from Tripp, her lawyer Jim Moody, Goldberg, or Justice Department officials who had been briefed on the subject before deciding to authorize Starr to investigate the matter. Moody, in fact, had allowed Isikoff to listen to one of the Tripp tapes before the story broke, though not the one in which Lewinsky discusses Jordan and the affidavit.

Goldberg publicly complained that Brill's article could have been written in the West Wing of Clinton's White House. Indeed, the president himself gleefully taunted reporters with a mock-up copy of the magazine at the annual White House Correspondents Dinner six weeks before publication. "I'm not the only one who is anxiously awaiting the release of Steve Brill's new magazine," he told several thousand reporters and their guests in attendance.

Brill admitted that he had had help from the White House—including a deluge of press clippings from Sidney Blumenthal and a "head start" from Kendall on his research for the article. Kendall, he said, supplied materials on the grand jury secrecy law, and Brill "went from there" to form his own judgments.

He adopted Kendall's controversial view of the secrecy law. Rule 6(e) of the Federal Criminal Procedure bars prosecutors from disclosing "matters occurring before the grand jury." In May, in an unrelated case involving Dow Jones, the federal appeals court in Washington had ruled that the ban included "what is likely to occur" before the grand jury. Brill used that portion of the opinion to claim Starr had violated Rule 6(e) because he admitted briefing the press and because he did not consider what witnesses say before they testify to be grand jury material. Kendall cited the same ruling in court, accusing Starr of grand jury leaks. "I don't know a lawyer on the planet who thinks that that doesn't violate 6(e)," Brill said on CNN.

Starr had sat on the same appeals court when the law was first defined. He believed the Dow Jones ruling did not alter the legal standard for the scope of Rule 6(e). The law always prevented prosecutors from discussing prospective testimony, but only if it revealed the inner workings of the grand jury. The test was not the timing of the testimony—before or after the grand jury. It was whether the information disclosed what the grand jury was doing. And Starr was not the only lawyer on the planet who saw it that way. Former Attorney General Richard Thornburgh sparred with Brill on CNN, saying some courts agreed with the independent counsel. "It is not as clear as Mr. Brill would have you believe," said Thornburgh, a colleague of Starr's in the Bush administration.

But there was no debating Brill. "It's a little embarrassing," he said, "to have to tell a distinguished attorney general such as Mr. Thornburgh this," but the Dow Jones ruling is "as clear as a bell that there is no legal argument that 6(e) does not include what might happen in front of a grand jury, what witnesses might say. I mean this really is not a terribly debatable legal proposition."

Judge Johnson agreed. Within two weeks, Kendall got most of what he had asked for. In a sealed opinion, Johnson ruled that there was prima facie evidence that Starr had made "serious and repetitive" disclosures of grand jury material, noting that his remarks to Brill "bolster the court's findings." She ordered Starr to appear on July 6 to show why he and his aides shouldn't be held in contempt. And she gave Kendall unprecedented power to demand documents from Starr's office and to interrogate him, Bennett and other prosecutors on their contacts with reporters. If she found direct violations of Rule 6(e), Johnson wrote, she could refer the violators for prosecution.

*　　*　　*

On June 26, the day Johnson issued her order, Starr summoned Bill Kelley, his former law clerk and a pillar of the legal team. "You've got to find a way to overturn it," he said. "This is a potential death threat to the investigation, aimed right at the heart," he said. It was time to prepare for Armageddon. Starr thought the license the judge had given Clinton's lawyers to turn the tables on prosecutors was a profound vote of no confidence in him. For her to justify it as necessary to protect the integrity of the grand jury undercut the ethical basis of his probe. It could not stand.

Starr conjured up one nightmare after another. Imagine the spectacle of his prosecutors summoned to Williams & Connolly for days of interrogation—investigators being investigated by the lawyer of their target. Imagine pugnacious Jackie Bennett forced to review every conversation he ever had with reporters. Imagine Kendall prying into the office's internal deliberations and raking up old press inquiries into the personal backgrounds of prosecutors. How could Starr and his aides deny violations of Rule 6(e) without revealing what the grand jury knew? Kendall could penetrate the very heart of the investigation. Starr wondered what would be left of his moral authority to pursue the most serious charges against a president in twenty-five years.

The staff was demoralized. Karin Immergut had arrived for work two weeks before the Brill article appeared. Now she questioned why she had ever left her prosecution job in Oregon. When Sol Wisenberg became a deputy in March, he had to sever ties to the San Antonio U.S. attorney's office. He recalled the pleas then of his old friends to come back because the Clinton probe would hurt his career.

Bennett drew back from the day-to-day affairs of the office, preoccupied with Brill's charges and how to rebut them. He wanted to mount a public defense, but couldn't because of the secrecy rule he was accused of flouting. He stayed away from the grand jury because of the charge that he had violated its secrecy. His withdrawal deepened the office malaise. Bennett was the seasoned pro who always knew what to do, the samurai who fended off attacks against colleagues. Kendall couldn't have hoped for a better outcome. The prosecutor most feared by the White House had been neutralized. Bennett's wife, Cindy, called longtime Bennett pal George Parks, an FBI agent in San Antonio, and asked him to call her husband to buck him up. "Pray for us," she asked.

The controversy highlighted what many of Starr's aides considered his greatest weakness: his lack of street smarts. They always respected his intellect and his sure footing in the country's highest courts. They admired how he took a punch and bounced back with civility; in his presence, it was forbidden to refer to the chief executive as anything other than "the president" or "Mr. Clinton." He never demanded more of his staff than he did of himself, and his sunny disposition made him approachable as a boss. But as a prosecutor, he had shortcomings even after four years in office and fourteen convictions. Staff veterans questioned his judgment in evaluating witnesses, not to mention his choice of magazine interviewers.

Nothing in Starr's life had approached the magnitude of this crisis. He had not had his integrity questioned since the sixth grade when a teacher falsely accused him of not paying twenty-five cents for lunch. The leaks accusation had come from the federal court, a place he revered and once made home. Moreover, the wound was self-inflicted and had hurt people he was supposed to lead. Before him lay the wreckage: an angry staff, rejoicing rivals, and an endangered investigation. Starr blamed himself. Alone in his corner office, he recalled the final words of Jesus. "My God, my God, why have you forsaken me?" His years had been filled with good fortune, he thought. Perhaps the divine scales were being balanced against him.

The Brill disaster made Starr realize more than ever that the office of the independent counsel was inseparable from the man appointed to lead it. He had brought it down. Only he could recoup its losses. He was more determined now to win. There would be no surrender, no retreat.

July 11 was marked "execution day" on Starr's calendar. On that Saturday morning, he, Bennett, and five current and former staffers had been ordered to appear at Williams & Connolly for a weekend of interrogation. If that wasn't dreadful enough, Judge Johnson had a hearing planned for Monday to review Kendall's findings and determine whether prosecutors should be held in contempt for violating the grand jury secrecy rule. To fire an independent counsel, the attorney general must have cause. A contempt finding would surely qualify. Within days, Starr could be tossed out of office, his probe thoroughly discredited.

There was no appealing Johnson's directive because it was a procedural step, not a ruling. But Starr did have a long-shot move plotted out by Kelley and Ronald Mann, a University of Michigan law professor recruited by the OIC to work on privilege litigation. On Thursday, July 9, Starr asked the appeals court for a writ of mandamus, a petition for extraordinary intervention to block an improper lower court ruling. Only a tiny fraction of such petitions are granted. Because Kendall's depositions were imminent, Starr sought an emergency stay until the court could hear the issue.

By Friday afternoon, with depositions set for the next morning, tension could not have been higher. With the courts about to close, Bennett, Emmick, and other worried lawyers hovered around the fax machines, hoping desperately for a reprieve. Finally, a machine whirred with the fateful news: The stay was granted.

Two dozen lawyers poured into the corridor near Starr's office, high-fiving and embracing like World Series victors. If Johnson's order putting Kendall in charge of the leaks investigation had been their darkest moment, this was among the brightest. Bennett and Emmick, frequent opponents, hugged like brothers. Starr got the news by phone in Bismarck, North Dakota as he was leaving a legal conference. He was exhilarated, yelling congratulations into the phone.

The victory restored the staff's faith in Starr's leadership. Emmick, who had often disagreed with his boss, stood in awe of his courage. When all the others were deeply demoralized, he had gone from office to office telling his aides "we have to keep our eye on the ball." What Starr had endured without complaint, Emmick thought, would have killed an ordinary man.

Starr concluded that the appeals court must have found Johnson way off base. It granted quick relief and saw no urgency to hear the mandamus petition, scheduling it for July 21. It was all the better, he thought, that the three-judge panel was chaired by Patricia Wald, a Carter appointee. No one could call this a trumped-up decision by Republican judges. He could get a fair hearing. It was a different theater for Kendall and his plans to kill the impeachment referral. He had Kendall where he wanted him. You're in my territory now, he said to himself. We beat the hangman.

Had the stay not come through, Starr might have defied Johnson's instructions. At his direction, Rosenzweig had drawn up a memo instructing the aides named by Johnson not to appear for their depositions Saturday morning. Starr himself, though not his aides, would have been in contempt of court with this directive. But there were benefits. He could appeal a contempt finding, which would get Johnson's deposition order reviewed by the court of appeals. It would have been a roll of the dice, though. If they didn't show up and Johnson found him in contempt, Janet Reno might have fired him on the spot.

The appeals court saved him and restored his confidence. When he appeared before it in late June to argue the Secret Service and government attorney-client cases, the clerk read off the roster of lawyers and introduced him simply as "Judge Starr." He won both cases. This was his arena, a place where fact trumped spin and political leverage. The other side had smart lawyers, journalists, spin doctors and even a good part of the public on its side. But Starr felt he had truth, his lifelong ally. The truth will out, Starr said to himself. Nothing can stand in its way.

Starr began to feel that when trouble called, the Justice Department was never far behind. Five days after Judge Johnson's order for him to show why he shouldn't be held in contempt, Deputy Eric Holder faxed him an alarming document. It was a draft pleading to Johnson, informing her that DOJ had received numerous complaints of prosecutorial misconduct by Starr's office and planned to look into eleven of them. Most of the accusations came from Democratic partisans or defense lawyers in the case. The attorney general could remove an independent counsel for good cause, but the department had never investigated one, and Holder knew it would look political. So, before notifying the judge, he asked Starr to concur with the plan. Instead, he received an angry reply.

The last thing Starr needed was a new batch of complaints sent to the judge who was weighing a contempt ruling against him. He wrote Holder that any intervention by DOJ at this critical moment in the investigation would be seen as a political strategy to aid the White House. He then rebutted each of the allegations, including Kendall's leak charges.

Holder's patience was wearing thin. Starr assumed everything Justice did was politically motivated. Holder countered in a letter that no one at DOJ was acting at the behest of the White House and that Starr's view of his own conduct was not sufficient to permit DOJ to discharge its responsibility. But he dropped the pleading and quietly asked the head of the office of professional responsibility to review the complaints.

Starr heard no more from Holder and assumed the issue was dead.

In an office that never stopped, a Sunday afternoon off was a rare treat. Starr authorized one on July 12, in observance of the World Cup Soccer final. The holiday lasted until 6 P.M., when Starr called his legal team together for a strategy session.

He opened with a warning to the thirty-two lawyers who had assembled, along with FBI agent Pat Fallon. They had to send the impeachment referral to Capitol Hill "at the earliest practicable time," and before July 31, when Congress left for summer recess. Starr had set deadlines before, but they had slipped by one after another. Now he was insistent. If they missed that date, he said, Congress would not see the report until Labor Day, dangerously close to the mid-term elections.

Everyone had read the 250-page referral draft, a work in progress since March. It had been put together by the special team of academics, polished legal writers, and former Supreme Court clerks Starr called his "brain trust"—a name as unpopular among its members as among the rest of the OIC staff. They included University of Illinois law professor Andy Leipold, who oversaw the writing team; Stephen Bates, a Harvard-trained lawyer who moonlighted as literary editor of the *Wilson Quarterly;* Craig Lerner, master of The Chron; and Julie Myers, the Generation X lawyer who had been brought in from the Little Rock office.

Early on, Starr and the referral team had decided to explain the scandal in narrative fashion, to help Congress absorb the facts much as the investigators had. Using material drawn from the testimony of Lewinsky's friends and coworkers, Vernon Jordan, Betty Currie, and retired Secret Service officer Lewis Fox, the draft told how Lewinsky's affair with Clinton had started and how they had tried to cover it up. One section laid out what the team argued were Clinton's impeachable offenses.

Leipold told the group the referral still cried out for the accounts of the principals, Lewinsky and Clinton. But his boss thought it already was a powerful document. The amount of "substantial and credible information" that could be grounds for impeachment was "over-whelming," Starr said. The law required that he report it to Congress, a view that went against his own innate desire for thoroughness. "I do not want any more Monica friends. That's not what's needed at this stage. Forget telephone records. Forget any more Betty Currie grand jury appearances. What is needed is to get this darn thing done," he said. The appeals court had removed the immediate threat to the inves-tigation, Starr said, but the Brill crisis had badly damaged the office in the public eye. "Since we are entirely ill-equipped to fight in the public relations arena, we need to get this into where it really belongs—the political arena," he said.

His plea launched hours of debate. Starr had the backing of Ron Mann, who argued that the standard for making a referral to the House of Representatives was low. Because Congress is not bound by the court's rules of evidence, he said, Lewinsky's handwritten admission in February could be incorporated into the referral. "We have substantial and credible information many times over," Mann declared. Support also came from an unexpected place. Hard-liner Steve Binhak had grown weary of the criticism and was ready to hand off to Congress.

"We're getting hammered," he told his colleagues; the office was doing the preparatory work for an impeachment and taking the heat for it, while Congress got a free ride. Let's just ship it, he said.

Such defeatism left Bittman incredulous. "I didn't come this far to quit!" he objected. The appeals court had rejected the claims of privilege for the Secret Service, and they were closing in on eyewitness testimony that could corroborate what was on the tapes and create a powerful incentive for Lewinsky to cooperate. This was no time to stop. Fallon agreed. Rushing the referral would seem panicky, he thought. "You're acting like you're running scared, like we don't have a strong case," he told Starr.

Brett Kavanaugh, a thirty-three-year-old member of the brain trust, had prepared a memo analyzing the strengths and weaknesses of the referral. There was a solid case that Clinton had lied under oath before a federal judge in his deposition in the Paula Jones case. It was strong enough to send to Congress now, he argued, although it would be bolstered with direct evidence from Lewinsky. By contrast, he said, the case on obstruction of justice was relatively weak without Lewinsky's testimony.

And what if she denied everything to Congress? asked Hick Ewing. "You're crazy sending this stuff up like this," Ewing warned. "She's in love with the guy. She can go south on you in a second."

By the time the meeting broke up at 10:15 P.M., everyone, including Starr, agreed they had to have Lewinsky's story before the referral went to Congress.

When they reconvened Monday morning, it was to decide the fate of Monica Lewinsky. Mike Emmick had spent six weeks weighing every possible option and outcome in a case against the young woman. His own views were no secret: Prosecuting her would be risky and time-consuming. But he put aside his bias to write a straightforward 150-page analysis of the possible charges, the strength of the evidence, the defenses she could present, and how a jury might react to Lewinsky as a defendant. If she did go to trial, Emmick would occupy the lead chair at the prosecution table. For now he was content to be a law school professor, using flip charts and the Socratic method to lead his colleagues through a five-hour discussion on a hot summer day.

Emmick presented a strong case against Lewinsky on charges of perjury, obstruction of justice, and subornation of perjury in regard to Linda Tripp. Especially persuasive were tape-recorded conversations in which Lewinsky pressured Tripp to lie about Clinton's dealings both with her and with Kathleen Willey. Lewinsky was heard offering Tripp half ownership in an Australian condominium and suggesting she fake a foot injury to get out of testifying. On the question of whether Lewinsky had something to conceal from the Jones team, eleven of her confidants had testified she told them of a sexual relationship with the president. Perjury and obstruction are normally hard cases to prove, but Emmick laid out the wealth of evidence against Lewinsky.

How would various pieces of the case hold up at trial? Emmick sought opinions from specialists around the room. They would have to call Currie as a witness against Lewinsky. "Will she waffle on us if we call her?" he asked Bittman. What about Vernon Jordan?

Emmick said Lewinsky would pull at the jury's heart strings. He sketched her as her own lawyers likely would: an immature and lovelorn young woman who bombarded her idol with insipid letters and gifts, who even positioned herself on Sixteenth Street near the White House so he might glimpse her from his passing motorcade.

Mary Anne Wirth jumped in. She was convinced a jury would loathe their star witness, Linda Tripp, who had befriended the pitiable Lewinsky, then taped and turned on her. Starr would end up playing the heavy who rummaged through Lewinsky's e-mail love letters and computer files. The jury would see Lewinsky as a pawn in a political power struggle between the president and Ken Starr. As the discussion continued, many of the prosecutors could see the case was not a guaranteed winner. They could lose it, in fact: A jury might simply ignore the evidence and refuse to convict Lewinsky. Juries in Washington, D.C., were famous for doing just that. Besides, it could take a year to bring the case to trial, given the crowded D.C. docket. They could try it in Virginia, perhaps in as little as three or four months, but then they'd be accused of jury shopping.

Don't do it, argued Ewing. He spoke from long experience with reluctant witnesses. "If you prosecute her, she's going to harden her heart. We've already got one like that—Susan McDougal. You prosecute her, you're going to drive her further away. You'll never get the truth." Ewing got people's attention. He had tried more than one hundred criminal cases, more than anybody in the room. "If you indict her, the whole White House defense team is going to come to her aid against big bad Ken Starr," he said.

Paul Rosenzweig left his seat to plot out a grid on the flip chart showing all the potential time frames and venues for charging Lewinsky. There were no clear paths to get her testimony promptly. Seeing it laid out this way moved Jackie Bennett off the fence. Bennett, who had regained his footing since the Brill attack, often called Lewinsky "a knowing multiple felon." But he could see the real cost of charging her. It would take anywhere from three months to two years before she would testify, too long for a boss bent on sending a referral to Congress as soon as possible.

A few prosecutors still had misgivings. Wisenberg, for one, wondered whether Lewinsky would ever give them the truth voluntarily. She only understood force, he believed. Trying her, even if a jury refused to convict, at least would get the facts out about the president's actions.

Leipold and his team were firmly against an indictment. They had to have Lewinsky's testimony. Otherwise, they faced the risk that Lewinsky and Clinton both would deny everything in Congress.

Starr listened carefully to both sides, although his mind was mostly made up. He had no intention of charging Lewinsky, though he thought she deserved it. She was not some lovesick teenager, but a college graduate who had worked in responsible government positions, and she had committed crimes and dragged out an investigation that was consuming the country. But he told the group that as a practical matter, it was impossible to charge her. He needed to get her story into the referral. And once her activities were made public in Congress, her lawyers would argue she could never get a fair trial. "We cannot both refer and indict," Starr concluded.

Starr said he was inclined to bring her before the grand jury and compel her testimony through a grant of limited immunity. Emmick responded that they would have more leverage to ensure a truthful and complete story if they made a deal. They just needed a little more time to put pressure on her.

"Haven't you heard?" Starr erupted, at last losing his patience. "We don't have time!" The July 31 deadline was nonnegotiable.

"You're wrong, sir!" retorted Jay Apperson, pounding the table. Apperson, who had been a federal prosecutor in Virginia and an investigator for a Republican congressman, had joined the office less than two weeks earlier. Not having lived through the frustrations of the past six months, he saw only the gaps in the case, not the obstacles the OIC had overcome to reach that point. Stephen Bates, Craig Lerner, and the rest of the referral team wanted more time, too. They had written the narrative and were acutely aware of its deficiencies. Julie Myers quietly panicked at the idea of finishing in two weeks.

Ed Page argued with uncharacteristic passion that there was an important piece of work that absolutely had to be done: Linda Tripp's tapes still needed to be sent to the FBI lab for authentication. Page knew what he was talking about. He had investigated former Housing Secretary Henry Cisneros and his ex-girlfriend for lying to the FBI, only to discover on the eve of trial that the woman had edited her recordings of Cisneros.

Litigation chief Roger Heaton weighed in, telling Starr they simply could not get the referral done by July 31. They were working seven days a week late into the night as it was. There were limits.

"I insist we begin to write," Starr decreed. He wanted the final draft ready for Congress.

The meeting ended in an uproar.

Several lawyers went straight to their offices and pounded out memos to Starr arguing for more time. Then commenced what Starr referred to as "visits from the Magi"—Bennett, Ewing, and, in memo form, Sam Dash. Bennett went in first, arguing they shouldn't give up nine-tenths of the way to the goal. Starr replied that he had no discretion; the law required him to turn over the information to Congress. But Bennett argued the Independent Counsel Act didn't specify when they had to make a referral. In his view, either they had met the standard for reporting to Congress months ago—in which case, why had Starr waited until now?—or they weren't there yet. "The only thing that remains is that which is within our grasp if we ignore the congressional recess," Bennett pleaded. "We're willing to take a pounding with you for another month. We've spilled a lot of blood and we're willing to spill a little more."

Ewing made his own pitch, then he and Bennett double-teamed their boss, imploring him to rethink the deadline. The only damage caused by delay would be incremental, they argued.

Sam Dash had not attended the meetings but had read the referral draft and Emmick's prosecution document. He weighed in from Georgetown in writing. The referral would be nothing without Lewinsky's testimony, he argued. Congress would struggle with inconsistencies in her handwritten admission, he said. Unlike his colleagues, he believed the "substantial and credible" standard was very high, akin to the "clear and convincing evidence" needed for civil cases involving fraud. He thought Starr needed to build an airtight case meeting the standard before sending anything to Congress, and that the only way to get there was with Lewinsky's testimony. That view put him in the same camp as the most hawkish prosecutors, though he told friends close to the White House that he was putting a brake on Starr's aggressive urges. He would resign in protest, he told Starr, if the referral went to Congress now.

On Tuesday, July 14, Starr sent a memo to his staff: He would move the referral date to August 15. In the interim, he would make a new overture to Lewinsky's lawyers to try to get her cooperation. And he was finally prepared to subpoena Clinton.

Starr had been reluctant to use the coercive power of a subpoena against the president. The referral, he thought, was strong enough so that he could leave that task to Congress. But his staff, including Dash, insisted the referral would be stronger with Clinton's testimony—no matter what he said—and they believed they were on solid legal ground in requesting it. Federal prosecutors are permitted to subpoena investigative targets if their testimony is essential and there is no other way to get the information. "You've got a record here," said Dash, after examining a half-dozen letters asking Clinton to testify voluntarily. "When you tried to be courteous, he refused. You're under no obligation."

But it was the private importuning of Charles Bakaly that persuaded Starr he had shown the president all the deference he was due. Bakaly, a tall man with slick-backed hair and aristocratic bearing, had spent a lot of time with Starr since the Brill episode. He knew the independent counsel was more worried about the separation of powers than he was about the evidentiary need for Clinton's testimony. He argued that even if the White House challenged Starr's authority to subpoena the president, the court fight wouldn't have to delay the referral. Starr could send the referral, then fight Clinton in court. In the meantime, Starr would have moved the impeachment issue to Congress.

The subpoena would signal Congress that though election season was near, an impeachment referral was on its way.

11

"QUEEN FOR A DAY"

FROM THE VERY START, Solicitor General Seth Waxman had been lukewarm about the Secret Service's effort to establish a "protective function privilege" to avoid having its officers testify in the Lewinsky matter. The service's safety concerns might have merit, he thought, but its legal arguments were weak. In a meeting with Secret Service director Lewis Merletti and Justice Department lawyers after the appeals court ruled against them on July 7, Waxman was even more reluctant. "It's over," he told Merletti. To keep going and keep losing would set legal precedent for precisely what Merletti feared. Better to get Congress to draft a law limiting officer testimony.

But Merletti argued back fiercely. "This will destroy the ability of the Secret Service to protect the president," he declared. "I will not back down." Waxman, his aides, and Jonathan Schwartz of the DOJ told Merletti bluntly he almost surely would not win. But Merletti was unmoved. "It's the fight that matters," said the director. If they gave up, he vowed, he'd go over their heads to the American people.

Waxman and Attorney General Janet Reno met with Treasury Secretary Robert Rubin on July 9 to tell him they wanted to drop the case. But Rubin insisted they support Merletti, and the attorney general reluctantly agreed. The department took the position that it had to defer to the Secret Service director if he believed that the president's safety was at stake. Privately, Schwartz told Bob Bittman: "We've got a bad client." On his behalf, however, DOJ was appealing the July 7 ruling, and doing so in a way that maximized delay—by seeking an en banc review by all eleven judges of the court of appeals.

Now the problem was back with Starr. Securing the right to question Clinton's guards was a vital part of the OIC strategy for netting Lewinsky's cooperation. Even without her, Secret Service accounts of her comings and goings would strengthen the referral and undermine denials by Lewinsky and Clinton. Mary Anne Wirth, who was in charge of Secret Service interviews, believed the agents and officers knew a lot. She was determined to put them in the grand jury.

Starr turned to Ron Mann and Bill Kelley, who had worked with him when he had been solicitor general. "How you handle this depends on how aggressive you want to be," advised Kelley. If Starr wanted to get tough, said Mann, "we can get rid of this in two weeks." Starr could send a new batch of subpoenas to Secret Service employees. The agency's only recourse would be to seek emergency stays, which would be denied up the line by the same courts that had already ruled on the question. Eventually—sooner, rather than later—the Secret Service would have to request a stay from Chief Justice William Rehnquist. That, in turn, would force Waxman to rush a petition on the underlying case up to the Supreme Court. Starr's office was confident the high court would refuse to hear it. The maneuver would shorten Waxman's filing deadline to days instead of months, explained Mann. It would be over in no time. "It's a pretty hard-nosed strategy," he conceded, "but it's the right one."

This was what legal tacticians like Mann did. They mastered the law's arcane procedures. Even to the academics at the table, the constitutional scholars and theoreticians, this was dazzling, although to Mann himself it was all in a day's work. He thought of himself as a relief pitcher, called in to quell a rally in the late innings.

Starr lit up as Mann laid out his strategy. Always solicitous of government institutions and their prerogatives, Starr had spent six months in futile negotiations with the Secret Service. He could have forced officers before the grand jury after his first victory in lower court, but he had held off. Now he believed DOJ was deliberately stalling. He was ready for hardball. "That's what we're going to do," Starr told Mann. He ordered up a half-dozen new subpoenas, including one to Larry Cockell, the agent who headed up Clinton's Secret Service detail. They went out Monday night.

Mann quickly churned out a string of briefs ready to be filed before the solicitor general knew what had hit him. They were rebuttals to legal arguments Mann assumed the department would make as it shopped a stay petition through the courts. For the next seventy-two hours, Starr and DOJ filed dueling briefs in a rapid-fire series of court showdowns. Waxman's lawyers were scrambling to keep up.

As Mann had predicted, the stay petitions fell like dominoes. One after another, judges denied them—first the district court, then an appeals court panel. Finally, on Thursday, July 16, the full court of appeals rejected Justice's request for a new hearing. It granted a one-day stay—until noon Friday—to give Justice time to file papers with the Supreme Court. The ruling was unanimous.

One of the appellate judges, Reagan appointee Laurence Silberman, issued a concurring opinion in which he called the protective function privilege "a constitutional absurdity." He excoriated Reno and her lieutenants in a statement that took note of "the terrible political pressures and strains of conscience that bear upon senior political appointees of the Justice Department." Silberman charged that "The president's agents literally and figuratively 'declared war' on the independent counsel," and that Reno had been "acting as the president's counsel under the false guise of representing the United States." Regardless of what her boss might want, Silberman wrote, the independent counsel law "limits the options that the Attorney General can legally pursue. Litigating against the Independent Counsel in this case is not among them."

At the White House, officials who had been heartened by their victory in the battle over grand jury leaks were rattled by the independent counsel's sudden offensive. They dropped their pose of disinterest in the

Secret Service testimony. The new subpoenas, press secretary Mike McCurry complained, were tactics of "an overzealous prosecutor" intent on getting the president's guards to betray his trust. The White House was especially upset that Starr was summoning Larry Cockell, who had extremely close proximity to the president as head of his security detail.

David Kendall understood the danger. He had learned through back channels what the Secret Service officers would say on the stand. None had witnessed intimate encounters between Clinton and Lewinsky, but they had seen the two alone in the Oval Office—something Clinton had told Paula Jones's lawyers under oath that he could not recall.

Clinton's Justice Department rushed its stay petition to Rehnquist. Waxman had little chance of winning the stay unless the high court was interested in hearing the underlying case, so his aides frantically drafted a petition for a review on the merits of the Secret Service privilege claim. They filed the petition with the Supreme Court clerk about 10 P.M. on Thursday, just fourteen hours before their temporary stay expired.

It was playing out just as Mann had anticipated. The Justice Department had expected to have ninety days or more to prepare an appeal; instead, it had only hours. Of course, the same was true of Starr's lawyers. Even before he saw Justice's petition for review, Starr assigned two lawyers to prepare an opposition brief. Brett Kavanaugh and a young associate, Joseph Ditkoff, wrote all night. As the sun rose over Pennsylvania Avenue, Kavanaugh was proofreading the twenty-five-page brief while an exhausted Ditkoff stretched out for an hour's sleep on a hallway floor. Starr arrived at 7:30 A.M. to edit it, and at nine o'clock, a paralegal jumped into a taxi to ferry it to the Supreme Court.

The next few hours were tense. Television crews stood by for an immediate feed of Rehnquist's decision. At four minutes before the noon deadline, Friday, July 17, the chief justice sent out a one-page ruling denying the stay. "The opinion of the court of appeals seems to me cogent and correct," wrote Rehnquist. "I believe my view would be shared by a majority of my colleagues." In arguing against a stay, Starr had pledged that until the case was resolved by the courts, he would ask Secret Service officers only about past events, not anything they were currently witnessing. Clinton would therefore have no reason to push away his guards. The idea was suggested at the last minute by constitutional consultant Ron Rotunda, and it was enough to persuade Rehnquist not to grant the stay. "Disclosure of past events will not affect the president's relationship with his protectors in the future," he wrote.

Starr's team cheered the news as it came across on CNN. Mary Anne Wirth threw on her backpack and rushed six blocks down Pennsylvania Avenue though the media mob outside the federal courthouse. Inside, Bittman was standing by with the subpoenaed agent and officers. Since the Lewinsky grand jury did not sit on Fridays, he arranged to borrow a grand jury and have transcripts made, a common practice when prosecutors want to get information on the record promptly. Within two hours, he and Wirth began taking testimony they had been seeking since January.

The Secret Service decision was a breath of oxygen for the independent counsel's office, reviving the investigation after its near-fatal encounter with *Brill's Content*. Starr was losing the public relations battle but out-lawyering the White House and the Justice Department. By summer, his appellate record in the Lewinsky matter was 6-to-0, but that was not known to the public: Many of his court victories were still under seal and would remain so for months.

Now Starr quietly opened a second front. Just before 6 P.M. Friday, a federal marshal delivered a subpoena to Kendall for the president's grand jury testimony. It required Clinton to appear at the grand jury at 9:15 A.M., July 28. With it was an "advice of rights" form indicating that Clinton was a target in a federal probe of perjury, subornation of perjury, obstruction of justice, and witness tampering.

For months, not even Starr's own staff had been sure whether he would be the one to issue the first grand jury subpoena to a sitting president. The Clinton lawyers were caught by surprise. Kendall had to figure out how to proceed. In the meantime, he kept the subpoena secret, even from senior White House officials.

The timing could not have been more delicate. Lawyers on both sides knew the Secret Service testimony would give Starr more leverage over Clinton and Lewinsky. No longer could the president claim that Lewinsky had fantasized their romance, or that they had never been alone. Starr was now in a stronger position to demand Lewinsky's cooperation—and to gauge the truth of what Clinton would eventually say.

On Tuesday, July 21, the leaks issue was back on the agenda, this time in a closed hearing of the U.S. Court of Appeals. Starr was appealing Judge Norma Holloway Johnson's instructions six weeks earlier that Starr and his aides must appear for questioning at Kendall's law firm. For Starr, the old appellate judge, pride was at stake. The lower court judge had rapped his knuckles. This was payback time.

Starr could not have found three people in America less likely to view him as irresponsible or devious. He had served with two of the judges on this very court. He'd been known as "Preacher Starr" then, and his only sin was talking too much.

The appellate judges didn't think much of Kendall's expansive interpretation of the grand jury secrecy law, Rule 6(e), the same view propounded in the Brill article. Kendall contended that the Dow Jones decision in May meant prosecutors could not discuss the "strategy of the investigation." But these judges, whose court had issued the opinion, suggested Kendall was reading too much into it. Dow Jones, in their view, set no precedent on grand jury secrecy. The position espoused by Kendall and affirmed by Johnson, said Judge Silberman, was "staggeringly broad." The judges indicated they disagreed with Johnson's finding of prima facie evidence that Starr's office repeatedly leaked stories to reporters. But the focus of their hearing was on how the leak probe should be conducted.

Starr argued that letting Kendall grill prosecutors would be unprecedented and dangerous. "You don't appoint the fox to go examine whether the chickens are doing just fine," he told the court. The judges agreed. Panel chief Patricia Wald said she couldn't understand how Clinton's lawyer was supposed to interrogate Starr on the question of grand jury leaks without forcing him to reveal the secrets themselves.

Lewinsky's lawyers, Jake Stein and Plato Cacheris, had joined Kendall in the leak pursuit as a way to weaken Starr and strengthen their client's position. Stein rose toward the end of the hearing to offer a vague endorsement of Kendall's argument. His appearance, though, reminded the court of the strange role his loose-lipped predecessor had played in the affair. Ginsburg had essentially forced Starr to keep correcting the public record. "There was enormous pressure put on the independent counsel because of the many, many, many statements by Mr. Ginsburg, some of which, I gather, were false," said one of the judges. "I'm not here to go into that," Stein responded lamely.

It would be two weeks before the judges issued their order, but it was obvious that morning that they intended to overrule Johnson. The president's lawyers would not interrogate the prosecutors. The sensitive job of probing leaks would be turned over to a special master. Kendall had overplayed his hand and lost. He came away with something, though: Getting reversed on a writ of mandamus is a major embarrassment for any judge, and Johnson now had even more reason to be angry at Starr's team.

For Starr, vexing the judge was a small price to pay for winning one of the biggest decisions of his career. He left the courtroom elated.

He had been disturbed, though, by the role of Stein and Cacheris. What were respected lawyers like them doing on the other side, Starr wondered. Why were they allied with the enemies of the truth, defenders of the darkness, spinners of the media? That's not their interest, he thought. Their interest lay in getting their client out of jeopardy.

The hearing let them know Starr wasn't going away. The judges had shifted the balance of power in his favor. If they hoped to protect Lewinsky, they would have to return to the bargaining table.

Just about the same time Starr was leaving the federal courthouse, Sam Dash sat down for lunch at the Cosmos Club. By coincidence, he had invited Stein's partner, Robert Muse. Old friends who had worked together in the Watergate probe, Dash and Muse had spoken by phone about the Lewinsky case. Now, as they dined under the brass chandeliers of the main dining room, they began to chip away at the logjam that had stalled the case since the last round of immunity talks had broken off in June.

Muse started off with a warning. Lewinsky wanted immunity, but she was ready to go to trial and had a good chance of winning. Starr could end up with nothing. Muse said distrust of Starr was rampant in the Lewinsky entourage. It was imperative that Starr take the initiative by calling Stein.

But what would it take to end the impasse? Despite initial hopes, Stein and Cacheris, unlike their predecessor, did not insist on an immunity deal first. But they demanded assurances up front that Starr would grant it unless he could prove she had been untruthful. Starr said he could give no assurances before interviewing her in person.

Dash got right to the point: Would Lewinsky give them an interview in advance?

Possibly, said Muse. Starr would have to ease her fear that prosecutors would use what they learned against her. She would want assurance that the interviews would not go on indefinitely, and some indication that she would walk away free at the end. Otherwise, Muse said, "You're holding the cards and we look like amateurs."

Dash said if Lewinsky agreed to be interviewed, he would recommend immunity, adding that Starr would likely concur.

Dash left the Cosmos Club and went straight to the office. He told Starr about his conversation with Muse and urged him to make the first move. Sol Wisenberg, the deputy most sensitive to this game of perceptions, feared that for Starr to take the initiative would be seen as a sign of weakness. Starr said he "cared not a fig" about image if there was any hope of a breakthrough. "Let's stop the posturing," he said. They had no immediate plans to indict her, so what was the downside? He called Stein and suggested a meeting. They settled on two days hence, at Dash's home in Maryland.

Stein hung up and walked into Muse's office. "The Eagle has landed," he said.

Despite Muse's bluster, Lewinsky's lawyers were worried. With

Secret Service testimony in hand, Starr wouldn't need her as much as he had before. Stein and Cacheris figured their client still was more valuable to Starr as a cooperating witness than as a hostile one, but they remembered the warning of her mother's lawyer, Billy Martin—that Starr was "hell bent" on indictment. They knew they would hold a weak hand at a trial, especially if Lewinsky were charged in Virginia. Secret Service officers and Lewinsky's friends would show she lied in her Paula Jones affidavit. She couldn't take the stand, even if it was the only way to dispute Linda Tripp's obstruction allegations. If she testified, she'd have to admit she had been alone with Clinton and had a sexual relationship with him, which would be tantamount to admitting perjury in the Jones case affidavit. On top of that, Stein and Cacheris already had hinted to Starr that she had the stained dress. If Starr subpoenaed it, it would be killer evidence. Then the independent counsel wouldn't even need her to prove Clinton lied under oath.

At 10:30 A.M. Thursday, July 23, the lawyers arrived at Dash's house. He led them to a glassed-in porch overlooking a pleasant garden. Brilliant sun streamed in as the men grazed from a lazy Susan laden with bagels and cinnamon rolls. Starr felt as if seven months of gloom had lifted, as if he had walked out of an alley fight into a summer picnic with old friends. There was no one-upmanship here, no strutting or haranguing.

The feelings were the same all around the table. Stein had worked with Starr during the Senate's 1994 sexual misconduct investigation of Bob Packwood, a Stein client. Starr was hired by the Senate Ethics Committee to screen the Oregon senator's diaries and tapes before they were turned over to investigators. Stein thought him fair and thorough, acting honorably in a sensitive job. Cacheris had known and respected Starr for years, and nothing in the Clinton probe had changed his mind. He believed that Starr had done a good job as independent counsel and that he had been maligned by the White House. He disagreed with those who claimed Starr's team had abused Lewinsky's rights at the Ritz-Carlton. He thought Mike Emmick and the others on the scene had done everything by the book.

Dash's wife, Sara, poured coffee as the foursome exchanged courthouse stories. When she left, they got down to business. Starr said he had a new offer he hoped would bring about a deal. Lewinsky would be made "queen for a day," which meant nothing she said could be used against her. If her remarks were "truthful and sufficiently complete," she would not be prosecuted. It was a pledge of immunity up front, replacing the more equivocal past promise to consider a deal if Lewinsky gave an interview and proved credible. Starr had reduced the process to a simple quid pro quo: candor for freedom. He ticked off other concessions. If she found a question too embarrassing, she could refuse to answer it. If Starr eventually did indict her, he wouldn't use her interview against her at a trial, even to rebut sworn testimony—a right prosecutors normally retain.

What he wanted in return was what he had sought since the first encounter seven months earlier. Lewinsky would permit the prosecutors to sample the merchandise before paying, the standard practice in immunity deals. If she turned out to be mendacious, they could walk away. Privately, Starr had no intention of charging her anyway.

Stein nodded assent, and Cacheris said "we'll recommend it" to Lewinsky. Behind their poker faces, they were thrilled. Cacheris asked Starr when he would like to interview her. "Now!" came the reply. Cacheris asked for the offer in writing. Lewinsky had such a jaundiced view of Starr it would take some convincing to get her to tell prosecutors what they needed to hear.

Starr suggested they conduct the interview at the New York apartment of his wife's stepmother, throwing reporters off the scent. "Are you going to be there?" Cacheris asked.

Starr didn't answer directly. He turned to Dash. "I definitely want you there," he said. He thought Dash would convey a sense of professionalism and integrity to Lewinsky's parents, who would remember his role in Watergate. Involving Dash in the interview would solve another problem, too. It would turn Dash into a champion of the process, rather than a critic.

Cacheris left the brunch and called Lewinsky, who turned twenty-five that day. "I've got a birthday present for you," he said.

"Do you trust them?" she asked. Lewinsky had spent the day fretting that Starr was deliberately waiting for her birthday to indict her.

"This is legitimate," Cacheris said. "If this works, it's what you want." He mentioned Dash to reassure her. She agreed to try it.

On Friday, July 24, a letter was hand-delivered to Bob Bittman. He couldn't believe his eyes. "The president is willing to provide testimony for the grand jury," wrote Kendall. He asked only that Starr withdraw the subpoena so Clinton could say he was testifying voluntarily, and that the questioning take place in the White House, sometime well in the future. Just as Starr's troops were closing in on Lewinsky's cooperation and the kind of direct evidence they needed to pin down the president, Clinton had agreed in principle to testify.

The subpoena had been issued in secrecy. No one other than Starr's office, Clinton, and his private legal team knew of it as the president pondered his options. There were three. He could assert his Fifth Amendment rights against self-incrimination. He could claim the subpoena violated the separation of powers doctrine and challenge it in court. Or he could agree to testify.

After seven months of hand-to-hand combat, few of Starr's assistants would have predicted such an easy outcome. Had Clinton known of the pending deal with Lewinsky, he might have chosen to run out the clock in a constitutional challenge. Bittman fired off a letter to lock him in. "We are pleased by the president's decision to provide testimony for the grand jury," he wrote. Bittman said Starr's office would discuss Kendall's requests after he committed to a date for the testimony. The office was not inclined, however, to withdraw the subpoena.

On the day Kendall's letter arrived, the *New York Times* had run a front-page story on presidential spokesman Mike McCurry's plan to leave his post soon, a development the *Times* read as "a sign of growing confidence at the White House that it is weathering the Lewinsky investigation." McCurry had waited for a calm moment to announce his resignation without appearing to desert a sinking ship. This timing seemed right. It was midsummer, and Congress would soon be in recess. The White House had no clue that Starr and Dash had met that morning with Lewinsky's lawyers.

Rumors of a subpoena reached the White House press room at midday Friday. Reporters pressed McCurry for answers. He had none. The scandal put him in the unenviable position of fielding press queries while getting little reliable information from Clinton lawyers. White House Counsel Chuck Ruff proved adamantly tight-lipped. He sent McCurry out with an oblique statement: "Mr. Kendall will work with Mr. Starr's office to try to ensure that the grand jury gets the information it needs." By Saturday night, several news organizations were reporting that Kendall had already received a subpoena. McCurry was furious and threatened to quit if Ruff didn't acknowledge it. McCurry would not stonewall or mislead the press.

That night it was Ruff who took calls from reporters, although they didn't get much out of him. "I am not now, and do not expect in the future to be able to talk about this in any respect," he told them. The next morning's *Washington Post* reported that Clinton would appear before the grand jury as early as Tuesday, July 28.

The story galvanized Bob Bennett, Clinton's lawyer in the Jones case, whom Kendall had elbowed out of the president's inner circle. Bennett told colleagues it was a huge mistake for Clinton to go before the grand jury unless he could testify honestly that there had been absolutely no sex with Lewinsky. He believed challenging Starr's authority on constitutional grounds would fail. The only other course was to take the Fifth. Bennett knew this would be seen as disgracing the office of the presidency, but he regarded it as preferable to risking perjury. Clinton could go on television and say that Starr had laid a sex trap for him, one that no American should have to face.

He passed along his thoughts to other lawyers, but he wasn't sure they were reaching Clinton. Former Commerce Secretary Mickey Kantor, one of the president's legal advisers, thought the definition of sexual contact used in the Paula Jones deposition was fortuitous, because it could be construed as excluding oral sex. Bennett was flabbergasted. He told colleagues that was never the intention of the definition. With Paula Jones making that very charge—that Clinton had asked her for oral sex—the idea that oral sex would be written out of the definition didn't pass the common sense test.

Bennett believed he still had the president's trust. So he tried to make his case directly. He met with Clinton for nearly an hour and emerged feeling defeated. Clinton was determined to testify. "He thinks he's so fucking charming he can handle it," Bennett told a lawyer friend. "No one alive can keep him from doing it."

One veteran lawyer who tried was William Hundley, who represented Vernon Jordan. At seventy-two, Hundley had been practicing criminal law long enough to believe anybody who let a target testify ought to lose his law license. Hundley had been a longtime pal of Kendall's mentor, Williams & Connolly founder Edward Bennett Williams. He told Kendall that if the president testified, he'd be courting disaster. "Don't let him do it," he said. Kendall was unwilling to show his hand and said little. Hundley, exasperated, berated him: "If Ed Williams were alive, Clinton would never be testifying!" Kendall finally blurted: "Quit yelling at me, Bill. I was overruled, okay?"

The client, not the lawyer, was running the case—as always, with one eye on the polls. A majority of the public might be able to live with a president who had an affair, but not one who took the Fifth Amendment. Hillary Clinton and Kantor advised the president to testify. So did Ruff. He had less information than Kendall because as a government lawyer, his communications with Clinton might not be shielded by attorney-client privilege. But he strongly believed the nation's chief law enforcement officer could not refuse to testify for fear of self-incrimination.

West Wing advisers wanted the president to testify as a matter of political survival. With an impeachment referral all but certain, they believed his most important constituency was the Congress. House Minority Leader Richard Gephardt reflected the pressure Democrats were feeling when he was asked July 24 by a reporter whether Clinton should honor a subpoena. Gephardt did not know one had been issued and tossed off a response. "I would hope that he would," he said. "I would think that he would."

Hours later, when rumors of the subpoena began circulating, Gephardt aides told the White House their boss didn't intend his comments to box Clinton in. But White House political aides worried that

Democrats would desert the president if he refused to testify, and they seized on Gephardt's comments to bolster their case.

The evening before Lewinsky was to be interviewed, Starr hopped on a train to New York, a baseball cap pulled low over his eyes as camouflage. He spent the night in what his children called "Grandma's Place," his mother-in-law's apartment on East 56th Street. The next day, the man who might determine the president's fate awoke early and went shopping for bagels and orange juice for the Lewinsky entourage. He scurried to get back before the notoriously punctual Jake Stein arrived at 9:15. Then Starr left, giving up a seat at the most important meeting of his investigation because he thought his presence would upset Lewinsky. As he pulled out of the horseshoe driveway at 9:12, a cab carrying Lewinsky and her lawyers pulled in.

Lewinsky had arrived Sunday from Los Angeles, wearing a blond wig, baseball hat, and reading glasses. She immediately met with her lawyers, including Sydney Hoffmann, a Cacheris associate brought in to work with Lewinsky because she was female and, at forty-six, a little closer in age and outlook.

The client was nervous. In just a few hours she would be telling a story that would forever define her life and that of a president. Hoffmann tried to calm her. She said Starr would get the story one way or the other, so it might as well be on her terms. Lewinsky had been bottled up for seven months, Hoffmann thought, and might say more than necessary. "Keep a lid on," she advised. "This is not your only opportunity."

The first to arrive at the meeting from Starr's team were Dash and three prosecutors chosen because they would make Lewinsky comfortable. Bob Bittman, who had made small talk with her on Martin Luther King's birthday, was there. So was Sol Wisenberg, the grand jury chief, who brought wide knowledge of the case and a good touch with witnesses. Mary Anne Wirth was invited for her expertise in sex cases, her empathic style, and her gender. The Ritz-Carlton debacle had been run by men. Starr wanted a female interviewer present for a female subject.

The three prosecutors were just as anxious as Lewinsky. This was the moment the team had been waiting for, the event for which they had passed up a deal with Ginsburg so long ago. For sixteen hours a day since then, they had struggled over a giant puzzle. They were about to meet the puzzle maker. Would Lewinsky tell all? Would she cavil and lie? Nearby in the Fitzpatrick Manhattan Hotel, Starr aides Mike Emmick, Karin Immergut, and Craig Lerner stood by to analyze her responses and advise. Starr had tapped Emmick and Immergut to debrief Lewinsky when a deal was struck.

When the Lewinsky team arrived, they were ushered into a dining alcove overlooking the East River. Everyone took seats around a glass table, with Dash observing from an easy chair about ten feet away. Lewinsky faced Hoffmann, who by prior arrangement started the questioning. She guided Lewinsky through a brief history of her relationship with Clinton and what led her to sign a false affidavit. The questions were designed to elicit a simple yes or no.

After thirty minutes, prosecutors got their chance. Wirth went first, asking what she intended as a softball question: What did Clinton do to indicate he cared about her? Lewinsky got teary and asked to leave the room. After composing herself, she said he had given her gifts, referred to her as "baby" and "sweetie," and told her "you are bright, attractive and make me feel young." He said he hoped to "have time in three years" after leaving office to see more of her.

Starr's team was not out to cover every detail in one day. Indeed, the one issue they wanted most to discuss—the stained dress—had been placed off limits by Lewinsky's lawyers. They knew there would be time for more facts. First they had to test her candor, so they probed areas they knew a lot about to gauge her replies.

Lewinsky recounted numerous sexual episodes with Clinton, usually in the windowless hallway between the Oval Office and a private study. Her version of a 1996 Easter Sunday encounter was tragicomic. She had just been fired from her White House job for shadowing the president too much. Clinton called to console her and invited her over. She showed up just as Clinton was getting off the phone with his wife, saying, "I love you." They went through a back door into the study, where Lewinsky performed oral sex, not stopping even as Clinton took a phone call to discuss politics. They decoupled only when they heard someone call "Mr. President!" at the front door of the Oval Office. Deputy Chief of Staff Harold Ickes was looking for Clinton. "Just a minute," Clinton yelled back. As he left, a topless Lewinsky threw on her clothing and ran out a back door.

The prosecutors mentally kept score: high marks for her Easter account. It provided fresh detail on Linda Tripp's diary entry, and was accurate down to the name of the person—pollster Dick Morris—whose call was noted in White House phone records.

Another test was how she explained inconsistencies in her February statement. Wisenberg asked how she could assert simultaneously that Clinton had never asked her to lie and that he advised her to tell Paula Jones's lawyers she only saw him during trips to drop off mail or visit Betty Currie. "I was pretty literal," Lewinsky replied. She said the cover story suggested by Clinton was "misleading," part of the fabric of lies that hid the affair. She had always promised to keep it secret and to deny it if the secret got out. Clinton didn't have to tell her to lie. It was implicit, she said.

The session broke for a lunch of sandwiches and awkward conversation. Starr, waiting nervously at the Fitzpatrick, assigned head paralegal Lindsey Matson to deliver the deli food and get a reading on Lewinsky's mood. On her return, Starr had Matson report by speakerphone to everyone left in Washington. She described what Lewinsky wore, what she had for lunch (roast beef), and how she appeared (relaxed and upbeat).

Questions resumed after lunch. By 3 P.M., Lewinsky began to say more than she had to. "She's tired," Hoffmann whispered to Cacheris. On cue, he looked at his watch and said, "We wanted to catch the four o'clock flight. You guys covered a lot of ground." Bittman motioned toward a bedroom for a conference. Monica remained at the table.

That was a "good start," Bittman said. "We're happy with the way things are going and probably would have some other things we want to follow up on."

"That's it," Cacheris said firmly. "You've seen enough to make a decision. If you want more, we want an immunity agreement."

"You mean a real one, signed and everything?" joked Bittman, referring to the aborted pact signed by Ginsburg but not Starr.

Stein made one of his characteristically cryptic observations: "You've got everything you want. If you ask more, you might get something you don't want. If I were you, I'd go back to my office and figure out what I want."

Bittman said Starr and the full office would have to review whether to take the next step. He would let them know the next morning.

Starr's corps trooped over to the Fitzpatrick in an upbeat mood. In a conference call to Washington, they gave a rundown of the interview and their impressions of Lewinsky. Each said she had pulled punches to protect Vernon Jordan on how much he knew of her relations with Clinton. But all felt she would be a credible witness. Dash was the most voluble. He pronounced Lewinsky truthful and precise. He was still singing her praises at LaGuardia Airport, as he and three Starr aides waited for the Washington shuttle. "I want to get this deal done," he kept saying, loud enough to let passersby in on the news. The meeting they had just left was so secret that Starr had ordered the three assistants to sit separately on the plane so as not to draw attention. Horrified by Dash's indiscretion, Immergut asked him to pipe down.

David Kendall knew nothing of the New York meeting. With Clinton slated to appear before the grand jury the next day, July 28, he sent a new, more strident letter to Bittman upping his demands. Kendall threatened to fight Starr in court if he did not withdraw the subpoena. And, he wrote, Clinton would not be able to squeeze Starr into his schedule for at least seven weeks, after his Martha's Vineyard vacation. "The first date the president could conceivably testify consistently [*sic*] with his other obligations would be Sunday, Sept. 13, although we would, in simple fairness, request that his testimony occur on Sunday Sept. 20."

From New York, Bittman dictated a letter refusing to accept a seven-week delay. He insisted that Clinton meet the grand jury the next day or commit to another date no later than August 7.

As the day proceeded, Kendall heard what everyone was learning from an NBC News scoop: that Lewinsky was in New York meeting with Starr's team. The legal landscape had suddenly changed. If Kendall had hoped for the president to testify first, creating a record for Lewinsky to follow, his hopes had vanished. Starr would have her story. He would be well prepared to question Clinton and catch any contradictions.

If Clinton did testify, White House aides wanted to push the date as far into the future as possible. The more time they had, the more they could find out about what Lewinsky and other witnesses had said. Any delay would force Starr to put off sending his referral until after the November election, when Democrats might strengthen their position in the House. Kendall got Bittman on the phone. He all but pleaded for extra time. There were a lot of people involved in this decision, he said, and he needed to consult them before responding. Bittman said no. Kendall said Bittman had forced his hand. He would ask Judge Johnson for help.

The meeting in Starr's office on Tuesday, July 28, was one of the smoothest all year. They were close to reeling in both key witnesses for the referral. The unpopular Linda Tripp was no longer the central witness and her tapes no longer such crucial evidence. Now, no one opposed an immunity deal for Lewinsky—not even the hard-liners who once had wanted to indict her.

Starr left to call Stein. "Let's get this in writing," he said, inviting him and Cacheris to the office to hammer out the terms. After an hour, they left with a ten-paragraph immunity agreement freeing Lewinsky and her parents of charges in exchange for her full cooperation. Her only liability would be perjury if she lied under oath.

While the agreement was being drafted, Cacheris let Starr know about the dress. Cacheris said he didn't know what had caused the stain, but would turn it over to prosecutors for testing.

The dress was a potential trump card, by itself worth the long wait for Lewinsky's cooperation. Six months earlier, Ginsburg had denied its existence. He and his co-counsel Nate Speights said a garment seized at her apartment was "the dress," though the FBI found nothing on it. Would Lewinsky have volunteered the real one as part of a February immunity deal? Looking back, prosecutors thought not. She was more enamored of Clinton then, less fearful of protecting him. Now they had certified her credibility in an interview, possessed independent evidence to keep her honest and were working with lawyers they trusted.

For Lewinsky, the ordeal had just begun. She had to reveal her most intimate dreams and moments with every likelihood of them becoming public. She had enlisted in Starr's army. When her lawyers presented the agreement for signature, she broke into tears. Her hand was so shaky that her last name was illegible.

The debriefing of Lewinsky would begin the next day. But first, the Starr team had to face Kendall at a hastily called hearing with Judge Johnson behind closed doors. Kendall complained that Starr was unfairly rushing him to decide how to respond to the two-week old subpoena. "There are no impending deadlines, no statute of limitations are about to run, and no trials are imminent. There is simply no justification for the OIC's deadline except for its own fiat," he argued. He warned that the president might "go to war" over the subpoena—then thought better of it. "We're not going to war," he said, but he might challenge the subpoena.

Six weeks after siding with Kendall in the leaks probe, Johnson had no sympathy for this argument. Clinton had been invited six times to give testimony, she said. The grand jurors have been working hard, and they have decided they need his testimony now. "If he can vacation for a couple of weeks, he can appear before a grand jury too, you know." The judge said she would decide on Kendall's request the next morning.

At 8 P.M., Kendall called Bittman. He was desperate. The White House didn't want a subpoena at all, much less a federal judge ordering a balky president to comply with it. Kendall said Clinton would testify voluntarily if Starr withdrew the subpoena.

Starr's lawyers were reluctant to give up their court-sanctioned authority over the proceeding. They worried that Clinton might assert privileges and refuse to answer questions. Kendall said that was not Clinton's intention. Bittman reluctantly agreed. Kendall insisted the session be at the White House; Bittman insisted it be broadcast live to the grand jury room, as well as videotaped. A date of August 17 was agreed upon.

In the week since his first call to Stein, Starr had lined up the missing pieces of his referral. Even Mary Anne Wirth, the office hand-wringer, was in awe. "It's amazing, with all the things we've gone through, the stars suddenly aligned," she told Bittman.

On Wednesday, July 29, Kendall announced the president's commitment to testify and the date. It was official: Clinton would be the first chief executive to submit to questioning by a grand jury investigating his actions. But history quickly took a backseat to news reports of a more stunning development: Lewinsky had agreed to hand over to Starr a dress that would be tested for traces of the president's DNA.

The sudden discovery of the dress shook Clinton's political aides. When FBI tests on the dress found in January had proven negative, they had dismissed the stories as scurrilous and ridiculed Starr for spending millions of dollars to prove a nonexistent affair. Even if Lewinsky came forward, the aides calculated the worst case would be a he-said-she-said disagreement. Now they confronted the possibility of independent evidence that Clinton had lied when he denied sexual relations. And no one in Clinton's inner circle was making the rounds assuring his aides that nothing was on the dress.

The president was in check. There was no backing out of his testimony now. And he would have little opportunity to evade the truth.

Lewinsky showed up in Cacheris's office on the afternoon of July 29, carrying one dark blue, front-button shift from the Gap, size twelve. It was wrapped in plastic and turned over to an FBI agent who came to pick it up.

Emmick came along to see Lewinsky. He had studied her like a biographer over the past thirty weeks, getting to know her moods, taste in books, spending habits, family relationships, and insecurities. He was barred from Grandma's Place for fear she might have bad memories of the Ritz-Carlton. Now with the agreement sealed, he could be reintroduced. He would be leading her debriefings, which would be lengthy and personal.

Emmick thought Lewinsky would feel less threatened if they met on her turf. When Cacheris led his client into the conference room, he said, "I think you two know each other." They smiled in recognition. Emmick said he had come to talk about her briefings, the first of which was in a few hours. He tried to demystify the process. "The most important thing is to tell the truth," he said. "If you're embarrassed about something, let it come out. It's almost like you're floating in ether, not really connected to the consequences of what you're saying." He said no one expected her to be perfect.

Emmick left Lewinsky convinced he would finally be able to work with her to get the truth. He still believed he could have gotten much of it in February. But it didn't matter now. He had a date with Lewinsky, and the blue dress—potentially the most important piece of evidence in a political corruption case since the Watergate tapes—was on its way to the FBI laboratory for testing.

12

"DID YOU HAVE SEX WITH THE PRESIDENT?"

IT TOOK A DAY for the FBI lab to learn that the stain on Monica Lewinsky's dress was semen. Starr's next step was a fateful one, made alone and in secret. He instructed Bob Bittman to get a sample of the president's blood to see if there was a DNA match. Starr could require a blood specimen only if he had a sound legal basis. So when Bittman sent a letter to Kendall July 31 saying "investigative demands" necessitate a sample, he tacitly confirmed DNA had been found on the dress.

If Starr had consulted his attorneys, they might have tried to discourage that move. Starr was throwing Clinton a lifeline as the president got ready for his grand jury appearance. Prosecutors could have waited until after the testimony to ask for a blood sample, keeping him in the dark. Then, if he stuck to his denial of any sexual relationship with Lewinsky, Starr would have an open-and-shut case of perjury.

But as Starr saw it, Clinton was not a normal witness. Taking the Fifth Amendment was not politically viable for a sitting president, and Starr did not want to set a trap for him in the grand jury. Instead, the independent counsel hoped Clinton would listen to some of his own advisers, who were using the press to anonymously urge a "mea culpa" strategy—admitting everything and throwing himself on the mercy of Congress.

Kendall had little room to maneuver once Bittman notified him of a "powerful predication for our request of the president"—legalese for "we have a good reason to ask for blood." On August 3, in a letter marked "to be opened by Mr. Bittman only," he offered to provide a sample of Clinton's blood that very evening, on condition of complete secrecy. Kendall stipulated that the blood had to be drawn by White House physician Dr. Eleanor Maricino. He proposed 10 P.M. in the White House Map Room.

Bittman and an FBI lab scientist arrived at the White House shortly before the appointed hour. They waited fifteen minutes in a small lobby before they were escorted to the Map Room. On the way, they caught a glimpse of Attorney General Janet Reno walking down a red-carpeted hallway toward the door. The president was hosting a small dinner for a group of youth-violence experts. Some of his guests found him uncharacteristically remote and distracted, leaving it to Hillary Clinton to engage the academics and religious leaders at the table. After dinner, Clinton chatted with a few of the visitors, including Cornel West, a Harvard professor. West asked Clinton how he could keep believing in the system when "right-wing gangsters in ties" were so busy trying to destroy him. "They've been at me for a long time," Clinton responded. "I'm prepared."

It was 10:10 P.M. when the president stepped into the dimly lit Map Room. He stuck out his hand and introduced himself to Bittman and the FBI agent. Kendall and Dr. Maricino were the only others present.

"How are we going to do this?" Clinton asked. Maricino had him sit in a chair, his right arm extended under a table lamp. She inserted a needle and drew four milliliters of blood. The room was tense and silent. Clinton's face was crimson. Kendall tried to break the mood with a bad joke. "I've always wanted to see a client in this position," he said. Clinton looked over his shoulder, annoyed, and snapped,

"What are you talking about?" Kendall mumbled something nervously.

Bittman stumbled, too, referring to Clinton as "your honor." He and the agent watched closely as the blood was drawn and the tube detached from the syringe. Maricino handed the vial to the agent, and Clinton cordially bade them a good night.

Bittman had a nagging thought as he reached his car with the agent. "I don't want to sound paranoid," he said, "but I lost sight of the tube for a moment. I'm worried there was a little switcheroo. I saw the needle go in and the blood come out, but the doctor's back was to me and I lost it for a moment."

The agent had had a better vantage point. "It never left my sight," she said, "and the tube was warm." She went straight to the FBI lab and handed the technician a vial of Clinton's blood.

It was at the Watergate that Monica Lewinsky began to arm Starr for the second impeachment fight of the twentieth century.

The independent counsel rented a two-room conference suite there—not for symbolism, but for convenience: Lewinsky was staying at her mother's Watergate apartment. By doing the first four of her seventeen interviews there before moving to Starr's office, prosecutors sought to relieve the jitters of her initial sessions. For one thing, she could avoid the pack of reporters who trailed her everywhere.

Lewinsky was accompanied by two of Plato Cacheris's associates, Preston Burton and Sydney Hoffmann, who had prepared her for New York. Mike Emmick and Karin Immergut led the interrogation for Starr's team.

Their first goal was to establish that Clinton, despite his sworn denials, had indeed had a sexual relationship with Lewinsky—a prerequisite to bringing charges of perjury or obstruction of justice. Illicit affairs are often hard to document, but this one was recorded on Lewinsky's Day-Timer calendars. She had circled dates she had seen Clinton or spoken to him by phone, totaling them in tiny numbers at the bottom of each month. Another set of numbers marked the days she had no sexual contact with him.

The immunity deal had opened a floodgate of memories. There was no stopping Lewinsky from talking, no subject too personal for her to discuss. She seemed to prime herself for each session, to pump herself up like an athlete before a decisive game. It wasn't that she had declared allegiance to Starr's side. At every session she vented her anger at the embarrassing process, and made clear her distaste for Starr himself. But she was also eager to document the central event of her life, a romantic liaison with the president.

She recounted nine episodes of oral sex (performed by her) and between ten and fifteen phone-sex encounters, beginning on November 15, 1995. Within a few sessions, Lewinsky was volunteering more than prosecutors sought—struggles with zippers and bras, efforts to muzzle sounds in the president's study, and interludes of "pillow talk" in the Oval Office. When it came to the most graphic details, she asked Emmick to leave the room while she spoke to female attorneys, but in a voice loud enough for him to hear. During one sidebar, she pulled aside Hoffmann, Immergut, and prosecutor Julie Myers to reveal a sexual practice performed on Clinton that only Immergut had ever heard of.

The sessions created an odd bond between the prosecutors and their erstwhile target. She arrived each day with bottled water and her knitting, a hobby she had taken up during her months of isolation. She joked ruefully about her weight, then happily gorged on the M&Ms they provided. Immergut was pregnant, and Lewinsky offered to knit a blanket for the baby. She and Myers, close in age, discussed hair in the ladies' room.

Other assistants came by for brief questions or to catch a glimpse of their famous witness. It never threw her off stride. But one prosecutor who never stopped in was the independent counsel. Immergut asked Starr if he'd like to. "Absolutely, if you think it would be helpful," he said. But Lewinsky seemed to harbor bad feelings, and Starr didn't want to spook her. Immergut let the issue drop. Neither of them thought it peculiar that the head of an historic investigation never saw his star witness in action.

Lewinsky's lawyers played a limited role. Hoffmann urged her to give yes or no answers and let prosecutors ask for more detail if they wanted it. "Why do you need this?" Hoffmann demanded from time to time. They replied that detail lent authenticity to her account. There was only so much Hoffmann could do. Lewinsky was their witness.

She still saw Clinton through a romantic haze, though less so than in the past. She had begun to question his sincerity. Many of his gifts to her had been recycled, she thought. His talking on the phone while she performed oral sex made her feel "cheap." She passed on an important insight: Clinton thought only intercourse counted as "sex."

Linda Tripp in her view was the great schemer. Tripp had proposed asking Clinton to involve Vernon Jordan in the job search. Tripp had urged Lewinsky to make sure the job was secured before signing the Jones affidavit. And Tripp had advised her to seal the semen-stained dress in a plastic bag and put it in a safe deposit box. Some of Lewinsky's most emotional moments came during the hours of listening to Tripp's tapes. She laughed at some passages and blushed at others, but mostly burned with anger.

Prosecutors devoted two interviews to the sexual details. The rest focused on the harder-to-prove questions of obstruction of justice: whether the president had tried to conceal gifts subpoenaed by Paula Jones, helped find Lewinsky a job to buy her silence, or orchestrated her affidavit to head off questions about her at his deposition.

One surprise was a note she had sent to Clinton after seeing the film *Titanic*. Folded into a book, it said she wanted to have sexual intercourse with him. The next day, they had spoken by phone about her affidavit. She brought up the letter and confessed it wasn't smart to put such things in writing. Clinton agreed. Three weeks earlier, Paula Jones's lawyers had requested any documents he had relating to Lewinsky. Prosecutors found out Clinton had never turned over the note—new evidence of a possible cover-up.

Lewinsky exonerated Frank Carter, the lawyer Jordan had chosen to draft her affidavit. Prosecutors initially had suspected Carter of participating in the cover-up, but Lewinsky told them she had lied to him, too. And she cleared up the mystery of the "talking points," the three pages she'd given Tripp with suggestions on how to answer questions about herself and Kathleen Willey. Since the early days of the scandal, it had been widely speculated that someone close to Clinton, possibly a lawyer, had drawn them up. Lewinsky said in her first interview that she wrote the talking points herself without help from lawyers or anyone close to the president.

Prosecutors interviewed Lewinsky for eight straight days. On the ninth day, August 6, they took her to the grand jury. She took the oath at 9 A.M., and within minutes was recalling how her affair had begun when she was a twenty-two-year-old White House intern. Immergut questioned her about the first sexual episode, eliciting concise responses. She gave a simple yes when asked if she had performed oral sex, and yes again to whether there had been "other physical intimacy." The prosecutor then pulled out the "definition of sexual relations" used at Clinton's deposition: purposely touching a person's erogenous body parts with an intent to arouse sexual desire. So defined, Clinton had denied sex with Lewinsky. Asked if the other intimacy included sexual relations "within the definition that I've just read you?" Lewinsky said, "Yes, it does."

Immergut went through a similar exercise for the next sexual encounter, then passed out a chart listing seven others. All fell within the definition, Lewinsky said.

The only time Immergut departed from this euphemistic style was to explore the staining of Lewinsky's blue dress. Lewinsky said it happened on February 28, 1997, the first time she was intimate with Clinton after a gap of eleven months. Betty Currie had invited her to attend the president's weekly radio address. Afterward, she testified, Clinton gave her a hatpin and a copy of *Leaves of Grass* as belated Christmas gifts, then had oral sex with her in a bathroom behind the Oval Office. She never noticed the stains until the next time she went to wear the dress. "It was just a little tiny spot down here and a little tiny spot up here," she said, pointing to her lower hip and chest. "Then I remembered that I had worn it the last time I saw the president, and I believe it was at that point that I thought to myself, 'oh, no.'" She had gained weight in the meanwhile and the dress no longer fit, so she didn't bother to have it cleaned. "It wasn't a souvenir," she told jurors.

The sex questions took up the first hour. Emmick then took over the questioning, focusing on the effort to find her a job. Lewinsky had been unhappy after being transferred out of the White House in April 1996. At the time, she recalled, Clinton said it had to be done for appearances' sake because it was an election year. He promised, "If I win in November, I'll bring you back like that," snapping his fingers. But long after the election, she still languished at the Pentagon. Frustrated, she wrote a nasty note to the president on July 3, 1997. Addressing him as "Dear Sir," she accused Clinton of breaking his pledge and warned if she were not given a White House job, she would "need to explain to my parents why that wasn't happening," a veiled threat to disclose the affair. It resulted in a 9 A.M. meeting with Clinton the next day, which she told jurors was "very emotional." After scolding her for threatening him, Clinton hugged her and was "the most affectionate with me he'd ever been." She left the meeting "emotionally stunned," she said, thinking he was in love with her.

But still nothing happened on the job front. In October, she finally decided to find work in New York and asked Clinton to enlist the help of Vernon Jordan. Clinton agreed and told her to prepare a wish list. She met with Jordan in early November, though he did not become fully engaged in the issue for another month—until Lewinsky was named as a potential witness in the Paula Jones sexual harassment suit.

On December 5, Jones's lawyers notified Bob Bennett that Lewinsky might be called to testify about Clinton's "pattern" of sexual advances toward female subordinates. The next day she had an unscheduled meeting with Clinton. She complained about Jordan's inaction as a headhunter. "Oh, I'll talk to him. I'll get on it," Clinton said. He did not tell her about the witness list, and maintained he found out about it later that day.

Five days later, Lewinsky was sitting in Jordan's office. He was suddenly much more forthcoming. "Well, you're a friend of the president of the United States," he said, explaining his sudden willingness to help. He gave her the names of potential employers in New York and advised her what to say in letters to them.

Emmick then turned to the December 17 call from Clinton informing Lewinsky that she was on the witness list. The president, she said,
called sometime between 2 A.M. and 3 A.M. and told her he had news
that "broke his heart." Lewinsky asked what she should do if subpoenaed. "He said, 'Well, maybe you can sign an affidavit.' At some point
in the conversation, I don't know if it was before or after the subject of
the affidavit came up, he sort of said, 'You know, you can always say
you were coming to see Betty or that you were bringing me letters.'"
Lewinsky said she took the statement as a "reminder of things we had
discussed before," cover stories that were part of the "pattern of the
relationship, to sort of conceal it." As Lewinsky construed it, the affidavit was intended to "prevent me from being deposed." She understood that Clinton expected her to describe their relationship innocu-
ously, or even go "as far as maybe having to deny any kind of a
relationship."

Two days later, she was served a subpoena while at work at the
Pentagon. The most alarming part of it, she told jurors, was its
demand for several items from Clinton, including a hatpin—the first
gift he had ever given her. Frantic, she called Jordan. He told her to
come to his office. While she was there, phone records showed, he
had a four-minute phone conversation with Clinton. Jordan hung up
and made an appointment for Lewinsky to see Frank Carter. Before
she left Jordan's office, she testified, he asked her two questions: "Did
you have sex with the president? Did he ask?" She interpreted them
as a test of how she would respond if asked by Jones's lawyers in a
deposition, and she replied no to both. She assumed that Jordan
actually knew the truth.

Lewinsky's last meeting with Clinton, on December 28, 1997, was
another key link in the obstruction case. Soon after her 8:30 A.M.
arrival, she testified, he gave her several Christmas presents, including a
marble bear's head—an Indian symbol of strength for her to hold
"when you need to be strong." He knew that nine days earlier Lewinsky had been subpoenaed and directed to turn over all her gifts from
him. They briefly discussed the Jones case, she said. He told her he suspected Tripp or his Secret Service guards had given them up. Lewinsky

expressed concern about the hatpin. Clinton asked whether she had told anyone where she got it. She said no.

"Maybe I should put the gifts away outside my house somewhere or give them to someone, maybe Betty," Lewinsky recalled saying.

According to Lewinsky, he replied, "I don't know" or "Let me think about that."

Several hours later, Currie called her at home and said, "I understand you have something to give me." Lewinsky packed the gifts in a large box and wrote on it, "Please don't throw away." She handed the box to Currie, who had driven to her apartment.

Emmick asked Lewinsky why she thought Clinton would give her gifts knowing there was a subpoena covering such items.

She replied that "from everything he said to me," there was no question "we were going to do anything to keep this [affair] private" and to "take whatever appropriate steps" were necessary to achieve that, including concealment of his gifts to her.

On January 7, Lewinsky signed the affidavit and took off for New York, where she had an interview the next day with McAndrews & Forbes, one of the firms picked by Jordan. She thought she did not handle the interview well and called Jordan, who said he would contact the company's chairman, Ronald Perelman. "I thought he was kidding," she testified. Jordan called back and told her not to worry. On January 9, she had an interview with a McAndrews subsidiary, Revlon, and within a few hours, was offered a job in public relations.

On the day Lewinsky told her story, the White House conducted business as usual. Clinton's spokesman said he was spending the day meeting with his staff. He did appear publicly, venturing into the Rose Garden to endorse a handgun control bill just after Lewinsky entered the grand jury room. In Starr's office, administrator Sandy Oldham watched the event on live TV and taped it. As she replayed the tape, she noticed Clinton's bright yellow necktie. It looked like one Lewinsky said she had given him. "I can't believe he wore it," Oldham shouted, and reported it to Starr. Prosecutors had been paying attention to neckwear ever since Lewinsky had observed that Clinton's steward, Bayani Nelvis, had worn one of her gift ties to Clinton to one of his own grand jury appearances. Was the president using her ties to send some kind of signal?

Someone got word to the courthouse. After lunch, Immergut showed photos of Clinton wearing the same yellow tie three times in recent weeks. Lewinsky testified she had noticed each occasion. The first didn't faze her. The second occurred on July 6, and she thought it might be a reminder of their emotional meeting the previous July 4. "And then when he wore it a few days later," she said, "I thought he's trying to say something. I mean, the president doesn't wear the same tie twice in one week, so—I didn't know what it meant, but it was some sort of reminder to me." As she explained, "I used to bug him about wearing one of my ties because then I knew I was close to his heart." He liked to point out every time he wore one, and knew that she was watching for it.

Six hours after she was introduced to jurors, Lewinsky left the stand. Prosecutors thought they had everything they needed.

Starr and two of his deputies learned something else as Lewinsky was testifying. The FBI laboratory reported on the first of two DNA comparison tests. The genetic markers of the semen found on her dress matched the president's DNA as sampled by his blood specimen.

As the day set for the president's testimony drew near, it was the consuming topic at the OIC: Who would be chosen to question him, the greatest responsibility any prosecutor could have? To Bob Bittman, the day-to-day manager of the investigation, the choice was obvious: He should be the one. He went to Starr to make his case, and Starr acceded.

Not everyone was happy with the choice. In the view of some colleagues, Bittman was better as an administrator than he was as a litigator. He was too deferential and not fast enough on his feet to question Clinton, they thought.

Some wanted Emmick to do the questioning, because he knew Lewinsky's story better than anyone. Another choice was Hick Ewing, a cagey interrogator who had interviewed Clinton in the Whitewater investigation. Emmick suggested Immergut, thinking a woman might throw the president off stride. But as a recent recruit, she was not familiar enough with the evidence. Mary Anne Wirth knew the evidence, but she wasn't regarded as a tough enough interrogator.

In the end Starr decided to stay with Bittman, but added his two other Washington deputies. Sol Wisenberg had encyclopedic knowledge of the case and a sense of nuance, Starr thought. Jackie Bennett was there to provide muscle. After he had rattled Clinton friend Harry Thomason before the grand jury on August 11, reports began to circulate that the White House feared Bennett would also be able to unnerve the president. That was enough to assure him a spot on the team.

As in the rest of the investigation, they had no road map. No president had ever been questioned before a grand jury. And this session was likely to be made public eventually. The framing of questions was a sensitive issue—how graphic should they be? How pointed? The deputies debated how to handle evasive and dilatory responses. Should Clinton be challenged as if he were an ordinary witness? Should he be confronted if he appeared to prevaricate? Bittman said the worst thing they could do was appear to be treating Clinton disrespectfully: "Let's not do anything that will feed our critics who say all we want to do is embarrass the president."

The team wrote a play book to cover every contingency. A few days before the testimony was to begin, they began to rehearse. Ewing came in from Little Rock to play Clinton. He had been with Starr since the start, and no one had studied the president more carefully. He had read all the Clinton biographies and speeches and had picked up the local lore from old Arkansas associates. He had seen Clinton up close in the earlier phases of the investigation, both in interviews at the White House and in his testimony at Whitewater-related trials. Clinton even related to him as a fellow Southerner. During one White House session, the president recalled mowing lawns as a boy in Hot Springs and finding all sorts of insects. "We even had centipedes," he said. "We'd tear them apart and watch them go different ways." When nobody laughed, he turned to Ewing. "Hick, I know you all probably did it in Memphis, didn't you?"

Ewing, dressed in a dark presidential suit for the moot court, was a perfect understudy. He greeted everyone with a handshake and sat down next to Paul Rosenzweig, playing David Kendall. Bittman fired the first question: "Did you ever give Monica Lewinsky any gifts?"

"Mr. Bittman, what you don't understand, down where we live, it's cultural for people to give gifts," twanged the mock president. "I mean, everybody gives gifts. My momma, growing up, specially around Christmastime, always kept a bunch of extra presents on the washing machine so that if somebody came by that brought you a present, she'd say, 'Billy, you go back there and get a present for Miss Daisy.' And so, I'd go back and get it."

Lesson number one: Don't ask open-ended questions. Bittman stood slack-jawed as Ewing chatted on, prevented by protocol from cutting off the president.

The deputy tried to recover. "Did you ever touch Ms. Lewinsky?"

"Look, where I come from, everybody hugs," came the reply. "We have funerals, we have weddings, I mean, this isn't up North now, we hug down South. Could I have possibly just hugged her one time? Well, yeah. I'm sure I hugged her one time."

Lesson number two: Even the most specific questions can be filibustered.

The witness disposed of another question about wearing one of Lewinsky's ties the first day she testified to the grand jury. "In fact, the tie I wore that day is one of Hillary's favorites," Ewing intoned unctuously.

Didn't Monica give you one like that?

"I really don't remember," he said. "I think I had three or four like that."

Ewing played Clinton to the hilt. He took refuge in semantics: "It depends on what you mean." He argued the literal truth of his sworn denial of sexual relations with Lewinsky: "Look, I didn't lie at the Jones deposition because if they'd have asked me did she perform oral sex on you, I'd have said yes. But the Jones lawyers never asked that."

Over time, the Starr questioners improved. Wisenberg braced the witness with a reminder that he was under oath. Bittman caught him at semantic hair-splitting. Bennett cut off a filibuster by asking him to answer the question because the clock was running. But during a break, two young lawyers who had just witnessed the first of the three moot sessions shook their heads. "Man, we don't have a case," one told Ewing. "You're better than Clinton."

Ewing thought a minute. "Naw," he warned. "I'm not better than Clinton."

Bill Clinton was in the tightest spot of his career—and the loneliest. His wife and partner in politics had too much invested personally to give him disinterested advice. He couldn't confide in anyone else in the White House, because their conversations were subject to subpoena. All he had were his private lawyers, David Kendall, Kendall's partner Nicole Seligman, and Mickey Kantor. But even they were not fully able to help him sort the legal and political costs of various options. If Clinton confided wrongdoing to them but decided to tell the grand jury something else, they would be ethically bound to correct the record or resign.

On July 31, the president had publicly pledged to testify "completely and truthfully." He had no choice but to retract his categorical denial of sexual relations with Lewinsky. Starr had made that decision for him by signaling the results of the lab test on the dress. But could the president afford to admit he had lied about an affair? A confession might take the bite out of Starr's report to Congress and lower the odds of impeachment. But it could backfire, too. It risked breaking his bond with a public that had seemed to accept both his denial of sex with "that woman" and also his supporters' portrayal of Starr as a right-wing hatchetman out to topple a popular leader. It also would be tantamount to admitting that he had lied in the Jones case, exposing him to an indictment by Starr—and, almost as bad, to the possibility that Jones's lawsuit would be reinstated.

Of the lawyers, Kantor was closest to the president. He had been Clinton's 1992 campaign chairman and played a role then in the effort to quell scandals from the past. In the days before the testimony, he seized on what he thought was the elasticity of the Jones definition of sexual relations. He thought the definition could be narrowly read to exclude a passive sex partner, such as the recipient of oral sex. "It gives the president a lot of wiggle room," Kantor told another Clinton adviser.

Gradually, a strategy began to emerge for the August 17 grand jury session: Acknowledge sexual intimacy with Lewinsky. Insist the sworn denial in January was technically truthful because the definition did not cover the precise form of intimacy they engaged in. Decline to elaborate.

Hillary Clinton wanted her husband to admit nothing and stick to his January testimony. But Kendall approved of the new approach. He was determined that Clinton must be truthful.

A trial balloon went up Friday, August 14. A front-page story in the *New York Times* reported that Clinton had been discussing a possible confession of misconduct but nothing criminal. At least some of his advisers, the story said, believed the Jones team's criteria for sexual relations could exclude oral sex.

The strategy relied on Starr's willingness to stand down, to recognize the president had come halfway, and not to trigger a constitutional crisis over the right to ask for more intimate details. Starr still would be able to interrogate Clinton on the potentially criminal questions of obstruction of justice, subornation of perjury, and witness tampering. It looked like the kind of deal Washington lived on—splitting the difference and allowing both sides to claim victory.

Clinton advisers set forth terms in the August 16 edition of the *Washington Post*. According to a story by Bob Woodward, the investigative reporter of Watergate fame, Clinton planned to admit sexual activity with Lewinsky and hoped that Starr would accept his recantation "magnanimously," without trying to "humiliate" him with intrusive sex questions. "Starr wins," one strategist told Woodward. "And we hope he wouldn't feel it necessary to drag the body around the arena."

After months of denouncing Starr as a fanatic, Clinton's team was ready to restore his good name. Now they portrayed him as a "righteous man" driven by justifiable moral outrage, or, alternatively, as the unwilling instrument of the flawed system created by the independent counsel statute.

Of course, it took more than planting a newspaper story to mollify a mortal rival, especially one now at the peak of his strength. So Clinton strategists tried a quieter form of diplomacy, as well, using perhaps the last man in Washington who had a foot in both camps: Sam Dash.

As Starr's ethics adviser and an old colleague of Clinton lawyers, he had played the role of intermediary for years. Now Clinton associates sought him out to convey a message to Starr. The president would tell the "truth," they said, if Starr didn't pry into the embarrassing details of his relationship with Lewinsky. Dash wasn't persuaded. The details of the relationship with Lewinsky were precisely what Starr believed Clinton had been lying about all along. How could they know he was telling the truth now if they couldn't question him? Dash always said Clinton should admit everything he had done.

He repeated that prescription to a nationally prominent lawyer and Clinton supporter who came to Washington and met Dash for lunch on the eve of the testimony. The lawyer asked Dash for an assessment of the legal dangers facing Clinton if he decided to tell everything. Dash figured the lawyer had been sent for a last-minute overture. A complete confession, he said, would "pull the teeth" from the referral and criminal investigation and might even lead Starr to shut down the probe.

Dash reported each overture to Starr. Starr said if the president made a clean breast of it, it could influence how he proceeded, but he was otherwise noncommittal. The prosecutors were now certain the President would make a qualified confession. If Starr agreed not to press him on his earlier sworn denials, Clinton would be home free. Perjury was the crux of their case. Starr's assistants were in no mood to capitulate. The weekend before the grand jury, their mantra was "no slack for the President." They drafted precise questions to pierce Clinton's legalistic parsings of the Jones definition.

First, they had to overcome last-minute struggles over logistics. The four-hour session was planned for the Map Room, allowing the president to avoid an unceremonious trip to the courthouse. The testimony would be transmitted to the grand jury over closed-circuit

TV. No provisions were made, however, for the jurors to ask questions. So Bittman made what he considered a routine request for a secure, two-way phone line. Deputy Counsel Cheryl Mills replied, vetoing the phone link, as well as plans by Starr's office to record the session with its own video camera.

When Bittman had negotiated terms of the testimony in July, he had insisted on a videotape to show jurors who missed the session. He didn't say so at the time, but he knew the tape would be an exhibit in Starr's report to Congress. Kendall made little of the issue then. But a week before Clinton's grand jury appearance, Kendall got his first look at the still sealed videotape that had been made of Clinton's deposition in the Jones case. He saw Clinton's evasions and his angry jousting with Jones's lawyers. Now Kendall wanted to stop the grand jury taping. "You're just doing it to embarrass the president," he told Bittman. The day before the testimony, Kendall suggested bringing jurors to the White House to obviate the need for taping. The Starr team refused. The logistics were set, and Bittman suspected that Clinton would try to charm the jurors by playing host.

Next, Kendall proposed to have the tape destroyed after it was shown to missing jurors. Again, he was turned down.

Bittman and prosecutor Jay Apperson, who was assigned to handle the logistics, thought the last-minute resistance was intended to get them to cancel the voluntary session. Then Starr would have to issue another subpoena, which Clinton could oppose on the ground that the prosecutors were out of control and trying to humiliate the president. Rather than take a chance on further delays, Bittman agreed to let the White House video team record the session and to use an unsecured line to the grand jury.

Meanwhile, Starr's crew was having technical problems of potentially greater significance. At Ed Page's urging in July, they had asked the FBI lab in Quantico, Virginia, to test Linda Tripp's tapes. Page was sitting in his cubbyhole a few weeks later when he received a call from Bruce Edward Koenig, the FBI's renowned expert in tape authentication. They had worked together once before, in the case against Henry Cisneros. "Ed, every time you and I get involved in a case together, your tapes have problems," Koenig said. Preliminary findings showed signs of duplication. Page was alarmed because Tripp swore the tapes were originals. He took the news to Jackie Bennett. "Holy shit," said the deputy.

The tapes represented the original material evidence in the case. If any suspicions were raised about their provenance, Bennett feared, the president's lawyers would have a pretext for canceling his testimony. "Keep this quiet," Bennett urged. Only Starr, his deputies, and Steve Binhak, Tripp's handler, were apprised of the problem.

Even before the Clintons moved into the White House, the state of their marriage was Washington's favorite parlor game. Did she know? Did she care? Whenever other women came forward—Gennifer and Paula—Hillary Clinton acted as if it was someone else's problem. But there was no hiding her feelings on the weekend before her husband's testimony. She disappeared into her second floor room in the family quarters, refusing visitors and taking calls only from her family.

White House officials told reporters Mrs. Clinton "learned" over that weekend the truth of her husband's relationship with Monica Lewinsky. Actually, she had had her talk with Clinton the previous Thursday night when Chelsea slipped out with friends. No one knew what transpired. But the president had rehearsed what he would say twenty-four hours earlier with a close friend from out of town. In his rehearsal, he said he had strayed over the line and was ashamed of it.

Hillary kept up appearances Friday, despite the story in the *New York Times*. She threw her husband a premature birthday party with spice cake and the Marine Band. Then she went to ground. She emerged Sunday afternoon, the day before the grand jury, meeting with lawyers and helping to shape strategy. At 10:30 that night, the Reverend Jesse Jackson entered the White House through a side door. He joined Mrs. Clinton and Chelsea on the second floor. They embraced, and discussed faith and "the storm." Jackson then took Chelsea aside for a talk about the temptations of the flesh.

13

"IT'S YOUR SPEECH;
SAY WHAT YOU FEEL"

ON A HOT, muggy August 17, precisely four years into his long slog through the Clinton scandals, Ken Starr set out for the long-awaited showdown before the grand jury. At last, the president and his accuser would confront each other over the issue of truth. Starr saw it as black or white; Clinton perceived a spectrum of grays. It was the central question, the fundamentally different way of seeing the world that had always divided them.

The independent counsel was unusually subdued as he climbed into the car shortly before 1 P.M. to ride up Pennsylvania Avenue. There were large crowds on both sides of the road. Bob Bittman, riding with him, was surprised to see that the public focused on this as a day of reckoning.

It was a make-or-break day for them all, Bittman believed. His father, who had squared off against Williams & Connolly three decades earlier, had offered some acerbic advice. "Don't worry about how you do," said Bill Bittman. "You're just going to have every litigator in the country picking apart your performance for the rest of your life."

As they were waved though the southeast gate of the White House, Jay Apperson was struck by the historic oddity of the palace guard welcoming prosecutors in to question the head of state. Sol Wisenberg, too, was swept up by the event. Famously disheveled, he had gotten a rare haircut for the White House proceedings, though he hadn't managed to see the shoemaker. A loose metal plate dangled from one heel.

They arrived at the South Lawn diplomatic entrance and were shown to the Red Room, their base of operations and point of telephone contact with grand jurors, who would call in their questions. Moments after they entered, David Kendall asked Starr to step into the hallway for a private conversation. He got right to the point. Clinton would make a statement, said Kendall, and would answer all their questions. But to preserve the dignity of his office, he would not go into detail about his relationship with Lewinsky. Starr replied he had no intention of treading on the dignity of the president. Kendall, steely-eyed and tense, underlined the point. If Starr transgressed, he warned, "I will fight you to the knife both here and publicly."

They were harsh words, but Starr saw no harm. He regarded Kendall as a tenacious lawyer protecting a singularly important client. The message he heard was the same one he had read in the paper: You've won. Don't drag the body around the arena.

Starr rejoined his team in the Red Room. Huddling in a corner of the empty chamber to avoid being overheard, he told them what Kendall had said. The veteran prosecutors took it as a threat. Now that they no longer had the power of a subpoena to enforce their questions, Kendall was trying to establish limits. But Bittman boosted their confidence with a report on Lewinsky's dress. No one besides him, Starr, and Wisenberg had known the results of the first test. That morning, Bittman told his colleagues, the FBI reported its findings of the second, more sensitive analysis. The president's DNA matched the stain on the dress, a match characteristic of one male out of 7.87 trillion Caucasians. Little was said, but they left for the Map Room relieved. There was less riding on the session now, less that they had to prove.

All the participants took their places before the president arrived. Mary Anne Wirth, Mike Emmick, Jackie Bennett, Wisenberg, and

Bittman sat at a table across from a small chair for the witness. Beside them was a podium for the questioner and next to that a table for the president's lawyers, Kendall, Nicole Seligman, and Chuck Ruff. Starr and Apperson occupied a sofa behind the prosecution table. Clinton arrived at 1 P.M. in a dark suit and gold and black tie. He shook hands and greeted everyone, then took his seat.

Bittman opened for the prosecution and wasted no time. "Were you physically intimate with Monica Lewinsky?" he asked.

Clinton pulled a statement from his coat pocket, unfolded it, and read: "When I was alone with Ms. Lewinsky on certain occasions in early 1996 and once in early 1997, I engaged in conduct that was wrong," he said. "These encounters did not consist of sexual intercourse, they did not constitute sexual relations as I understood that term to be defined at my January 17, 1998 deposition. But they did involve inappropriate intimate contact. These inappropriate encounters ended at my insistence in early 1997. I also had occasional telephone conversations with Ms. Lewinsky that included inappropriate sexual banter. I regret that what began as a friendship came to include this conduct, and I take full responsibility for my actions. While I will provide the grand jury whatever other information I can, because of privacy considerations affecting my family, myself and others, and in an effort to preserve the dignity of the office I hold, this is all I will say about the specifics of these particular matters." He then volunteered to answer questions about what he understood "sexual relations" to mean in the context of the Jones case.

Starr's team called a break, and adjourned to the Red Room. The president had conceded little. Clinton was admitting to a sexual relationship, but not to lying under oath. Since they had withdrawn the subpoena in exchange for his voluntary testimony, they could not compel his responses. They quickly hashed out their options: They could walk out; they could press on and see how far Clinton would let them go; or they could forgo any detailed questions, then issue a new subpoena. Bittman had one in his breast pocket for just this contingency.

Starr was torn. If they walked out, Clinton could claim they had been unreasonable and mount a time-consuming challenge to a new subpoena. If they stayed and allowed him to refuse to answer key questions, they would not get the information they needed. After a few minutes of discussion, Starr decided they should go forward with the testimony. He was inclined not to be aggressive, but to evaluate the questioning as they went along. They filed back into the Map Room.

Bittman returned to the podium to test the truth of Clinton's statements in the Jones deposition. During that deposition, Bob Bennett had tried to head off questions about Lewinsky by introducing her affidavit, containing the by-now notorious assertion that "I have never had a sexual relationship with the president." Bennett had told Judge Susan Webber Wright that Lewinsky had sworn "that there is absolutely no sex of any kind in any manner, shape or form with president Clinton." Then he had turned to Clinton and asked if Lewinsky's affidavit was "true and accurate." Clinton said it was "absolutely true." Lewinsky's statement said she had met Clinton at the White House and seen him at functions, but "there were other people present on those occasions."

Now, Bittman pointed out, Clinton was acknowledging being alone with Lewinsky and having inappropriate intimate contact. Why did he allow his lawyer to introduce a false affidavit and tell a federal judge "there is absolutely no sex of any kind?"

"Well," said Clinton, "in the present tense that is an accurate statement. At the time he said that, and for some time before, that would be a completely accurate statement." Clinton was trying to hide behind semantics and verb tenses, as Ewing had predicted. Wisenberg, taking the podium a bit later, took another crack at it: "That statement is a completely false statement . . . an utterly false statement. Is that correct?"

"It depends on what the meaning of the word *is* is," replied the president. "If *is* means is and never has been, that is not—that is one thing. If it means there is none, that is a completely true statement."

Apperson jotted down a question and passed it to Wisenberg.

"Do you mean today that because you were not engaging in sexual activity with Ms. Lewinsky during the deposition, that the statement of Mr. Bennett might be literally true?" Wisenberg asked.

"No sir," said Clinton, "I wasn't trying to give you a cute answer. . . . I was trying to tell you that generally speaking in the present tense, if someone said that, that would be true. And I don't know what Mr. Bennett had in his mind." He had not paid any attention to the discussion, said Clinton, and was not responsible if his lawyer misled the court. "He was representing me, I wasn't representing him," he said.

Of Lewinsky's affidavit, the president acknowledged that he hoped it would free her from testifying, but denied advising her to lie. "I felt quite comfortable that she could have executed a truthful affidavit which would not have disclosed the embarrassing details of the relationship that we had, which had been over for many months by the time this incident occurred," he said.

At the courthouse, the grand jurors wanted to know how that was possible, relaying a question by phone that was handed to Wisenberg. "The grand jurors want you to be more specific about the inappropriate conduct," he told Clinton.

But Clinton refused to discuss "something that is intensely painful to me. This has been tough enough on me and my family, although I take responsibility for it. I have no one to blame but myself." He was willing to answer questions about what behavior was included in the Jones case definition of sex, but he said he would not answer questions that seek to "criminalize my private life."

The definition stated "a person engages in sexual relations when the person knowingly engages in or causes contact with the genitalia, anus, groin, breast, inner thigh or buttocks of any person with an intent to arouse or gratify the sexual desire of any person."

Wisenberg relayed another question from the grand jury: Was oral sex included in the definition? "As I understood it, it was not, no, if performed on the deponent," said Clinton. "Let me remind you, Sir, I read this carefully. And I thought about it. I thought about what 'contact' meant. I thought about what 'intent to arouse or gratify' meant. And I had to admit that under this definition that I'd actually had sexual relations with Gennifer Flowers. Now, I would rather have taken a whipping than done that." During the 1992 presidential campaign, Clinton had denied Flowers's claims of a twelve-year affair.

Clinton agreed that touching and fondling by him would be included in the Jones case definition of sexual relations. If Lewinsky said Clinton had fondled her, Wisenberg asked, "would she be lying?"

"That's not my recollection," said Clinton. "My recollection is I did not have sexual relations with Ms. Lewinsky and I'm staying on my former statement about that."

Even as he denied lying in his deposition, the president flatly contradicted a number of points in his earlier testimony. Whereas in January he'd had no recollection of being alone with Lewinsky, he now admitted being alone with her about fourteen times, up until three weeks before his Jones testimony. Clinton also changed his accounts of whether he had ever talked to Lewinsky about testifying in the Jones case and whether he had given her gifts.

On the question of whether he conspired with Lewinsky to conceal the gifts, the president recalled a discussion with Lewinsky about turning over subpoenaed items. But his account differed from that of Lewinsky, who had said he was noncommittal when she suggested hiding them. "I myself told her if they ask you for gifts, you have to give them what you have," he testified. He denied asking Currie to pick up anything from Lewinsky on December 28, the day Currie took the box of gifts from Lewinsky and hid it under her bed.

Wisenberg kept focusing on Clinton's testimony the previous January, looking for evidence of perjury. In his Jones deposition, Clinton had minimized Vernon Jordan's role in advising Lewinsky how to handle her subpoena. He'd said he could not recall discussing the subpoena with anyone but his lawyers and Bruce Lindsey. Didn't Clinton know that Jordan had met with Lewinsky about her subpoena? the Jones lawyers asked. "I thought that he talked to her about something else," Clinton replied. But the grand jurors knew better. Jordan had already told them he'd had "a continuing dialogue" with Clinton about the Lewinsky subpoena. And Jordan's lawyer, Bill Hundley, had kept Kendall apprised of Jordan's testimony, so Clinton knew that this time, he'd have to come up with a better answer.

"Why didn't you tell the court when you were under oath and

sworn to tell the truth, the whole truth, and nothing but the truth, that you had been talking with Vernon Jordan about the case, about the affidavit, the lawyer, the subpoena?" Wisenberg asked.

"Well," answered Clinton, "that's not the question I was asked. I was asked, 'Has it ever been reported to you that he met with Monica Lewinsky and talked about this case.' I believe—and I may be wrong about this—my impression was that at the time, I was focused on the meetings. I believe the meetings he had were meetings about her moving to New York and getting a job. . . . " In other words, Clinton was saying, he had answered a question about meetings between Jordan and Lewinsky, not telephone conversations.

But there were meetings as well as phone calls, Wisenberg reminded Clinton. "Are you saying, sir, that you forgot when you were asked this question that Vernon Jordan had come on December 19th, just three and a half weeks before, and said that he had met that day, that day that Monica got the subpoena?"

Clinton said he was a busy man, and "It is quite possible that I had gotten mixed up between whether she had met with him or talked with him on the telephone in those three-and-a-half weeks."

The president had a few set pieces to denounce the Jones team as his political tormentors, justifying his misleading answers. "Now, I will admit this, Sir," he said. "My goal in this deposition was to be truthful but not particularly helpful. I did not wish to do the work of the Jones lawyers. I deplored what they were doing. I deplored the innocent people they were tormenting and traumatizing. I deplored their illegal leaking. I deplored the fact that they knew, once they knew our evidence, that this was a bogus lawsuit. But I was determined to walk through the minefield of this deposition without violating the law, and I believe I did." He bitterly noted Linda Tripp's role in arming Jones's lawyers for the deposition and went so far as to accuse Starr of also being in league with the Jones lawyers. "You seem to be criticizing me because they didn't ask better questions, and as if you didn't prepare them well enough to sort of set me up or something," he said.

Clinton ran out the clock, painting himself as the target of a political witch hunt. He was passionate in the belief he had been wronged, and his demeanor was confident and challenging. But at the defense table, Kendall was agitated throughout the session. He had complained to White House aides and other defense lawyers that he didn't have enough time to prepare Clinton for the questioning. There was no real role for him this day because lawyers are normally not allowed into grand jury sessions. Ruff and Seligman sat by him, silently scribbling down the questions and Clinton's answers.

Starr, too, sat on the sidelines. He found it demeaning for the president to dodge questions and filibuster, but just as demeaning for the prosecutors to have to corner him. He put only a brief series of questions to the president, legalistic queries about whether Clinton had authorized his aides to invoke executive privilege. Yes, the president answered—not because he was worried about what people would say under oath, but out of an "honest difference of constitutional principles" between the White House and Starr.

Jackie Bennett fired off a few parting shots in his characteristically blunt style. Had Clinton purposely worn a tie from Lewinsky on her first day of testifying to send a message? As if borrowing a page from his understudy, Ewing, the president said he had "no earthly idea" it was a tie she had given him.

Why had his steward, Nelvis, worn one of her ties at a grand jury appearance?

"May I explain, Mr. Bennett? It won't take long," said Clinton. "Every year since I've been president I've gotten quite a large number of ties, as you might imagine. I get, I have a couple of friends, one in Chicago, one in Florida, who give me a lot of ties, a lot of other people who send me ties all the time, or give them to me when I see them. So I always have the growing number of ties in my closet. What I normally do, if someone gives me a tie as a gift, is I wear it a time or two . . ." Clinton chatted on for several more precious minutes describing how he distributed them to aides.

As closing time neared, Bennett threw deference to the winds, lobbing pointed challenges about Kathleen Willey.

"You did grab her breast as she said?" asked Bennett.

"I did not," Clinton replied.

"You did place your hand on her groin area, as she said?"

"No, I didn't."

"And you placed her hand on your genitals, did you not?"

"Mr. Bennett, I didn't do any of that, and the questions you're asking betray the bias of this operation that has troubled me from the beginning."

When the four hours expired, the prosecutors asked Clinton to extend the questioning. His reply was directed to his unseen audience back in the courthouse. "I wish the grand jurors would have been allowed to come here today as we invited them to do," he said. The grand jury knew nothing of Kendall's eleventh-hour suggestion the day before. "I wanted them down here. I wanted them to be able to see me directly. I wanted them to be able to ask their questions directly. But we made an agreement that was different, and I think I will go ahead and stick with the terms of it."

The moment it was over, the president bolted from the room, looking angry. As prosecutors prepared to leave, he returned, composed and gracious in his farewells.

As Starr and his team drove off at 6:30 P.M., Kendall stood outside the diplomatic entrance to announce that Clinton would give a speech that night. He said nothing about the grand jury session, but conveyed its tone. "We're hopeful that the president's testimony will finally bring closure to the independent counsel's more than four-year and over forty-million-dollar investigation, which has culminated in an investigation of the president's private life," he said. The $40 million price tag represented the work of Starr's multiple investigations; the cost of the Lewinsky probe was $4.4 million.

The prosecutors returned to their offices to disappointed reviews from staff members who had watched the testimony from the grand jury room. Clinton was very charismatic, they said. "He kicked our ass," agreed Emmick. Wisenberg felt the president had handled himself masterfully. Only Starr and Bittman were satisfied with how things had gone. They felt Clinton had made significant admissions, a view some others in the office began to share the next day after they read the grand jury transcript.

Clinton sat down in the nearby infirmary to reprise his testimony with lawyers. He was angry and depleted. For the first time in his career he had eaten his words, and he had done it before a bitter rival. He was in no mood to be contrite. Political advisers had been pushing hard for a televised address, warning that any delay would look like he was hiding something. That was before they had found out, in fact, that he did have something to hide. The news, delivered to them at noon Monday, shattered the illusions of those who had believed him and mortgaged their own credibility. But all of them were angrier at Starr for driving Clinton into a corner and forcing him to pay a price they thought was far in excess of his crime. Now, they agreed, it was all the more important to condition the public before his testimony began leaking.

At 6:40 P.M., political aide Doug Sosnik wandered in and asked Clinton how he was feeling. "I'm fine. Let's do it," he replied.

The speech had been in the works since late the previous week. Paul Begala drafted it at home on Saturday, then came to the White House on Sunday to tune it up. He had seen enough in the papers to know that the president's penitence would have to be the centerpiece, undiluted by criticism of Starr. Consultant Bob Shrum sent in his ideas, as did Sidney Blumenthal, who was traveling in Italy. Linda Bloodworth-Thomason, the Hollywood producer and old friend of the Clintons, helped polish the language.

But on Monday morning, Clinton handed Begala an outline of his own draft—in effect, a screed against Starr. After Clinton began his testimony, Kantor called a meeting of political and legal advisers in Ruff's office. Begala and other aides argued against the harsh tone of what was supposed to be an apology. But Kantor indicated that was the tone Clinton wanted, as did the first lady.

"Mea culpa" had always been the toughest words for Clinton. The only time he had come close was when he ran in 1982 to regain the Arkansas governor's office he had lost two years earlier. His consultant then, Dick Morris, wanted him to apologize for unpopular actions in his first term, most notably raising the car license tax. They argued for hours about the need for the word "apology" in his statement, and in a last-minute switch rephrased a television ad simply to say he would not make the same mistake again if voters gave him a second chance.

In his second term, Clinton had no more electoral chances. But he did have a legacy, and he knew this night would profoundly influence it. He was in a fighting spirit when he sat down with his lawyers and wife in the Solarium three hours before the speech.

His political staff and James Carville arrived at 8 P.M. and picked up a working draft that started with personal contrition, then turned on Starr. They pleaded with Clinton to give the first part only. Even Carville argued this was no time to blame Starr. But Clinton insisted that no other prosecutor would have waged a war on his personal life and that if he didn't make that clear, no one else would. He agreed to a few softeners. But there was no stopping him. Everyone turned to Hillary Clinton. "It's your speech, say what you feel, what you want to say," she said, then left the room.

One missing adviser was Mark Penn. Kantor had barred the pollster to avoid charges that the speech was a political exercise. But Penn quietly made his views known. Two audiences would be watching Clinton, he said. The public was weary of scandal, looking for some explanation and a quick exit. The public opinion elite—legal moralists, editorialists, political figures, and academics—wanted more. To satisfy them, Clinton had to accept responsibility and ask forgiveness. Penn knew it would be tough to win over both groups in one speech. But the worst thing the president could do was hammer Starr, he told one adviser who sneaked in a call. That would anger the elites and eliminate any chance of giving the public what it most desired: closure.

At 10 P.M., the president returned to the Map Room, where Franklin D. Roosevelt had directed Allied efforts during World War II. This battle would be fought alone.

He sat in the same chair from which he had addressed the grand jury, an ordeal that still showed in his face five hours later. He began contritely, but rushed through his remarks so swiftly that they seemed pro forma. He acknowledged a relationship with Lewinsky that was "not appropriate" and represented a "critical lapse in judgment and a personal failure on my part." He said his public comments gave a "false impression," and he "misled people, including even my wife. I deeply regret that." But he drew a line between human frailties and criminal acts. He had given "legally accurate" answers in the Jones deposition, he insisted, and never asked anyone to "lie, to hide or destroy evidence or to take any other unlawful action." His transgressions, Clinton seemed to be saying, boiled down to illicit conduct hidden to protect Hillary Clinton.

The statement lasted four and a half minutes. About halfway through, his gaze hardened like a prizefighter's. The deposition, he said, had arisen from a "politically inspired lawsuit" and had led to a probe by an independent counsel appointed to look into twenty-year-old Arkansas business dealings. Starr, he asserted, "moved on to my staff and friends, then into my private life," and now his "investigation itself is under investigation"—a reference to the probes of leaks and payments to David Hale. "This has gone on too long, cost too much and hurt too many innocent people," he said. "It's time to stop the pursuit of personal destruction and the prying into private lives and get on with our national life."

What political Washington heard in his 543 words was vintage Clinton. He was intimate with the camera and conveyed a sense of personal failure. But the scapegoating and selective truths of his statement enraged his critics. Was his finger-wagging denial of January simply a "false impression"? Was he being "legally accurate" in excluding oral sex from the definition of sexual relations? Or in claiming he couldn't recall being alone with Lewinsky? Was it true he had never asked anyone to lie, even though he acknowledged asking Betty Currie such leading questions about Lewinsky as "We were never alone, right?" Was it appropriate for him to blame Starr for the "pursuit of personal destruction" when his own aides and supporters had so effectively discredited Starr and trafficked in rumors about his assistants?

Clinton didn't need his pollster to find the public's pulse. He touched on every reason Americans disliked Starr's investigation—its intrusiveness, length, and cost. The public registered neutrally to his speech. But as Penn had predicted, Clinton lost the very people he needed to extricate himself. Democratic Senator Dianne Feinstein of California, who had stood by him at the White House the day he denied having sex with "that woman," said, "My trust in his credibility has been badly shattered." She was an influential voice among Clinton's large female political following. Democratic Congressman Paul Hale of Pennsylvania called the affair "morally repugnant" and said the president should resign. Republican House leaders were quick to agree.

That night, about a dozen prosecutors went to Sam & Harry's, a downtown restaurant, to unwind over a steak dinner. When Clinton appeared on television to speak to the nation, they gravitated to the bar to watch. After the intensity of the afternoon, the president seemed remote and disembodied. No one was quite sure what to make of his speech or how it would be received.

The next morning, Hillary Clinton's spokeswoman told reporters "she's committed to her marriage" and "believes in the president." Then she and the president, looking painfully estranged, walked with daughter Chelsea between them across the White House lawn to the helicopter that would ferry them off for a Martha's Vineyard vacation. On Air Force One, Clinton picked up the *New York Times* crossword puzzle. At 46 down, the clue was a four-letter word for "meal for the humble." "Well," he said, "here's one that's appropriate for today." The answer was "crow." When they landed, he observed another now awkward ritual from pre-scandal days. Vernon Jordan embraced him and invited him for dinner that evening with their wives.

The president's most important review was written in an apartment on Manhattan's Upper East Side. Lewinsky watched his speech alone and was crushed. There were no kind words for the woman who had protected him when Starr's team tried to turn her into an informant. None for her family despite its great pain. She felt violated. Even worse, Clinton had raised so many questions in his testimony, she was called back to the grand jury herself.

On August 20, Lewinsky marched back into the jury room with a new attitude. She said Clinton had hurt her by failing to recognize her pain and her decency. She was even angrier over sketchy news accounts of his testimony, especially his characterization of their relationship. What he suggested was one-way sex that made it sound like she had a "service contract, that all I did was perform oral sex on him," she said. She felt it had been more. "I don't know what the truth is anymore," she said.

But her version of events grew sharper. She gave fuller accounts of Clinton's instructions to deny their affair and his chagrin over the subpoenaed hatpin. Lewinsky also insisted he knew the origin of the yellow tie he put on for the first day of her testimony, saying the president had thanked her for it in a note.

While jurors questioned Clinton's motivations for wearing ties on certain days, the public was looking for hidden agendas in his air strikes against Afghanistan and Sudan—a measure of the president's growing credibility gap. Talk radio was flooded with callers comparing the surprise military moves to *Wag the Dog*, a film featuring a president who fakes a war to divert attention from a sex scandal. Was life imitating art?

By the end of her second day of testifying, Lewinsky had won the jurors' hearts. One asked her to describe Prom Night, a subject she conjured into a scene from a Solzhenitsyn novel. She tearfully recalled being asked to record conversations with Betty Currie, Vernon Jordan, and possibly Clinton. She told of being threatened with prosecution of her and her mother, being discouraged from calling Frank Carter, and being made to feel that if she left the hotel, she would be arrested.

Emmick had left the jury room at her request, leaving behind Immergut, who knew little of the event. Had others been present, Lewinsky might have been asked whether there had been a direct request to record Jordan and Clinton, or whether that was something she had inferred. They might have asked if prosecutors had threatened her or merely informed her of the risks of not cooperating. And they might have asked why, if she had really been held hostage, she had been allowed to roam the nearby mall unaccompanied.

But Lewinsky got her story out and wrapped up her testimony with the assertion that "nobody told me to lie" or promised her a job for silence. She said she was sorry for "everything that's happened" and added a final thought: "I hate Linda Tripp." One of the jurors said of Tripp's future: "What goes around comes around." The forewoman said the jury offered her a "bouquet of good wishes."

The president's testimony prompted the prosecutors to do something they had not done in two grand jury sessions: record details of the Lewinsky-Clinton trysts. It wouldn't have been necessary if Clinton had confessed to having sex with Lewinsky and to lying in the Jones case. Instead, he denied both under the prevailing definition of sexual relations. Starr believed his "hands-off" defense was untrue, but only Lewinsky could provide the evidence. Her debriefings, explicit as they had been, did not have the authority of sworn testimony.

Lewinsky had seemed embarrassed when the grand jury asked her to explain a particular encounter with the president. "Can I hide under the table?" she asked. So Starr aides let her provide sworn testimony of the most intimate details outside the grand jury room, in a deposition conducted by Immergut and Wirth.

In the session, held August 26, Lewinsky gave graphic descriptions of each sexual encounter. All told, her testimony described nine occasions on which the president had fondled her. The prosecutors tried to make sure that Clinton's speech had not tainted her testimony. "Do you, for any reason now, want to hurt the president?" Immergut asked.

"No," said Lewinsky. "I'm upset with him right now, but I—no, that's the last thing in the world I want to do."

14

"IT'S NOT TIME FOR
THE FAINT-HEARTED"

WHENEVER PART-TIME consultant Bill Kelley came to Starr's office, he couldn't help but notice how inured the lawyers had become to the underlying sexual facts of the Lewinsky case. They barely flinched at subjects that were racy—if not taboo—in places like South Bend, Indiana, where Kelley spent most of his time. It was an occupational hazard that worried him as he moved in for the final phase of the Lewinsky investigation: drafting an impeachment referral for Congress.

After the testimony of Clinton and Lewinsky, the draft referral had to be radically overhauled—and quickly, to meet Starr's new deadline of September 9, the day Congress returned from its summer recess. There was plenty of new material to fill the gaps in what had been a circumstantial case. But the details were inescapably salacious. The president had forced the issue with his insistence that the "inappropriate intimate contact" he had enjoyed with Lewinsky had not constituted sexual relations as defined by the lawyers in the Jones case. The only way to prove he had lied in his deposition in January, and then before the grand jury in August, was to document in explicit detail the nine sexual episodes claimed by his partner. If that made the narrative section read like a Henry Miller novel—well, the president had no one to blame but himself.

Kelley, thirty-five, a baby-faced Harvard-trained lawyer, agreed that the case had to be drawn in sufficient detail to eliminate any doubts. But as successive drafts reached his desk, some passages struck him as unnecessarily lurid and repetitious. He recorded his objections in a large scrawl: "TAKE THIS OUT" and "YOU CAN'T DO THIS." When they kept resurfacing, he questioned the drafters. Why mention masturbation if the criterion for sex was touching the other person's body parts? What is the relevance of Clinton's comments to Lewinsky on the state of his marriage?

After six months of being ridiculed and abused by the White House, saving the president from public embarrassment was not high on the OIC's list of concerns. But there also were compelling legal reasons for putting in all the details, and they were argued most fervently by the women who had debriefed Lewinsky. Karin Immergut, Mary Ann Wirth, and Julie Myers maintained that the specific details of what had gone on between Clinton and Lewinsky were necessary to put the charges in context and to bolster the credibility of Lewinsky's testimony. To disbelieve her was to assume, for instance, that she'd made up the incident with the cigar—and who could imagine a young woman inventing something so personally degrading? The female prosecutors saw sexual exploitation in Clinton's behavior—having Lewinsky service him while he chatted on the phone with a congressman, just to cite one case. They found it sad that Lewinsky had to ask, in one of their early trysts, if he remembered her name.

In Starr's male-dominated office, the women's view carried great weight. It assured Starr that Congress would agree the salacious details were indispensable.

Kelley had pressed his case with Starr several times. "The world isn't ready for this," he pleaded. He found an ally in Brett Kavanaugh, who was writing the grounds section of the referral. Kavanaugh thought the narrative was duplicative. If it couldn't be cleaned up, he argued, they might as well eliminate it.

That was a radical recommendation. The narrative section of the referral had been in the works since March, an enormous, labor-intensive project that incorporated all the relevant facts in easy-to-follow story form. But Kelley and Kavanaugh viewed it as largely superfluous now that they had direct testimony from the principals. In late August, they appealed directly to Starr. Kavanaugh contended that the narrative gave the impression that this was a sex tale, not a serious legal matter. He and Kelley urged Starr to scrap it, subordinate it to the grounds section of the referral, or put it in an appendix.

Starr, whose personal tastes ran to PG-rated movies, was predisposed toward discretion. His first hope was that some of the key moments in the affair could be described inoffensively. "Will it write?" he kept asking his drafters, using a judge's line to gauge whether the logic of an oral opinion will hold up when rendered in black and white. But when vague terms or euphemisms were substituted for some sexual practices, they just raised more questions. And generalized accounts of "sexual activity" between Clinton and Lewinsky failed to test Clinton's definitional defense. There was no escaping mention of oral sex if Starr hoped to challenge Clinton's sworn denial in January of sexual relations with Lewinsky. Nor could he challenge Clinton's grand jury denials of fondling her without citing specific cases recalled by Lewinsky. "You can't go making accusations if you don't prove your case," Starr said.

To him, this was no more a sex case than Watergate had been a third-rate burglary. It was a test of the rule of law, a challenge to Clinton's mockery of it. He told his staff it was their "duty" to present contradictory facts from other witnesses to prove the presidential lies. "We cannot afford the luxury of blinking," he said.

The bar already was high for referring the nation's top elected official for impeachment. Starr and his staff believed they needed to set it higher still because their own judgment and motivation were under such public assault. "If there's the slightest defect, this is going off to the scrap heap," Starr told aides. "If you state a conclusion without airtight facts, then why did you state the conclusion? It's not time for the faint-hearted. We have to prove our case and prove it as lawyers."

The referral, he said, had to be "usable" by members of Congress. It had to be a document they could rely on to judge the need for an impeachment inquiry. Only a chronological narrative of the affair and its cover-up would give congressmen the foundation to understand the grounds for impeachment. Starr wanted all relevant evidence within easy reach of busy lawmakers, not packed away in an appendix. The referral should stand on its own, as a summary of the entire case.

Down the hall from Starr's office, Andy Leipold supervised the referral writing. His wall was covered with easel paper listing assignments. After months of carefully piecing together evidence in drafts, Stephen Bates and Craig Lerner had to rewrite the narrative with huge chunks of new testimony from Clinton and Lewinsky. Early on, Leipold had roughed out the charges in the grounds section in point-counterpoint fashion. But Kavanaugh, in revising, forged forceful conclusions about Clinton's actions. The very fact that they were sending a referral implied a judgment that their information was substantial and credible, and the legal writers wanted to present their charges assertively.

The sometimes fractious office turned into a model of teamwork. Lewinsky's debriefers—Wirth, Immergut, Myers, and Mike Emmick—fed pieces of her testimony to the drafters and helped shape the grounds. Sol Wisenberg, with an overview of everything that had been presented to the grand jury, added his insights. He was the first to see obstruction of justice in Clinton's assertion during the deposition that Lewinsky's affidavit was "absolutely true," and in allowing his lawyer to assert that it showed "absolutely no sex of any kind in any manner, shape or form with President Clinton."

On Monday, August 31, Kavanaugh circulated drafts of his grounds, renewing debate over the standard for charges. Starr argued against a pure prosecutorial test. The law and history of impeachment, he said, showed that transgressions such as abuse of the public trust qualified as reasons for removal from office. "We should not intrude into Congress's evaluation by erecting a bar that must be provable as a crime," he said.

For two weeks, the lawyers worked nearly around the clock. Pizza boxes and coffee cups littered the office. Amid the chaos, Ed Page injected a new challenge. The FBI lab had evidence that nine of the seventeen tapes Linda Tripp had submitted as originals might actually be duplicates. As they entered the final drive on Labor Day weekend, drafters scoured the referral, deleting quotes derived from the tainted tapes.

White House lawyers analyzing the president's grand jury testimony knew just how the Starr team would read it. They feared Clinton had given Starr new grounds for perjury charges—and license to include details about his sexual encounters with Lewinsky. Some advisers privately worried about what exactly those details would reveal of his sexual tastes. Leaving aside the truthfulness of his testimony, could he win a political fight if every time he took to the podium, his listeners were thinking "cigar"?

They had reason to worry. While the president traveled the world in August and early September, from Martha's Vineyard to Moscow, even his allies criticized his failure to apologize forthrightly for lying to the American public. Clinton insisted that he had asked for forgiveness in his August 17 speech. But New Jersey's Robert Torricelli, the Senate's most partisan Democrat, responded curtly: "It wouldn't work in my family."

Even more damaging was the Senate floor speech of Connecticut's Joseph Lieberman. A longtime friend and ally of Clinton's, the senator described him as "immoral" and deserving of "public rebuke." Lieberman was a moderate, a man of eloquence and integrity who commanded respect on both sides of the political aisle. White House aides feared his denunciation could start a stampede, especially when two other influential Senate Democrats, New Yorker Daniel Patrick Moynihan and Nebraska's Bob Kerrey, endorsed his words. And Senator Russell Feingold, a maverick Democrat from Wisconsin, said

Clinton's regrets were not enough: "What he has to answer is [how] he said one series of things and then changed his story."

At every foreign stop, Clinton was asked about Monica Lewinsky. Presidential aides told reporters their boss was deeply stricken by what was happening, and his appearance—drawn and baggy-eyed— suggested they were not exaggerating. In Ireland, his last stop before heading home, Clinton moved a little closer to contrition: "I've already said that I made a big mistake, it was indefensible and I'm sorry about it."

Meanwhile, his wife was barely speaking to him. Clinton told a friend she even brought up the Ten Commandments, saying: "You've done more to give adultery a bad name than anyone since Moses." Hillary Clinton's concerns went beyond his extramarital adventure. Her husband had made it almost impossible to demonize Starr, she told a political adviser. He had given Starr credibility. The president's aides weren't much friendlier, though some focused their anger on David Kendall, blaming him for inventing Clinton's "legally accurate" defense of his deposition.

Kendall returned from vacation to a capital buzzing with anticipation of Starr's report. On Monday, September 7, he called Bob Bittman and asked to have the referral a week before it was delivered to Congress. If not, Kendall warned, he might go to court to try to block it. But when his request was rejected, he turned instead to drafting a rebuttal.

On Tuesday, September 8, Starr's office teemed like a campaign boiler room on election day. Every lawyer and adviser except Sam Dash, Charles Bakaly, and Starr himself worked through the night, checking every detail in the referral. They flanked the long conference table, plowing through thousands of pages, checking spelling, footnotes, and legal citations against stacks of grand jury transcripts and FBI interviews.

Starr arrived early Wednesday morning. He had read and edited the entire referral. Leipold stepped into his office to get a small change approved. Was he okay with the package? asked Leipold.

"I'm at peace with this," said Starr.

At noon, Leipold and Kavanaugh were ready to hit the print button when Dash rushed in and asked to examine the final draft. He took exception to the wording of one of the grounds: that Clinton's assertions of executive and attorney-client privileges constituted an impeachable abuse of power. He demanded changes, threatening to resign. Dash wanted mention of the attorney-client privilege excised, and the executive privilege charge made stronger, to say the president had "unlawfully" abused executive privilege to conceal his misconduct from the grand jury.

Kavanaugh and others lawyers thought Dash's language went too far and were outraged at his last-minute interference. But Starr agreed with Dash's argument and ordered the final count rewritten to accommodate his demanding ethics adviser. Ninety minutes later it was ready to be printed.

The referral to Congress listed eleven possible grounds for impeachment. Five of them accused Clinton of lying under oath in the Jones deposition or the grand jury about his sexual relationship with Lewinsky, about being alone with her, about exchanging gifts with her, about discussing the Jones case with her, and about his contacts with Jordan over her involvement in the Jones case. Three charged him with obstructing justice by concealing gifts subpoenaed by the Jones lawyers, scheming with Lewinsky to have her submit a false affidavit in the case, and helping her to get a job in New York at a time when her testimony could have hurt him. The remaining grounds accused him of trying to tamper with a witness, Betty Currie, in the days after his deposition; trying to obstruct the OIC investigation by lying to his aides, knowing they would repeat those statements to the grand jury; and abusing his authority and impeding Starr's investigation by lying to the public and the Congress and unlawfully directing his aides to assert executive privilege to avoid testifying before the grand jury.

At 1:30 P.M., Leipold brought the signature page to Starr, and as half a dozen staffers looked on, he authorized the second impeachment report to Congress in the nation's history. Leipold handed the page to paralegal Lindsey Matson. "Let it rip," he said. A cover letter identified the materials as highly confidential, but contained no warning about sexual explicitness. It never occurred to Starr that lawmakers would release grand jury material unedited. He assumed that there would be a process of choosing what to make public, and that the president's lawyers would be involved. Starr—like everyone else—was in uncharted political waters.

Paralegals assembled two copies of the referral and attachments—eighteen boxes each for Democrats and Republicans—and turned them over to FBI agents. Watching the boxes loaded into vans, Craig Lerner realized he was still wearing the same T-shirt he had worn the previous Friday night when he left the office to have a beer and watch Mark McGwire hit his sixty-second home run. Kavanaugh was equally unkempt. As he drove home to Bethesda that afternoon, he began to drift into sleep. He pulled over and flagged a cab. He had not been home to sleep for three straight nights.

The vans pulled out of the garage, with administrator Sandy Oldham driving and Bittman riding shotgun in one of them. As they turned onto Pennsylvania Avenue for the ten blocks to the Capitol, media vans were in hot pursuit, cameramen hanging out of windows for a close-up. "Don't worry about these guys," Bittman counseled Oldham. "The last thing you want to do is get in an accident with us carrying the referral." He could imagine boxes tumbling into the street.

They arrived intact, and Bittman was greeted by the House sergeant-at-arms, Wilson Livingood. "I understand you have something for us," Livingood said. Bittman was carrying cover letters from Starr to House Speaker Newt Gingrich and Minority Leader Richard Gephardt. He found Gingrich across the street at the Library of Congress. "Mr. Speaker, I have an envelope from Judge Starr," he said. Gingrich, accompanied by a photographer, scowled and thanked Bittman. Bittman then repeated the ritual at Gephardt's office. The minority leader responded with a cordial smile.

The report's arrival created pandemonium. Members of Congress returning from summer break were jolted by the news. Gingrich, Gephardt, and their whips met to decide how to proceed. While they had waited in trepidation for the referral all year, they had no knowledge of what Starr would send and no plans for handling the explosive material.

Pressure immediately built to make it public. Republicans, of course, were eager to have voters see Clinton in all his perfidy, two months before the mid-term elections. Democrats figured the worst parts would leak out anyway. Gingrich and other GOP leaders had hoped the referral would contain Whitewater or travel office charges— something more than the sex-based Lewinsky matter. Now that it was clear it was only about Lewinsky, they feared it would backfire on them. Better, they thought, to put it out now while it was still Starr's product, not theirs.

Late Wednesday, leaders of both parties met and agreed to put the referral on the Internet without so much as cracking the cover. The only delay would be a pro forma Rules Committee approval Thursday and a full House vote the next day.

Starr and his team were stunned. They hadn't expected all of it to stay secret in the hands of 435 House members. But with a wholesale release, the OIC would be blamed for publishing some of the most explicit nonfiction material in modern times. Kavanaugh, Bittman, and Jackie Bennett urged Starr to press Congress to keep the material under seal. Kavanaugh drafted a letter to Gingrich and Gephardt saying some of the contents were highly sensitive and might never be suitable for public dissemination.

Starr thought the letter was a good idea until someone raised the question of whether it would be seen as intruding on Congress's prerogatives. Members knew from press reports it would be full of graphic details, Starr reasoned. If he sent the letter now he would throw the House into upheaval. "It is their business," he said. He decided to hold off, and the House voted overwhelmingly to publicly release the referral.

Despite all his years in Washington, Starr had misread Congress. Sam Dash kept reminding him that its members were driven above all by self-preservation, not by reason or fair play. Yet Starr had sent his referral to Congress expecting it to get the same judicious handling a sensitive brief would receive at the Supreme Court. He failed to see that both parties would find it expedient to release it unread. Focusing exclusively on his legal obligations, he neglected to protect the document on which he would be judged from the reckless demands of politics.

As Congress prepared to release the Starr Report, Clinton called an old friend. What do I do? he lamented. The friend urged Clinton to heed his political advisers, who were urging frankness, not his lawyers, who wanted him to go down, if not precisely fighting, at least splitting legal hairs. Clinton said he feared a perjury indictment. "You're not going to jail," said the friend. "You may be impeached, but you are not going to jail."

On Friday, September 11, Clinton issued a new apology, telling a prayer breakfast, "I have sinned" and vowing to repent. As he spoke, the House clerk loaded a computer file onto the Internet. The Starr Report had gone public.

Clinton told religious leaders that "legal language must not obscure the fact that I have done wrong." But Kendall was circulating a seventy-eight-page rebuttal attempting to do precisely that, describing the referral as "nothing but the details of a private sexual relationship told in graphic details with the intent to embarrass."

Kendall aimed his criticism not at House politicians but at Starr. He called the report "little more than an unreliable, one-sided account of sexual behavior." Some of the media followed his lead. One column referred to the independent counsel as the "Porn Starr." But the *New York Times* opined that until now no citizen "could have grasped the completeness of President Clinton's mendacity or the magnitude of his recklessness." The *Detroit Free Press* and *Philadelphia Inquirer* called on Clinton to resign, as did Atlanta's *Journal-Constitution*, the *Des Moines Register*, the *Denver Post*, and the *Orlando Sentinel*.

In Congress, Democrats were on the defensive as the countdown to the election began. At first, they criticized Starr for unfairly refusing to let the White House review the referral in advance. But the more they read it, the less appetite they had for Clinton's defense. Gingrich, with his well-known instinct for the jugular, called Clinton to discuss terrorism and ended the conversation with some political advice. The Republicans were riding high in the polls and could pick up dozens of seats. Soon, he said, the president would be hearing from worried Democrats who would want him to step down.

For ten days after the report was released, the presidency wobbled. Presidential lawyers Kendall and Chuck Ruff made it worse on the Sunday talk shows, insisting that Clinton's sworn denial of sexual relations with Lewinsky might have been misleading, but that it was not perjury. Gephardt and Senate Minority Leader Thomas A. Daschle publicly urged Clinton to put a halt to this semantic charade. At a Democratic meeting on September 15, Delaware Senator Joseph R. Biden Jr. told colleagues that the party might be better off if Clinton resigned. He didn't recommend it, but House Democrats were starting to call for a full impeachment inquiry.

Clinton supporters, though, were a long way from giving up. The Internet magazine *Salon* revealed that House Judiciary Chairman Henry Hyde had had an extramarital affair in the 1960s. "The only purpose for this being dredged up now is an obvious attempt to intimidate me and it won't work," said the seventy-four-year-old Hyde. His allies suspected the White House had planted the story. Sidney Blumenthal, who frequently dealt with *Salon* reporters critical of Starr, denied putting out the Hyde story. But during this period, Blumenthal told at least one reporter that his mother had recently been reminiscing about seeing Hyde with his girlfriend at a Chicago hotel.

The *Salon* story angered Republicans. Gingrich spoke of investigating other Clinton scandals. In October, with the support of thirty-one Democrats, the House approved an open-ended inquiry similar to the one undertaken for Watergate twenty-four years earlier. Then its members headed home for the election, in which the GOP expected to pick up at least thirty new seats because of the scandal. In the final week, Gingrich approved $10 million in ads highlighting the president's moral lapses.

But Democrats had polls suggesting that voters were tired of Lewinsky, of Starr, and of impeachment. Days before the election, a confident Blumenthal was savoring the prospect of settling scores.

Talking to a guest at a British Embassy dinner party, he said Clinton supporters intended to "fix Starr," and "we want to put Ken Starr in jail."

The GOP's strategy backfired on election day. The Republicans lost five seats in the House, leaving them a razor-thin majority. Three days later, Gingrich resigned his post and hinted that he would quit Congress.

As the hearings approached, Hyde dropped his ambitious plans to take testimony from many of the key players in the scandal. His Republican colleagues wanted Starr out in public to explain and defend his report. Democrats had been waiting all year for the chance to confront Starr. Hyde decided to give both sides what they wanted.

Starr had always distrusted the political arena, and the last ten months of confrontation had left him more disillusioned than ever. He saw Hyde's call for him to testify as further politicizing his investigation, an opportunity for more sound bites and finger-pointing. He had done his statutory duty. Now Congress should meet its constitutional requirements by examining the evidence.

But he did recognize an opportunity to tell his story. All during the Lewinsky probe, and for the forty months that preceded it, he had been a largely silent observer of his own downfall. Seldom does a public figure drop in public esteem as far and fast as Starr.

A man once considered a likely future Supreme Court justice was now the subject of a D.C. Bar Association ethics probe. A Republican who had enjoyed wide respect from members of both parties was now reviled as a latter-day Joe McCarthy. The righteous son of a preacher was now ridiculed for wallowing in prurience. The same polls that showed overwhelming approval of Clinton put Starr's numbers at the level of Saddam Hussein's.

The censure had spread to his staff, collectively know as "Starr's cowboys." Many had suffered—Bruce Udolf had left the office in a state of great distress, and Mike Emmick and Jackie Bennett had seen their names tarnished. Others felt the sting socially. Steve Binhak, the aide assigned to Linda Tripp, was chatting with friends at a reunion at Rye Country Day School in New York when a French teacher he'd known accosted him. "I'm ashamed of what you're doing," he said. Wirth compared the Starr stigma to the one facing Vietnam veterans. "Nobody gives you credit for what you've done," she said.

In the House hearing, Starr saw a chance to put right what had gone wrong. But once again his contentious ethics adviser found reason to dissent. After reading Starr's prepared statement, Dash told Bittman it sounded as if Starr was advocating impeachment, not simply laying out facts that "may" amount to impeachable offenses. Bittman replied that the remarks reflected the conclusions of the referral. "Why do it again?" Dash retorted. "He's already done his job." Dash didn't mind if Starr gave the committee an accounting of his probe or replied to charges against him and the office, but he thought it was going too far to explain why Clinton's actions amounted to impeachable offenses. Starr had asked Dash to join him at the witness table, as a bipartisan gesture. Dash said he could not do it if Starr insisted on making the statement.

Bittman reported Dash's concerns to the independent counsel. Starr believed all he was doing was defending the methods and conclusions of the referral. But for once, he refused to be drawn into a debate with Dash. His ethics adviser was a man of strong beliefs and he would make them known. He might even resign, Starr realized. He had threatened to quit at least five times since January and was planning to leave at year's end anyway because of a pay cut imposed by the Justice Department. His liberal colleagues at Georgetown University considered him a sellout for going to work for Starr in the first place. Starr wasn't going to lose any more sleep over Dash's opinion.

But there was one person whose views mattered a great deal, and that was Attorney General Janet Reno. Starr asked to meet with her before his testimony to clear up an oversight dating back to the first days of the Lewinsky probe. When Reno was first deciding whether to assign the Lewinsky investigation to him, Starr had neglected to remind her of his prior contact with Jones's lawyers. Clinton's supporters had made much of the omission, and Starr was planning to set the record straight at the hearing.

He also wanted to give Reno a heads-up about another twist in the same story. Starr's view that a sitting president could be sued was well known. And in 1994, his predecessor as special counsel, Robert Fiske—who was considering a civil lawsuit against Clinton—had asked him to write an amicus brief. Starr had been mulling the idea when he was named to replace Fiske. He had never mentioned the conversation, which he considered confidential.

The meeting with Reno took place on November 15 in Reno's conference room, a majestic wood-paneled chamber topped by a ceiling mural depicting Justice Granted and Justice Denied. For what Starr had expected to be a courtesy call, Reno had assembled a high-powered retinue, including her deputy, Eric Holder, and the heads of both the criminal division and the public integrity section. Starr noted that his hearing was coming up and he was anxious about it. He then described his four-year-old talks with Fiske. Reno said he was "very thoughtful" to alert her. She nodded appreciatively as he updated her on the leaks litigation.

When he finished, the mood shifted. "I want to raise a point with you," Reno said. She picked up a page of talking points and began reading, without expression. She had received numerous complaints of prosecutorial misconduct, she said, some easy to dismiss, some not. The office of professional responsibility (OPR) had recommended further inquiry. Reno said she had a duty to investigate the allegations. She had no authority to supervise the independent counsel, only the right to fire him for serious transgressions. She excluded leaks as a subject for examination, noting that the department, like Starr, disagreed with Judge Johnson's view of grand jury secrecy rules. But she did not specify which of the many allegations would be investigated.

Reno knew Starr saw her every move as part of a White House plot to derail him. "I want to reassure you the timing of my decision has nothing to do with your testimony," she said. The OPR recommendation had just reached her, and Starr did not have to respond to the inquiry until after the hearing. "I want to emphasize," she said, "neither OPR nor I have formed any conclusions about these allegations. We're acutely aware that allegations such as those we have received present only one side of the story and that knowledge of your view of them may cast a very different light on them."

"We do have answers," blurted Bob Bittman, who had accompanied Starr.

Starr shifted in his chair, leaning away from Reno. He glared at her. He was furious, unable to comprehend how an attorney general could launch an investigation of the author of the impeachment referral just as Congress was getting ready to act on it. Starr saw only one explanation: a cowardly deferral to the interests of the president.

"If I get a phone call from OPR," he said, glowering, "I will take steps to protect the integrity and independence of the investigation." Reno had determined the timing was "appropriate," Starr said indignantly. "From the independent counsel's perspective, we are under unmitigated assault." He said the attacks are "daily, unremitting, of a personal nature. It's part of our operating environment. I believe the department should assist the independent counsels."

Reno said she wanted to do "anything possible" to help. Holder jumped in, noting Jackie Bennett had complained the department did nothing while the personal lives of Starr's staff were being raked over. "Had we known, we might have taken steps," said Holder. "We didn't know. To the extent you possess information, you should share it."

Starr said it was critical that OPR's plans be kept secret. He had little faith that they would, given the shots he had been taking from the department. Starr brought up an October National Public Radio report, in which an unnamed senior Justice official claimed Reno "would never have agreed to expand his jurisdiction if she had known" of his earlier interest in the Jones case. The report had given Starr's critics a new issue.

"We've heard privately the NPR report is not the position of the department. If it is, I'd like to hear about it in person," said Starr.

"It is not the position of the department," Reno responded.

Starr was not reassured. He thought Reno was both weak and stubborn. A leak of OPR's intentions to investigate him, he warned, would be "inimical to the appearance of justice."

"If it's public," Reno said, "the only person madder than you is me."

The meeting ended soon after the exchange. Someone had been trying to page Bittman while he was inside. It was press spokesman Charles Bakaly calling to say that *Newsweek* would report on Monday that Justice was "close to launching a formal ethics probe into at least one episode" of Starr's investigation: Lewinsky's complaint that she was discouraged at the Ritz-Carlton from calling her lawyer, Frank Carter.

Starr was outraged. He had barely left the building with Reno's assurances of confidentiality only to be undermined again. Four days before his long-awaited public debut, Justice was broadcasting that it shared the concerns of Starr's severest critics. For Starr, it was the equivalent of Pearl Harbor, a sneak attack at a critical moment. It was one thing for Clinton's personal lawyers and supporters to make wild charges, he thought, and another for the nation's top law enforcers to take them seriously.

He called Holder to protest the leak, and the deputy said he'd look into it. Starr thought he seemed indifferent. What Starr didn't know was how the misconduct issue had roiled Holder and his staff since October 29, when OPR counsel Marshall Jarrett had called for a harder look at some of the allegations. Reno and Holder had agreed. The question was when to tell Starr of their plans.

A majority of Reno's advisers thought it was only fair to alert Starr to the inquiry, in case the subject came up at the hearing. Otherwise, if asked about the allegations, he might say that Justice had found no cause for concern—which would be both untrue and embarrassing when the truth came out. A few of Reno's aides recognized the danger that Starr would take it as an attempt to rattle and undermine him just before his crucial appearance. Reno came down in favor of full disclosure. She knew he would be angry. And now the leak to *Newsweek* had made it much worse.

Reno had learned of the leak even before Starr. Her chief of staff had entered the conference room as Starr was leaving and passed on the news. Distressed, she said she wanted to find out how the information had found its way to *Newsweek*. Her aides knew it would just confirm Starr's dark view of the department. They could hardly blame him this time.

As a consolation, Justice agreed to downplay the issue in a statement to reporters. Jonathan Schwartz, Holder's assistant, worked out the language with Bittman. "The Department of Justice has not launched an investigation of the Office of Independent Counsel," it began, and went on to say that while DOJ had received allegations of misconduct against Starr's shop, many had been dismissed. For the rest, it said, DOJ is seeking additional information from the OIC.

His face-off with Reno made Starr all the more wary of the House Democrats lying in wait. Now they had new ammunition. He consulted his former deputy, Democrat Mark Tuohey, who warned the questioning would be very nasty and test his composure. Starr had to prepare, but there was only so much he could anticipate. A House hearing was no orderly courtroom. It was a messy realm with idiosyncratic rules and players.

At 10 A.M., November 19, Starr entered Room 2141 of the Rayburn Office Building. It was swarming with spectators. Starr had argued twenty-five cases before the Supreme Court, but he had never had to make a case in his own defense. He knew his professional life was on the line, along with the fate of his impeachment referral.

On a raised mahogany rostrum facing Starr at the witness table was the House Judiciary Committee, perhaps the last place in America to find an open mind. Its thirty-seven members, among the most ideological in Congress, had the partisan impulses—and the manners—of a Elizabethan theater audience. The sixteen Democrats, a balanced ticket by religion, gender, and race, but a liberal monolith politically, had come prepared to sling mud. The Republicans—all white, all conservative, and all but one male—had brought armloads of bouquets. On controversial votes, the committee typically split along strict party lines. That was how they had divided on the preliminary votes they had taken so far, on the release of Starr's evidence and the video of the president's grand jury testimony. Looking down on the proceedings was the oil portrait of Peter Rodino, the revered New Jersey congressman who had chaired the committee during Watergate.

Starr stood to take the oath, then patted the pocket where he had tucked the "go Dad" letters from his children. For the next two hours he gave the closing argument of a prosecutor summing up eight months of testimony. He didn't vary from the facts of the referral, but added editorial markers to guide the jury through the complex case. He took pains to separate the moral and legal issues. "The propriety of a relationship is not the concern of our office," he said. Rather, the referral dealt with criminal offenses and "cannot be understood without appreciating this vital distinction." The president's affair had been an "issue of private contact" until December 17, when Clinton advised Lewinsky to use a cover story if she were subpoenaed. "At that moment," Starr said, "the president's intimate relationship with a subordinate employee was transformed into an unlawful effort to thwart the judicial process."

In the final minutes, he praised his staff and tried to redeem his own image. He said he was not a "man of polls, public relations or politics" but a "product of the law and the courts" who has a "deep respect for the legal process that is the foundation of our Republic. President Lincoln asked that 'reverence for the laws be proclaimed in legislative halls and enforced in courts of justice.' Mr. Chairman, my office and I revere the law."

Starr knew if there were minds to change, they were in the television audience. He refused makeup but listened to one theatrical tip. His public relations friend, Merrie Spaeth, had said that people seated behind him would influence the way viewers saw him. She was proven right not long after he started talking. Well-wishers called Starr's office saying he was doing great, but who was the guy sleeping behind him? It was Wisenberg, who sat slouched in his chair, his eyes half closed from boredom. He kept getting notes from GOP staffers, "Sol, you're on TV. STAY AWAKE." He drank coffee, but it didn't help. Finally, he gave up his seat and watched the rest of his boss's testimony on closed-circuit TV in an anteroom.

The Democrats got their turn after lunch. Their strategy was to portray Starr as so lawless in his pursuit of Clinton that his referral shouldn't be believed. Minority Counsel Abbe Lowell got into a cross-examiner's crouch, throwing out accusations in place of questions. He sought to cast Starr as a conniver who had tricked Reno into authorizing his probe, dispatched Linda Tripp to brief the Jones lawyers on the eve of Clinton's deposition, coerced Lewinsky into the Ritz-Carlton, deprived her of her right to counsel, and omitted exculpatory details from the referral. Wrapping up, Lowell asked why those actions don't "undermine the substantiality and credibility of the evidence on something as weighty as impeaching a president of the United States?"

Starr held his ground in the hour-long fusillade, then accused Lowell of dealing in characterizations, not fact. And none of Lowell's charges constituted evidence that the president "was not involved in serious offenses that now is your responsibility to evaluate," he said.

For the next several hours Starr played the role of a political Humpty Dumpty. Democratic congressmen tried to break him apart with charges of prosecutorial abuse; Republicans rushed in to restore him. Not a single question was asked about the facts or charges against Clinton contained in the referral. This was more theater than truth-seeking, a contest to see whether Starr would leave the hearing as tarred-and-feathered as Clinton. The parrying and posturing warmed up the room for the main event.

At 8.30 P.M., David Kendall took a seat. He and Starr were twenty feet apart, Washington superlawyers for whom four years of legal jousting had become mortal combat.

After sparring with Starr over the significance of Judge Johnson's rulings on alleged grand jury leaks, Kendall asserted, "Mr. Starr, in fact, there has been no case remotely similar to this in terms of the massive leaking from the prosecutor's office."

"I totally disagree with that," Starr replied heatedly. "That's an accusation, and it's an unfair accusation. I completely reject it."

When Hyde admonished Kendall to stick to the facts, Kendall gave a glimpse of his strategy: "These are the facts," he declared. "The campaign to disseminate information against the president is very much a part of the fairness of the document which your committee is having to consider." Starr took umbrage, saying the most sensitive evidence against Clinton—FBI test results on the dress—did not leak only because no one in Kendall's defense network knew about it.

The sparks kept flying when Kendall moved to the January night when Starr's agents had "held" Lewinsky at the Ritz-Carlton. He didn't complete his question before Starr interjected "that premise is false."

Kendall: "I was not meaning to be offensive."

Starr: "That is false and you know it to be false. . . . She was not held."

Kendall: "Her own psychological state will speak for itself as to how she felt. It's in the record in her testimony."

Starr: "You said she was held. You didn't say how she felt. You said she was held. And I think that's unfair to our investigators."

Kendall: "During her sojourn with your agents."

Starr: "Well, the Ritz-Carlton is a very pleasant place to have a sojourn."

Kendall was supposed to have thirty minutes but Hyde gave him an hour. When it was up Kendall pleaded in vain for more time. Starr had been fielding questions from the witness chair for almost twelve hours when the microphone then passed to Majority Counsel David Schippers, the burly former mob prosecutor who agreed to take the job for his old friend, Hyde. He lobbed a few easy questions, then leaned forward and asked Starr how long he had been practicing law. He replied twenty-five years. "Well, I have been an attorney for almost forty years," said Schippers. "I want to say I am proud to be in the same room with you and your staff."

Everyone on the Republican side of the rostrum stood and applauded Starr. It was a rare moment of public acclamation for the battered prosecutor. He and his team had suffered their obloquy in isolation.

It was eleven o'clock. Starr's eyes welled up, but he was almost too numb to absorb the praise. He couldn't get out of his mind an earlier question from California's Mary Bono. What had been the personal toll of the probe?

Starr received more applause from his staff in the anteroom. He hugged Bittman, looked upward, and said, "To God be the glory." The room filled with GOP committee members. Among them was Lindsey Graham, the South Carolinian who would become the folk philosopher of the impeachment debate. He pulled Starr aside for an essential question. "Can impeachment of a president be sustained without popular support?"

Starr paused, feeling a surge of energy for a question of "first principles," as he put it. He told Graham the answer was basic to his view of leadership. Was he an "echo chamber representative"? asked Starr, or a leader sent to Washington to "come to your judgment and call it the way you see it"? It was a question Starr had long ago decided for himself. "It's your view of what your role is, and only you can answer that," he said.

By any measure, Starr had performed well. The Republicans left the hearing buoyed and united. Starr's staff took pride in his besting of Kendall. The next morning Sam Dash stepped on Starr's victory by quitting, saying Starr improperly acted as an advocate for impeachment. But even inside the White House, Dash's move was widely viewed as meaningless. Starr's testimony was no stronger than the referral. Starr, who learned of the resignation from television, had no hard feelings. But his staff was enraged at what they saw as Dash's naked effort to regain the good graces of his liberal friends.

But this one disappointment would be offset by a steady stream of congratulatory calls. "I want you to know, I used to teach trial law," said one old friend from the Justice Department. "You were the perfect witness." It was New York's Republican Mayor Rudolph Giuliani— still months from learning that he might face Hillary Clinton in the race to represent New York in the U.S. Senate.

Then there was Abbe Lowell, who had grilled Starr for House Democrats. He commended Starr for handling himself well. Lowell was not quite the fierce partisan he had seemed during the hearing. He was an aggressive litigator making the most of his moment in the sun. This was Washington. Lowell knew that someday, on another big case, he would likely cross paths with Ken Starr again.

* * *

Despite the plaudits, Starr was not in a celebratory mood when he got home. He watched his own reruns on C-Span, transfixed by the image of himself at the crossroads of his career. He didn't like everything he saw. Oh, my goodness, how could I have said that? he wondered. Why couldn't I have put it this way? He focused on the tiny flaws, not on the overall sweep of his presentation.

It was the start of a long period of self-criticism and introspection for a man unaccustomed to both. Before long, Starr would chastise himself for ever taking on the Lewinsky investigation. By the time it began, he realized, he had already taken on too much. Much of the public was already confused about his work and distrustful of his motives. The Clinton White House had seen to that, and he had not tried hard enough to counter it. His authority derived not just from the law, but from the American public. There is only so much baggage one can carry, he would say, and he should have known he'd already reached his limit. When Linda Tripp had showed up, he should have shown her to the door of the Justice Department and let the attorney general worry about how to investigate the president.

But he had not. Instead, he had pressed doggedly ahead, despite the terrible personal cost to him and his staff, because it seemed at the time the right thing to do. Asked toward the end of his tenure as independent counsel what lessons life had taught him about courage and strength in adversity, Starr began to speak of his late father, diagnosed at the age of eighty-two with fast-metastasizing stomach cancer. Believing that his time had come, the highly religious elder Starr refused surgery. As Starr told his father's story, his voice cracked. He swallowed hard, trying to recover, but was quickly overcome. He removed his glasses and wept inconsolably into his hands.

It was as if his father's illness was a medium for his own suffering, as if in grieving for him, he lamented his own fall from grace and the limits of his own endurance.

He had been cast as the leading man in a national political drama. Was he a man of courage, holding up time-honored virtues at great personal sacrifice? Or was he a man obsessed by his own righteousness, fighting for ideals few shared and, in the process, deepening the public's cynicism?

Ken Starr himself had no idea how history would judge him. For now, he held close a verse from Proverbs sent by a friend.

These are also sayings of the wise:
To show partiality in judging is not good:
Whoever says to the guilty, "you are innocent"—
Peoples will curse him and nations denounce him.
But it will go well with those who convict the guilty,
And rich blessing will come upon them.
An honest answer is like a kiss on the lips.

EPILOGUE

In mid-January 1999, a month after the historic House of Representatives vote to impeach Bill Clinton, Ken Starr called a meeting to discuss the last pressing issue of the Lewinsky case: whether to indict the president.

During the investigation, the independent counsel had concluded that he had the authority to prosecute a sitting president. At the time, however, he had no interest in doing so. He decided to press ahead with impeachment and consider the criminal issues later. After testifying before the Judiciary Committee, he assigned Mike Emmick to draft a sample indictment and a prosecution memo outlining the pros and cons of charging Clinton. The January meeting was intended to raise issues Emmick should consider.

The prospect of an indictment forced the prosecutors to shift from the fluid standard for an impeachment referral to the higher bar the Justice Department sets for bringing criminal charges: evidence strong enough for a fair-minded jury to convict. But they had deeper questions to confront as well. Just what were their responsibilities to the rule of law? Was it right to have undertaken this enormous investigation, to have amassed powerful evidence of wrongdoing—then to bring no criminal charges? On the other hand, if they went ahead with an indictment and a jury refused to convict Clinton, wouldn't that be a blow to justice and the rule of law?

The only consensus was that if they chose to indict, they would have to wait until Clinton left office. Indicting a sitting president would be too disruptive for the country—and in any case, he would simply seek a continuance until after his term ended. They concluded they could not seek an indictment under seal, to be made public when Clinton left office, because Justice Department guidelines allow secret indictments only when there is a risk of flight or concern that a public indictment would alert other suspects.

In the end, Starr's team decided to put off deciding. They would continue preparing the prosecution memo, then reevaluate whether they should go forward.

On February 12, the U.S. Senate, sitting as a Court of Impeachment, acquitted President Clinton, allowing him to serve out his second term. And not long afterward, Starr began to believe that he had become too tainted in the public eye to do his job. His indictments of Susan McDougal (for criminal contempt in refusing to testify about Clinton) and of Julie Hiatt Steele (for perjury in testimony about Kathleen Willey) ended in setbacks; in both cases, the OIC was widely criticized for being heavy-handed, and in both, the juries refused to convict.

In June, Starr decided to drop two cases against Webster Hubbell in exchange for a guilty plea that resulted in no further jail time. A consensus had been building among Starr's prosecutors: if there was any chance that they would eventually indict the president, they must not squander what little was left of the public's good will.

The OIC did get good news in the form of vindication from some of the most serious charges against it. In July, a yearlong investigation of the allegations that Starr Whitewater witness David Hale had been paid off to discredit the president ended, finding that the charges were untrue. Then, in September, the Court of Appeals ruled definitively that Starr's office was within its rights to communicate with the media as long as prosecutors did not reveal the grand jury's deliberations.

Starr made plans to return to private life in the fall of 1999. Jackie Bennett, Bob Bittman, Sol Wisenberg, and many other veterans of the Lewinsky investigation had already moved on. The three-judge panel that had appointed Starr looked to senior members of his staff to find a successor.

Starr called a final summit meeting for his last discussion of Clinton's fate. The entire staff—including recently departed aides—assembled in Washington on a weekend in October 1999. Starr did not know who his successor would be, but all the candidates were in the room. Before Starr and his team disbanded, the next independent counsel would have the benefit of their views.

Mike Emmick and Andy Leipold presented four possible charges in a Clinton indictment: perjury, subornation of perjury, conspiracy, and obstruction of justice. No one doubted the strength of their evidence, at least in a perjury case. The issue before them was a matter of prosecutorial discretion.

For every argument that no jury would convict a popular president, there was a counterpoint. In deciding to indict, prosecutors are not supposed to factor in fears of a runaway jury. The group also addressed whether prosecutors could take into account ways other than criminal indictment that the rule of law could be vindicated.

Along with impeachment, for example, Clinton had suffered the not insignificant consequences of the Paula Jones case. In late 1998, he had agreed to pay $850,000 to settle the suit, forestalling any chance of its being reinstated because of his false deposition. Then, in April 1999, Judge Susan Webber Wright had found Clinton in contempt of court, pointing to "clear and convincing evidence" of "false, misleading, and evasive answers that were designed to obstruct the judicial process" in the Jones deposition. The president, she said "undermined the integrity of the judicial system." Wright ordered Clinton to pay $90,000 in legal expenses incurred by Jones's lawyers in connection with the deposition. His law license was also at risk.

Some at the summit meeting argued that Clinton had suffered enough. Others insisted that he had gotten off lightly because politics had short-circuited the impeachment process.

Starr himself left office calling on the president to acknowledge his wrongdoing and "get right with the law." Wright's contempt ruling, he said, had vindicated the rule of law and surely foreshadowed the way history would ultimately judge Bill Clinton.

Clinton, in turn, hardened in his views of Ken Starr. "I don't regret that I fought the independent counsel," he said in a television interview in January 2000. "What they did in that case and generally was completely overboard." He agreed, he said, with Starr's critics, who talk about "what an abuse of power it was and what a threat to the American system it was."

Starr's successor, Robert Ray, had a reputation as a tough, experienced prosecutor. He joined the office of the independent counsel in 1999, well after the impeachment referral had been sent to Congress. He was present during the October summit meeting on whether Bill Clinton should be indicted. During those proceedings, he kept his own counsel.

Ray will face some of the same challenges his predecessor endured. As soon as he was appointed, for instance, he came under fire from James Carville. Carville claimed Ray was tied to Rudy Giuliani, Hillary Clinton's rival for the U.S. Senate seat from New York, because he had worked in the New York district attorney's office for a brief period when Giuliani was its chief.

If Ray decides to indict Clinton, he will begin building the case well before January 2001, when the president leaves office. Evidence gathered for the impeachment referral would form the basis of any charges, but it would have to be reconfigured for a criminal proceeding. New activity at the federal grand jury would be one sign of an indictment in the works. The OIC also would have to bring in new agents and lawyers to prepare their case and to get witnesses ready to testify.

During his first four months in office, the new independent counsel gave no indication of nailing the door shut. He hired four new lawyers. Three of them have backgrounds in investigation or prosecution.

NOTES

CHAPTER ONE

The pressure had been building for weeks . . . Discussion of Starr's preparation for his House testimony comes from interviews with Ken Starr, Alice Starr, Merrie Spaeth, Ted Olson, Judy Nardella, and members of Starr's staff at the Office of Independent Counsel.

Discussion of Starr's early life and educational background from Ken Starr, Alice Starr, San Antonio minister Terry Sumerlin, former Starr high school teacher Roberta Mahon, and Duke classmate Walter Manley.

It was hardly the last time Starr was to witness . . . Starr's career in the Justice Department, from Ken Starr, and former colleagues Terry Eastland, John Roberts, Tom Merrill, Chuck Cooper, Richard Seamon.

After Clinton swept . . . From Starr and staff members he hired in his early days as independent counsel. Starr told the lawyers he would need them for a few months.

The education of Ken Starr. . . Foster and others in the counsel's office had arranged for the replacement of the veteran White House travel office workers with Clinton friends. They said there were financial irregularities in the travel office, and tried to initiate an FBI investigation to justify the firings. The travel workers knew reporters who traveled with presidents and the story was soon out. Foster and others in the counsel's office were widely criticized for abuse of power.

Fiske had subpoenaed Foster's office files and conducted an extensive four-month forensic investigation of his death. He had even interviewed Clinton for clues to Foster's frame of mind. The White House disclosed the existance of the travel notebook to the OIC in the summer of 1994, and to the public in early 1995.

A sensational "soul cleansing" memo authored by David Watkins, the White House administrator who'd carried out the travel office firings, surfaced 18 months after the Foster notebook appeared. In it, he said he acted at the insistence of Hillary Clinton, though she had denied any role in the firings in written responses to Congress. Watkins confessed that he had hidden the truth from congressional and law enforcement officials. Starr had long before subpoenaed all White House documents on the travel office firings as part of the Foster death investigation. A clerk unearthed the Watkins memo from storage boxes that belonged to administrative chief Patsy Thomasson, a transplant from Clinton's state government in Arkansas. The memo's contents were so explosive the OIC obtained a search warrant for Thomasson's apartment. Deputy White House counsel Jane Sherburne refused Thomasson's entreaties to protest the search.

Each time an important piece of evidence . . . Testimony by Kendall and Sherburne before the Senate Whitewater Committee, Feb. 8, 1996. According to two former White House lawyers, Kendall and Sherburne also were summoned before Starr's grand jury in Washington to explain their handling of the billing records. The episode created lasting distrust. Two years later, in the midst of the Lewinsky investigation, Starr deputy Robert Bittman recalled the fingerprint episode in a letter to

Kendall when the president's lawyer insisted Clinton had done everything possible to cooperate with Starr. "Of course, you know that this
is not true. You and the president have failed to produce financial
records that have been under subpoena for several years," wrote
Bittman. "The forensic value of the records was in fact compromised
after handling by your office." Kendall wrote back saying Bittman's
"smear is simply false." Sherburne went along with his desire to copy
the records and, he said, the OIC had been able to obtain fingerprint
evidence from the records. The letters are contained in an appendix of
Starr's referral to Congress.

From Starr's point of view . . . Local prosecutor Mark Stodela
threatened to arrest David Hale, who had plead guilty to federal
charges and was set to testify in Starr's probe. Stodela wanted to take
him into custody on state insurance fraud charges but abandoned that
course amid public criticism that his actions could be seen as interfering
with a federal witness.

An important Starr witness lost his administrative job at the Little
Rock airport. Former Madison loan officer Harry Don Denton testified at the Tucker-McDougal trial, then told Starr's grand jury and
bank regulators of Hillary Clinton's legal work for McDougal. He
was later fired by airport commissioners who once employed Hillary
Clinton as their counsel. William Watt, another witness in the
Tucker-McDougal case, testified that some of the witnesses had
joined forces with Kendall to resist Starr's investigation. Watt and his
lawyer met with Kendall, and Watt urged Denton to call the Clintons' lawyer too. "I was making sure that Don knew if he made the
decision to resist, that he had avenues available to him to call and at
least would have a place to start," Watt told the court. "[I] Mentioned that a Mr. Kendall . . . is representing some of the Clinton
interests out of Washington" and that he was ready to offer "legal
assistance and informal advice." Watt ultimately pled guilty and
cooperated with Starr's investigation.

To see the president allied with . . . Federal judge Susan Webber
Wright made an evidentiary finding in the summer of 1996 that

Bruce Lindsey was part of a criminal conspiracy, though he was not charged. Starr expressed amazement to aides that Clinton allowed Lindsey to remain on the White House staff.

At 1600 Pennsylvania Avenue . . . Description of the Clintons' attitude toward Starr and the evolving strategy of how to deal with his investigation comes from interviews with three former White House lawyers and a political advisor involved in the damage control effort.

Carville organized his own Education and Information Project . . . EIP internal documents detail its mission and methods. They were turned over under subpoena to Judicial Watch, a conservative organization that has sued the Clinton White House for allegedly misusing government files in violation of the Privacy Act. EIP files contained a copy of a five-page FOIA request to Starr on a disc marked "Kendall FOIA." In a deposition in the case, Carville declined to discuss Kendall's dealings with EIP, saying Kendall was his lawyer. In an interview for this book, Carville said he is primarily represented by Kendall's partner, Robert Barnett, who acts as his book agent, not as a lawyer for EIP.

EIP files contain memos on research to be done on Starr ("federalist society/letters—GOP praising Starr as judge or solicitor general/FOIA his days of William French Smith/foloup on S&L/National Security Archives/did he say anything about BCCI, HUD, Iran-Contra . . . public records/voting, driving, court records, deeds, mortgages . . . ").

EIP files contain talking point documents linking Scaife to Starr and various Republicans, including Rep. Henry Hyde and Newt Gingrich, as well as 8th Circuit Court of Appeals Judge Pasco Bowman, who served on panels that overturned a string of rulings from Little Rock judges that went against the independent counsel. EIP materials claim Bowman, like Starr, is tied to Scaife and a tool of conservative North Carolina senator Jesse Helms.

EIP's predecessor was a group called the Back to Business Committee, which ran newspaper ads that tried to discredit Whitewater investigations conducted by Congress and the independent counsel. The group was run by Ann Lewis and Lynn Cutler, who later took jobs in the White House. They kept their donor list secret, though one contributor was Johnny Chung, whose lavish and as it turned out illegal gifts to the Democratic National Committee bought him regular entrée to the White House.

Scaife's Pittsburg-area newspaper promoted conspiracy theories about Vincent Foster's death being the possible result of foul play in the White House. The stories accused Starr of ignoring or covering up evidence. They gained currency on the Internet and were promoted in national newspaper advertisements bankrolled by Scaife. Scaife's foundations have contributed hundreds of millions of dollars to institutions and charities, including many conservative think tanks and advocacy groups.

Carville and other Clinton allies portrayed instances when Starr and Scaife had dealings with the same group as evidence of Scaife's control over the independent counsel. Carville branded Starr "an extreme right-wing partisan" who was "working for" Scaife. Scaife's donations are so ubiquitous even the Clintons could not avoid them: He contributed to a fund for White House renovations and was a guest for dinner there January 21, 1998, the day the Lewinsky story broke.

Some Clinton aides mounted private campaigns . . . Blumenthal's efforts were described by former White House aides. Lyons' e-mail to Carville was turned over to Judicial Watch in its lawsuit over use of government files. Lyons, in an interview, said he never put any credence in the rumor.

Every legal argument that could be made . . . Discussion of the strategy to resist Starr is based on interviews with three former participants in the White House damage control effort.

Despite the combat he was engaged in . . . From interviews with former Starr Justice Department colleague Terry Eastland, Starr friend Robert Vagley, and Alice Starr.

CHAPTER TWO

Description of lead-up to Linda Tripp's first call to the OIC from interviews with Starr and members of the OIC staff.

Details of Linda Tripp's first interview with Starr's team taken from FBI 302 report included in Starr's impeachment referral to Congress.

Tripp's feelings about the Ritz-Carlton meeting with Lewinsky Jan. 13 are taken from her handwritten diary included in impeachment referral.

Details of what was said on FBI "sting" tape from transcript of the tape included with impeachment referral.

Details of Jan. 14 meeting from Starr and OIC staff.

Bennett said little . . . Interview with John Bates.

CHAPTER THREE

Jackie Bennett telephone conversation with Eric Holder at the Wizards game is taken from contemporaneous notes the IOC turned over to the House Judiciary Committee.

Details of the meeting with Holder from OIC notes supplied to House Judiciary Committee.

At 6 P.M. the next day . . . Description of meeting in Holder's office based on interviews with OIC staff and Justice Department officials. Details about Holder's thinking and his conversation with Ohlson based on interviews with senior Justice officials.

The Justice Department would later . . . Josh Hochberg's views drawn from his meeting notes, supplied to House Judiciary Committee.

Reno's January 16 meeting based on interviews with three senior DOJ officials.

Jim Moody views based on interview with source in Tripp camp.

Michael Isikoff's dealings with Jim Moody and the OIC taken from Isikoff's book *Uncovering Clinton: A Reporter's Story.*

Tripp's handing over of talking points and her comments to FBI drawn from FBI interview contained in impeachment referral.

Lewinsky's view of Tripp as she was taken to room 1012 of the Ritz-Carlton recounted in Lewinsky's book, *Monica's Story.*

Description of prosecutors' approach to Lewinsky at the Ritz-Carlton is based on FBI 302, sworn declarations provided by participants in previously sealed litigation over whether attorney Frank Carter could be compelled to testify, and interviews with OIC staff.

The scene of Lewinsky running into Tripp at the Pentagon City Mall, and of Lewinsky's attempt to call Betty Currie are from *Monica's Story.*

Meeting at Tripp's house, rendezvous at Four Seasons Hotel, meeting at Howard Johnson's based on interviews with several participants, and on declarations and testimony provided in a December 1999 evidentiary hearing on illegal taping charges against Linda Tripp in Maryland state court.

Wesley Holmes said in an interview that the Jones lawyers learned sometime before Jan. 16, either from Moody, Conway, or Jerome Marcus, that Starr was investigating Tripp's allegations.

Clinton lawyers' initial view of the Jones questions about Lewinsky from interviews with the president's legal team.

Testimony during Jones deposition taken from a transcript of the proceedings.

CHAPTER FOUR

Betty Currie pages to Lewinsky: Currie testified she was calling Lewinsky about the Jones case deposition but could not recall exactly what she was trying to find out or impart on Clinton's behalf.

Vernon Jordan got on the phone . . . From Jordan grand jury testimony and Bruce Lindsey grand jury testimony. On talking to Mills and Lindsey about his efforts to find Lewinsky a job: Jordan testified June 9 that prior to Clinton's deposition, he had conversations with Mills "in a very general way" about the job search, "just expressing my frustration that her calls are pressing me on this, and just an exchange of conversation about that." He said he told Mills "I was trying to help Ms. Lewinsky find employment." He talked to Mills often, he said. "I'm sure that somewhere in the process of my conversations with her I told her that I was helping Monica Lewinsky. Now that was no secret, I don't think, around the White House, that I was helping Monica Lewinsky. . . . I'm fairly certain that Bruce Lindsey knew it, that Betty Currie knew it and that Cheryl Mills knew it." He was asked whether he discussed the job search with Lindsey. "No discussion so much as an acknowledgement casually that it was happening . . . a mutual acknowledgement." He said he assumed Lindsey had learned about the search from Clinton or Currie. Mills, in her August 11 grand jury testimony, said she first heard of Monica Lewinsky after the president's deposition. On Jan. 19, Martin Luther King Day, she testified, Jordan told her he'd been trying to get Lewinsky a job. Lindsey denied in his grand jury testimony knowing about the job search prior to Clinton's Jones case deposition.

Jordan told the grand jury he talked to Clinton about the Drudge Report naming Lewinsky on the King holiday, and they were both "incredulous" over it. They also talked about Lewinsky's job, and the motion to quash her testimony, he said.

Bennett went to see Jordan . . . From sources with knowledge of the meeting and Jordan's grand jury testimony in which he discusses the call from Clinton.

But there was hemorrhaging all around . . . Details of White House mood in the initial days of scandal are based on interviews with five White House aides and lawyers for the president.

CHAPTER FIVE

Currie had said "right" in response . . . The timing of Clinton's second discussion with Currie remains murky. During her grand jury testimony, Bittman confused the day it may have taken place, and Currie's muddled response then put the second session at a point in time before Clinton knew Starr was investigating the Lewinsky matter. If Clinton had had the session with her after he knew about the Starr investigation, it would suggest obstruction. If it was before he knew about Starr, it could be less damaging, suggesting that Clinton may have been trying to obstruct the Jones civil case, rather than a criminal probe.

Betty Currie grand jury testimony is contained in Starr's impeachment referral to Congress.

Wechsler meeting with Mills, Ruff, and Breuer. From Mills and Breuer grand jury testimony, August 1998.

Details of immunity talks from OIC interviews and a transcript of sworn testimony from Ginsburg, Emmick, and Bittman March 5, 1998 before Judge Norma Holloway Johnson. The subject of the previously sealed hearing was Ginsburg's claim that Starr's office reneged on an immunity deal with him.

CHAPTER SIX

Campolo statements from interviews with each of the two friends he encountered at the February 5 prayer breakfast. Independently, the OIC received a similar report traced to a theological colleague of Campolo in Philadelphia, though the office did not pursue it. In an interview, Campolo said he did not recall such a conversation with friends, though he acknowledged telling others about his struggle with the Nathan and Barnabas roles. In a later written response, he wrote, "Regardless of what anyone said I said, I never told anyone that the president confessed to me. If there had been a confession, I would not have had to be an accusing Nathan—would I?" The biblical Nathan did more than accuse. He convinced the King to repent.

Campolo said after the President's public confession, Clinton began to compare himself to David.

From the moment . . . Mood of the White House from interviews with White House aides.

On Tuesday, Feb. 3 . . . Details on privilege meeting between Ruff and Starr come from OIC notes of the session and interviews with OIC staff and White House lawyers. Correspondence after the session between Ruff and Starr taken from Starr's impeachment referral.

Discussion of differences between Ruff and Kendall legal strategies based on interview with a member of Clinton's legal team.

Polling data on impact of the Lewinsky story provided by White House advisers.

Marcia Lewis at the grand jury based on grand jury testimony and FBI report attached to Starr referral.

Marna McLendon call to Jackie Bennett recounted in Bennett's sworn testimony in a December 1999 evidentiary hearing on illegal taping charges against Linda Tripp in Maryland state court. Tripp was charged with illegally recording a conversation with Lewinsky Dec. 22, 1997, and illegally disseminating the tape to *Newsweek* magazine. "She indicated that she was under pressure that was becoming unbearable to her . . . There was political pressure to bring an indictment," Bennett testified. He said McLendon told him the OIC's immunity agreement with Tripp would make prosecution "difficult." McLendon, who was not called as a witness in the hearing, told reporters afterward that she never discussed "the effect of federal immunity on a state prosecutor," and said Bennett's statements were an "absolute mischaracterization" of what she said.

Bob Bennett's views of attacking Starr from White House advisers.

Blumenthal's conspiratorial outlook . . . Interviews with White House aides and reporters. His distribution of materials about Emmick and Udolf from Blumenthal's grand jury testimony. His "assets to the enemy" list included reporters for the *New York Times,* ABC News, and author Schmidt of the *Washington Post.*

Carville's operation, the Education and Information . . . Carville published some of the erroneous material about Emmick in his 1998 book attacking Starr titled . . . *And the Horse He Rode in On.* Information about Carville taping comes from documents referring to subpoenaed tape recordings in the Judicial Watch lawsuit. In a deposition of Carville in that case, Carville lawyer William McDaniel asserts that one of the subpoenaed recordings "concerns Mr. Starr," and that both of the audiotapes in question "contain unverified rumors about people. They have never been disseminated by Mr. Carville. He would like you not to disseminate them." In a subsequent letter to the court, Judicial Watch chairman Larry Klayman filed the tapes under seal because they contain "scandalous material" of concern to Starr's office. Carville said in an interview that he would not discuss the tape recordings, but that they showed "just the opposite" of the claim made by Klayman that he was "probing into the sexual and personal backgrounds of investigators."

Finally, Starr broke his usual public . . . Details of *U.S. News* incident from OIC staff and *U.S. News* staffers. Harry Evans said he occasionally spoke to Blumenthal and often made story suggestions to the staff, but he had no recollection of the incident. Evans was a signatory on an ad in the *New York Times* in October 1998 urging Congress to censure rather than impeach Clinton.

Mike McCurry had been assured . . . Interview with McCurry.

The White House had an important ally . . . In an interview Becker said he did not believe there was any conflict in investigating Starr as he was seeking a post that would by filled by Clinton appointees at the Justice Department. He said he thought of the OPR job as "a career job" rather than a "political job," though Deputy Attorney General Eric Holder ultimately made the selection.

As Clinton allies . . . Clinton lawyers insisted any arrangements among lawyers were informal and oral, most times ad hoc. They preferred to describe their dealings with defense lawyers as recognition of "common interest privileges" rather than informal joint defense networks.

The questioning of Ashley Raines . . . From Raines FBI interviews and grand jury testimony, and from previously sealed Breuer declaration in privilege litigation with OIC. "Over a two-day period in approximately late January 1998, I had three conversations with a White House employee, Ashley Raines, who I understand was a friend of Monica Lewinsky. During these conversations, I provided legal advice to Ms. Raines in her capacity as a White House employee with respect to obtaining counsel. In the course of those discussions, I also obtained information about the Lewinsky matter."

The White House counsel's office . . . From FBI interview with Alex Nagy.

Ruff lined up defense lawyers . . . From White House lawyers and defense lawyers, including Gerard Treanor.

Lawyers for other important witnesses . . . From grand jury testimony of Currie, Lindsey, and Blumenthal.

Starr tried to make sure the grand jury . . . From Lindsey grand jury testimony.

CHAPTER SEVEN

Lessons of the Warren Commission, from interview with Ken Starr.

Starr background, youth and college years. Interviews with Starr, and his friends and acquaintances from childhood, college, and law school. Justice department background from Starr, former associates at DOJ.

Details of Tripp's debriefings from FBI reports.

At the White House . . . Lindsey's possession of the Willey letters from grand jury testimony of Oval Office administrator Nancy Hern-reich. Clinton calls Carville for advice on whether to release Willey letters, from Carville deposition in Judicial Watch lawsuit.

Broaddrick FBI interview summarized by congressional sources based on FBI interview accompanying impeachment referral. Broad-drick interview and many other OIC materials were available for members of Congress to examine but have not be publicly released.

Jordan began by minimizing . . . Phone records show Jordan called Bennett and Kendall late in the day Nov. 5, and when pressed about the calls he said he may have been calling to tell them to settle the Jones case. But he said he never talked to Kendall about Lewinsky and talked to Bennett about her only on Jan. 22. Jordan did not say anything in his testimony about going to Bennett's house one evening around Nov. 5 and urging him to settle the Jones case. (From interviews with Clinton adviser and source close to Jordan.)

Complaints about Wisenberg's scheduling of witnesses from defense lawyers.

But there was no criticizing . . . From grand jury testimony of Neysa Erbland, Catherine Allday Davis, and Lewis Fox, and deposition of Gary Byrne.

In a closed court hearing seven days earlier . . . White House Counsel Charles Ruff said the president personally had ordered the invoking of executive privilege. Ruff's declaration filed in federal court on March 17, seven days before the president's dismissive reply. He informed Johnson he "had discussed the matter with the president, who had directed the assertion of executive privilege."

CHAPTER EIGHT

The tip came from a source . . . The source said he heard the Oval Office story described in the presence of Merletti. In an interview for this book, Merletti vehemently denied he'd received any directive from Clinton. "There is absolutely no truth in that whatsoever. There is not one shred of truth in it," he said. "Throughout, the Secret Service stood on principle."

Background of Justice Department's support for protective function privilege in the Jones case from senior DOJ officials. On January 6, 1998, Hunger wrote Associate AG Raymond Fisher, informing him of plans to resist subpoenas from the Jones lawyers. He said DOJ planned to argue that complying with the subpoenas would impair the relationship between the Secret Service and the president.

Holder's reasons for favoring the Secret Service privilege based on interviews with senior Justice officials. How he and Schwartz handicapped it from OIC interviews.

Polling input on Secret Service privilege provided by White House advisers.

Bob Bittman's reasons for subpoenaing Kelleher came from a March 6, 1998 letter he sent to DOJ's Gary Grindler.

Description of March 29 meeting from a senior DOJ official.

Merletti's dealings with DOJ from senior DOJ officials.

Details of April 17, 1998 letter from Jackie Bennett to Holder, in referral documents.

Description of Holder's meeting at OIC from senior DOJ official.

On flow of information from Secret Service to White House, a senior White House official and a senior DOJ official.

Questioning of Lindsey from his grand jury testimony contained in impeachment referral.

But Holder didn't let the matter drop . . . Asked about communications with Johnson, a department spokesman said "At no time did Eric Holder ever encourage the judge to forward the matter involving the alleged leaks to the Justice Department."

Description of animosity of white collar defense bar in Washington toward Jackie Bennett drawn from interviews with several of those lawyers, as well as current and former DOJ officials. Description of Texas cases from interviews with lawyers and other participants in them, and from DOJ officials.

The normally placid Holder was agitated . . . Description of meeting from OIC interviews and senior DOJ official.

Holder's letter to Starr seeking an investigation of the allegations about David Hale was drafted by Bob Litt, Holder's principal deputy assistant and a former law partner of David Kendall. Litt said in an interview the reference to a potential conflict for Starr and offer by DOJ to conduct an investigation was not intended to embarrass Starr. The department had not passed judgment on any conflict, and was merely giving Starr an option if he felt he had one. He said the allegation concerned an important witness in an important case, leaving DOJ little choice but to make sure it was examined. Litt said Jackie Bennett did not object to release of the letter, though he had not been told of the Scaife reference.

Correspondence on Hale matter between Starr and DOJ, and Starr and Kendall is included in impeachment referral.

Description of how Starr weighed his duty to report to Congress from OIC interviews.

CHAPTER NINE

Starr's political background from interviews with Ken Starr, Robert Vagley, Alice Starr, etc.

Mark Penn's assessment of Starr's public opinion rating from a White House adviser.

Description of public relations rescue effort from Vagley, Holly Rudkin, Alice Starr, Ken Starr, OIC staff.

The conversation was overheard . . . Al Kamen, *Washington Post,* April 8, 1998, "In the Loop" column.

They shared another powerful experience . . . Information about Jerry Starr from Texas court documents, newspapers, and interviews with lawyers and one of the victims. Exploits of Hickman Ewing's father from OIC interview and *Wall Street Journal* profile of Ewing by Glenn Simpson, July 31, 1996.

One of the loudest opponents . . . Interviews with Sam Dash and OIC prosecutors.

Letters from OIC seeking president's voluntary testimony and responses from David Kendall are included in impeachment referral documents. Description of March 20 courthouse meeting from two participants.

Kendall changed the subject . . . Various media organizations had reported that the Jones legal team had been aided by Richard Porter, a lawyer in the Chicago office of Kirkland & Ellis, Starr's law firm. Porter denied doing legal work for Jones. Other lawyers involved with the Jones team confirmed in interviews that Porter did not do legal work, though he made phone calls and put people in touch with one another to help Jones' case.

Details of the *Vanity Fair* shoot and Ginsburg comments from *Time* magazine, June 16, 1998 edition.

For months Starr's team . . . Judge Johnson's previously sealed order on immunity issue, May 1, 1998. Ginsburg's admission of lying to media from transcript of March 5, 1998 closed hearing on the immunity issue before Johnson.

Description of handwriting and fingerprint session from OIC interviews and FBI report attached to impeachment referral.

The deleted portion of Ginsburg's "Open Letter to Kenneth Starr" recounted in Lewinsky's book, *Monica's Story.*

Conversation between Lewinsky and Ginsburg over dinner at Legal Sea Foods from *Time* magazine, June 16, 1998 edition.

Lewinsky's unhappiness that Ginsburg had to tap the criminal expertise of Speights, from *Monica's Story.*

Lewinsky's firing of Ginsburg and hiring of Plato Cacheris and Jake Stein from interviews with Cacheris, Lewinsky sources, and *Monica's Story.*

Description of initial meetings between Lewinsky's new legal team and OIC came from interviews with Cacheris and OIC staff members. In addition, we relied on contemporaneous notes taken by a participant in the meetings.

Lewinsky tells her lawyers about the dress, from interview with Cacheris.

White House reaction to new Lewinsky legal team, from interviews with two White House officials. Speights-Seligman discussions were extremely closely held, known to a few presidential advisers, one of whom provided the information for this book. Speights, in an interview, denied sharing information with the Williams & Connolly lawyers. Seligman had no comment about the back channel to Speights.

Mark Penn's analysis of Lewinsky from a White House aide and an adviser.

Clinton had no choice but to wait . . . Lenzner's background investigation of Monica Lewinsky reported in the *Washington Post,* June 21, 1998.

CHAPTER TEN

Brill said in response to written inquiries that it was fair for him to infer that Starr had leaked grand jury secrets on the basis of his admission that he occasionally had background briefings with reporters. Brill said any background briefing was improper for Starr, though reporters should always try to get one. Brill said before his interview with Starr, he disclosed his plan to write about his dealings with the media.

Brill said he based his account on more than the six news organizations whose journalists had challenged parts of "Pressgate." He said he was not at liberty to disclose them, though he identified the *New York Times* as one. Brill said he only suggested that Starr had a monopoly on "certain, specific information." Brill said Kendall provided him a public court opinion.

Judge Johnson's June 15 comments and those of Kendall and Bittman came from a transcript of the hearing unsealed by the court.

Information on the July 1 draft pleading to Judge Johnson came from senior DOJ officials.

Description of OIC summit meetings on setting referral date and how to proceed with Lewinsky come from interviews with many participants plus contemporaneous notes taken by one of the lawyers present.

CHAPTER ELEVEN

Discussions about protective function privilege from senior DOJ officials and Secret Service officials.

David Kendall understood the danger . . . That Kendall knew what Secret Service would say is based on interviews with one of the president's advisers and a lawyer for another witness who kept in contact with Williams & Connolly.

Description of July 21 mandamous hearing from participants and hearing transcript.

Starr's negotiations with Lewinsky lawyers described by participants, as well as proposals and counterproposals. On June 15, Cacheris and Stein sent the OIC an offer to deliver Lewinsky for questioning on condition that "at the conclusion of the proffer, we should be advised as to the decision of your office regarding whether or not Ms. Lewinsky and Ms. Marcia Lewis will be prosecuted. If your office concludes that the proffer is not truthful, we require a demonstration by you as to what items or statements are untruthful. The untruthfulness must be demonstrated by evidence other than that contained in the Tripp tapes."

On the same day, Bittman replied that the proposal "gives us fewer assurances of Ms. Lewinsky's reliability than the proposal we rejected in our negotiations with Ms. Lewinsky's previous counsel. Indeed, we spent months litigating the earlier proposal before Chief Judge Johnson in order not to be forced to accept the terms of the previous proposal." The letter went on to say "we will not consider any agreement as to Ms. Lewinsky's legal jeopardy without first hearing from her in an in-person proffer."

Correspondence between OIC and Kendall concerning Clinton's testimony is contained in impeachment referral documents.

Description of Mike McCurry's efforts to confirm subpoena to Clinton from interview with McCurry.

Bob Bennett's views from a White House adviser and Bennett associates.

One veteran lawyer . . . Interview with a lawyer privy to Hundley-Kendall conversation. The views of others close to the president about whether he should testify comes from interviews with White House advisers.

Information on the Dash brunch came from interviews with Starr, Cacheris, and Sara Dash.

Lewinsky's worries of a birthday indictment from *Monica's Story*.

Details of OIC interview with Lewinsky from participants on both sides, as well as FBI 302.

Details of arguments before Judge Johnson about whether the president should have more time to respond to subpoena from hearing transcript.

CHAPTER TWELVE

White House dinner and president's conversation with Cornel West from *Newsweek* article, Aug. 17, 1998.

Details of Lewinsky debriefing sessions from FBI 302s and interviews. Grand jury sessions from testimony transcript.

Views of Hillary Clinton and Clinton's lawyers about how he should handle grand jury testimony from interviews with White House advisers and a defense lawyer close to members of Clinton's legal team.

Even before the Clintons moved to Washington . . . Description of Hillary Clinton's reaction to her husband's admissions from *Time* magazine, Aug. 31, 1998.

CHAPTER THIRTEEN

Clinton's grand jury testimony from transcript included in impeachment referral.

Wisenberg kept focusing on . . . Lanny Breuer told the grand jury that Hundley also kept the White House counsel's office apprised of Jordan's testimony.

Clinton's preparations for speech after his testimony from interviews with White House aides and advisers.

Description of Clinton's trip to Martha's Vineyard aboard Air Force One, from *Time* magazine, Aug. 31, 1998.

Lewinsky's deposition and statements to the grand jury from transcripts in impeachment referral.

Lewinsky's reaction to the president's speech came from her grand jury statements and *Monica's Story.*

CHAPTER FOURTEEN

White House lawyers analyzing the president's grand jury testimony . . . From interviews with a lawyer for the president and a presidential adviser.

Meanwhile his wife was barely speaking . . . Ten commandments comment from interview with Clinton family confidant; Hillary Clinton's chagrin about being unable to demonize Starr from a White House adviser.

Clinton's worries about the possibility of his being indicted came from an interview with the friend.

Newt Gingrich call to Clinton described in an interview with a presidential adviser. Gingrich declined interview request.

Clinton supporters, though . . . Blumenthal made the comment about Henry Hyde to *New Yorker* writer Jeffrey Toobin, who disclosed it two years later in his book *A Vast Conspiracy.*

Blumenthal comments about Starr from confidential interviews with two guests at British Embassy party.

Description of Starr-Reno meeting Nov. 15 from participants on both sides, from contemporaneous notes taken by a Staff staffer at the meeting, and from Reno's written talking points. Discussions among Reno advisers about when to alert Starr to their pending inquiry from senior DOJ officials.

Congratulatory calls to Starr from interviews with Starr and Abbe Lowell.

EPILOGUE

On Sept. 7, 1999 the D.C. court of appeals sided with Starr on the issue of what information falls under grand jury secrecy rules. The court ruled that Judge Norma Holloway Johnson misread what it said in the 1998 Dow Jones case about "matters occuring before the grand jury." In that ruling, the court noted the phrase encompasses "not only what has occurred and what is occurring, but also what is likely to occur," including "the identities of witnesses or jurors, the substance of testimony as well as actual transcripts, the strategy or direction of the investigation, the deliberations or questions of jurors, and the like." But despite its seemingly broad nature, the appeals court judges said, "we have never read Rule 6(e) to require that a 'veil of secrecy be drawn over all matters occurring in the world that happen to be investigated by a grand jury.' Indeed, we have said that "the disclosure of information 'coincidentally before the grand jury [which can] be revealed in such a manner that its revelation would not lucidate the inner workings of the grand jury' is not prohibited." The phrases "likely to occur" and "strategy and direction of the investigation," the court said, must be interpreted within the overall context of the grand jury secrecy rules.

The distinction of "utmost significance," the judges said, is between statements by prosecutors about their own probe and those about a grand jury's. That does not permit prosecutors to disclose testimony about to be presented to the grand jury. But it does provide latitude for other discussions of an investigation. "Thus, internal deliberations of prosecutors that do not directly reveal grand jury proceedings are not Rule 6(e) material," the court said, not even if they involve discussions of whether an indictment should be sought or whether a person is potentially liable.

The news story that led to the appeals court ruling was a report by the *New York Times* in the midst of the Senate trial that said Starr was considering indicting Clinton. While it was well known Starr had to decide the question one way or the other, the timing of the *Times* story suggested he was trying to supersede Congress and it set off a political furor. David Kendall filed another motion for a leak investigation. To quell concerns, Starr initiated a leak investigation of his own, calling in the FBI when he could not readily discover the source of the information in the *Times* story. OIC spokesman Charles Bakaly was subsequently forced to resign over statements he made to investigators.

The appeals court disagreed with Judge Norma Holloway Johnson, who concluded that a paragraph of the *New York Times* story revealed grand jury material: "Inside the Independent Counsel's Office, a group of prosecutors believes that not long after the Senate trial concludes, Mr. Starr should ask the grand jury of 23 men and women hearing the case against Mr. Clinton to indict him on charges of perjury and obstruction of justice, the associates said. The group wants to charge Mr. Clinton with lying under oath in his Jones deposition in January 1998 and in his grand jury testimony in August, the associates added."

The court said while such statements are "troubling" because they could damage the reputation of an innocent suspect, they do not implicate the grand jury. That the timing for seeking an indictment was disclosed—after the Senate trial—did not indicate what is likely to occur before the grand jury, the opinion said. All it reflected was the desire of some prosecutors to seek an indictment then, not a decision to do so, it said. Nor was it a problem to disclose the general grounds for an indictment as long as no secret grand jury information was disclosed.

At this writing, Judge Johnson has not yet ruled on Kendall's original leak motion, filed two years ago, though the special master appointed to look into the leaks was reported to have completed his investigation in mid–1999. Nor has the Justice Department concluded its inquiry of misconduct allegations involving Starr's office, though with Starr gone it is not clear the department has standing to continue to investigate.

On July 30, 1999, Linda Tripp was indicted in Maryland on state charges she taped a telephone call without consent and disseminated the recording to *Newsweek* magazine. She pleaded not guilty and is scheduled to stand trial in July 2000.

After a yearlong investigation of the allegations Hale was paid off to discredit Clinton, Michael Shaheen concluded the allegations were false. In June and July 1999, Shaheen received a confidential correspondence from Little Rock federal judge William R. Wilson, who recused himself early on in Starr's investigation because of his friendship with the Clintons. Wilson said he was "writing on behalf of our Court (the District Judges for the Eastern District of Arkansas), pursuant to a discussion we had at our last judges' meeting concerning the David Hale/Dozheir Bait Shop investigation." Wilson said the court was interested because "it is my understanding . . . that your report addressed specific crime, and did not address possible ethical violations by lawyers." The judges, he said, might try to obtain transcripts of grand jury proceedings conducted by Shaheen.

In January 2000, the Arkansas Supreme Court, acting on a citizens' group complaint pending for sixteen months, ordered its professional conduct committee to decide whether Clinton's law license should be revoked or suspended as a result of his false statements in the Jones case.

A NOTE ON THE SOURCES

THE LEWINSKY INVESTIGATION of 1998 presented one of the great journalistic challenges. The demand for new information was relentless, and the possibilities of getting it finite. The customary difficulties of reporting a sensitive story were compounded by the silence, half-truths, or diversions of many of the principle players.

We set out to clear the fog of this extraordinary moment in American politics. Although emotions remained strong in the months after the Starr Report, we found people on all sides willing to give their own clear-eyed accounts. We tried to immerse ourselves in the personalities and decision making of the various camps, and in doing so interviewed more than 150 people. Much of our energy was devoted to pulling back the veil of secrecy that surrounded Starr and his team.

While we made use of a trove of records made public with the impeachment referral, much of this book is oral history based on hundreds of hours of interviews with the key participants, among them Starr and twenty-five of his assistants in the Lewinsky probe, including Sam Dash. Starr sat for ten sessions of several hours each, resulting in nearly three hundred pages of typewritten transcripts.

Many staff members granted us multiple interviews, and our sessions with them spanned more than two hundred hours. For biographical sections of the book, we spoke to Alice Starr, two of Starr's maternal aunts, and more than thirty friends and professional associates.

On the Clinton side, we interviewed fourteen of his lawyers, aides and advisers, including his White House Counsel Charles Ruff. Other interviewees included nine Justice Department officials; four Secret Service officials; and fourteen lawyers and advisors for Paula Jones, Linda Tripp, Monica Lewinsky, and other key players. We also interviewed officials of Congress, among them Henry Hyde, who were involved in the impeachment process.

Virtually all the events in our book were described by more than one source and often by several. We benefited from the contemporaneous notes and diary entries of several participants, internal documents, private correspondence, and previously sealed transcripts of court hearings. Many of these records are referenced in the chapter notes at the end of the book. In the rare instances where factual discrepancies among parties could not be resolved, we have tried when possible to reflect the differences in the text and in the chapter notes.

Starr's referral is a reporters' windfall of documents that normally never see the light of day—thousands of pages of grand jury transcripts, FBI interviews, phone records, correspondence, and other materials. We used that record as our basic framework to reconstruct what investigators were learning outside the public eye during the year of Lewinsky.

ACKNOWLEDGMENTS

To cover the news is to write the first draft of history, it's said. We have been fortunate enough to get a crack not only at the first draft, but the second, just as the participants of this story were taking stock of what they'd lived through. We are deeply appreciative of the many hours they spent with us before their memories faded.

We wouldn't have gotten very far without Joni Evans, the most dedicated and artful literary agent. She was determined to find the right publisher for us, and she did. She read every chapter and offered countless suggestions and ideas to make our book better. Joni hooked us up with David Hirshey at HarperCollins, whose talent is exceeded only by his sense of humor. David saw the value in a clear-eyed account of Ken Starr's investigation of Bill Clinton, and he helped us navigate the shoals of writing about events so polarizing to the country. We are grateful, as well, to Merrill McLoughlin, whose deft touch sharpened our prose.

We asked a few people to read our manuscript, and are grateful we did. Their ideas improved this book. Susan Schmidt's husband, Glen Nishimura, a fine editor, and her father, George Schmidt, offered sage advice that we valued and followed. *Time*'s Washington bureau chief, Michael Duffy, and the *Washington Post*'s David Maraniss, both esteemed authors, guided us as if they were polishing one of their own works. *Post* writer Sharon LaFraniere offered thoughtful advice and encouragement.

In the year it took to produce this book, we had a luxury most authors could never imagine—help from some of the most skilled reseachers in the business. Washington Post researchers were an enormous help to us, and we would like to thank them here, beginning with the indefatigable Mary Lou White, who has been finding gold in her databases on this story since Martin Luther King Day 1998. Others generous with their time include Jennifer Belton, Melody Blake, Bob Lyford, Madonna Lebling, Alice Crites, Kim Klein, Nancy Shiner, Karl Evanzz, and Bobbye Pratt. At *Time* we enjoyed the skilled research assistance of Anne Moffett, Karen McCree, AnnMarie Bonardi, Kathleen Dowling, Angela Thornton, Sandra Jamison, and Charlie Lampach.

Both of us covered the Lewinsky investigation for our news organizations. We have drawn on our work as well as that of our editing and reporting colleagues. From the *Post* they included Ruth Marcus, Peter Baker, Dan Balz, Lorraine Adams, Bob Woodward, Karen DeYoung, Bill Hamilton, and Susan Glasser. At *Time,* they are Michael Duffy, Jef McAllister, Priscilla Painton, Stephen Koepp, Margaret Carlson, Eric Pooley, Nancy Gibbs, Richard Lacayo, Chris Ogden, Karen Tumulty, Viveca Novak, Jay Branegan, Elaine Shannon, Mark Thompson, John Dickerson, Jay Carney, Lissa August, Ratu Kamlani, Elizabeth Rudulph, Barbara Burke, and Marta Dorian.

We would also like to thank Olwen Price, who ably transcribed interviews for us.

From Susan Schmidt:

I am grateful to my bosses at the *Post* for their help in making this book possible. Executive editor Leonard Downie could not have been more accomodating when I asked for a year off, and Tom Wilkinson was generous with arrangements. Managing editor Steve Coll, who had experience in coauthoring a book, shared his system for organizing materials that proved invaluable to us. Publisher Don Graham's regular encouragement has been a great source of support.

Several other *Post* colleagues helped us navigate the world of book publishing. Ben Bradlee's advice and enthusiasm gave me the confidence to plunge forward. He and his wife, Sally Quinn, generously helped us find our agent, Joni. Roberto Suro and Glenn Frankel, both authors of successful books, offered helpful advice and contacts.

I feel incredibly lucky to have teamed up with Michael Weisskopf on this book. His creativity and his dedication to truth propelled us all year.

Special thanks must go to my family, who have lived with the story of Ken Starr's investigation of Bill Clinton for as long as I have. My father, George Schmidt, and my brother, David Schmidt, have been willing sounding boards for many of its twists and turns. I have been buoyed by their love and support, along with that of the rest of the Schmidts—my stepmother, Catherine; my brother Gary; and my sisters-in-law Susan and Linda—and by my Nishimura relatives in California, especially George and Hazy, and Kathy and Nick Bryan. My cousin Beth Alberts and her husband, Rich Lemoyne, have offered fun and respite during the writing of this book. Though my work over the past few years often has disrupted family plans, both the Schmidt and Nishimura clans have been unfailingly supportive of it.

My love and gratitude go especially to my children, Kate and Lacey, who have been so patient, taking only pride in my labors, and to my husband, Glen. It would have been a lesser book without his many sacrifices, his high tolerance for domestic chaos, and his wise counsel about presenting this story.

From Michael Weisskopf:

My thanks begin at the top of *Time*. Managing editor Walter Isaacson and deputy managing editor Jim Kelly gave me the time to write this book. But their contributions began as soon as the political story of a generation broke. They set a standard for excellence, style, and enterprise unmatched in the news business. Assistant managing editor Priscilla Painton generated so many story ideas that more than a few were left over for this book.

In an entire career, few reporters are fortunate enough to find a partner who improves every facet of their work and turns every day into an adventure. I'm far luckier than most. Michael Duffy made me a better reporter and writer in 1998 and pushed me to take on this book. The only consolation to working without him were his calls of guidance and encouragement during the year. He redefines the word *mensch*. David Maraniss has never stopped being my partner since we met at the *Washington Post* in 1977. He informed this book with insight and excellence as he has virtually everything I've done in the past quarter of a century. Susan Schmidt was an inspiration and joy in this project.

No one can survive a book without the comfort of great friends. I am grateful to Judith Stoler for her summer tomatoes and her loving support. My oldest friend, Mark Plotkin, kept nostalgia alive. David Aikman supplied important help. And my spirits were kept high by Linda Maraniss, Bill Hamilton, Valerie Strauss, Mark Levy, Otto Mannheimer and Cecelia Udden-Mannheimer, Jan Rothschild and Mike Philips, Janet Barnes and Rex Blankenship, Ted and Nellie Bristol, Sheila Resnick, and Tom Beller. Don Collins kept my computer humming right through the Millenium New Year.

This book is co-dedicated to the three most important people in my life. My wife, Judith Katz, believed in me and pushed me to swing for the fences on this book. She did at great personal sacrifice, which is a small measure of her heart. I'm in eternal debt for her support and steady stream of cappuccinos. My kids, Skyler and Olivia, kept my loft filled with artwork and love. My father, Warren Weisskopf, never lived to see his son publish a book. I am grateful for the ideals he planted. My mother, Marcella Stillerman, is an author who cultivated those ideals. She and my stepfather, Jack Stillerman, provided me great encouragement as did my oldest support system—sister Leslie Flesch, brother Richard Weisskopf, brother-in-law Michael Flesch, and his two sons, Warren and Ben. My mother-in-law, Sabina Katz, has been a secret weapon for years, giving me confidence and courage. My brother-in-law Ben Katz and his wife, Debbie Hager-Katz, added their love.

INDEX